SO YOU
A THEATRE DIRECTOR?

Since leaving Cambridge University in 1981, Stephen Unwin has directed over fifty professional productions, initially at the Traverse Theatre in Edinburgh, where he was Associate Director until August 1988. All of his productions there were new plays from Scotland, England and abroad. Six transferred to London theatres, including the British premieres of two plays by Manfred Karge, *Man to Man* and *The Conquest of the South Pole*. Actors he worked with at the Traverse include Tilda Swinton, Simon Russell Beale, Ken Stott, Katrin Cartlidge, Kathryn Hunter, Ewan Bremmer and Alan Cumming.

In June 1993 Stephen launched English Touring Theatre. His many productions for ETT include *Hamlet*, *A Doll's House*, *As You Like It*, *Hedda Gabler*, *The Taming of the Shrew*, *The Master Builder*, *The Cherry Orchard*, *Ghosts*, *King Lear*, *John Gabriel Borkman* and *Romeo and Juliet*. Actors he has worked with at ETT include Alan Cumming, Eleanor Bron, Michael Pennington, Timothy West, Kacey Ainsworth, Diana Quick, Prunella Scales, Michael Feast, Samuel West, Alexandra Gilbreath and Kelly Hunter. His work has been seen at the Old Vic, the Royal Court, the Donmar Warehouse and the Lyric Hammersmith. He has also directed in repertory theatre and in Europe.

Stephen has directed a dozen operas including *The Decision*, *The Marriage of Figaro*, *Lucia di Lammermoor*, *Cosi Fan Tutte*, *Gianni Schicchi* (ENO), *Il Barbiere di Siviglia* (ROH), *Albert Herring*, *Falstaff*, *Die Entfuhrung*, *Le Nozze di Figaro* and *Don Giovanni* (Garsington).

Stephen was the Joint Winner of the 2003 Sam Wanamaker Prize awarded by the Shakespeare Globe and was the Judith E Wilson Visiting Fellow at Cambridge University in Autumn 2003. He has co-authored three *Pocket Guides* for Faber and Faber: *Shakespeare*, *Twentieth Century Drama* and *Ibsen, Chekhov and Strindberg*.

To the actors

The publisher gratefully acknowledges permission
to quote from the following:

'The Friends' in *Poems 1913-1956* by Bertolt Brecht, translated
by Michael Hamburger; *Glengarry Glen Ross* by David Mamet;
Saved by Edward Bond: all published by Methuen Publishing Ltd.
No Man's Land and *The Caretaker* by Harold Pinter; *A Piece of
Monologue* by Samuel Beckett; *Juno and the Paycock* by Sean
O'Casey: all published by Faber and Faber Ltd. *Men Should Weep*
by Ena Lamont Stewart: published by Samuel French © 1983.
Chekhov's *The Cherry Orchard* and *The Seagull*; Ibsen's *John
Gabriel Borkman* and *Ghosts*, translated by Stephen Mulrine;
Ibsen's *Hedda Gabler*, translated by Kenneth McLeish:
all published by Nick Hern Books.

Contents

SO YOU WANT TO BE
A THEATRE DIRECTOR?

'Speak the speech, I pray you, as I pronounced it
to you, trippingly on the tongue.'

Hamlet

'The truth is concrete.'

Bertolt Brecht

1

What it takes

Directing plays is difficult.

Putting together a coherent evening of theatre requires many skills. The aim of this book is to describe what those skills are, and give some sense of how a person wanting to become a theatre director might acquire them. The emphasis is on the professional theatre, but the book should be useful in other contexts – amateur dramatics, university, secondary schools and so on. Directing is directing, wherever you do it. If the emphasis is on text-based theatre, it's because it's the area that I know best. It's also the one that the young director is most likely to encounter.

But have you got what it takes?

Skill

The first skill you need to acquire is how to read a play. This isn't always as easy as it sounds. A director needs to be able to read dialogue, hear different voices and sense the dramatic action within the text. This isn't taught at university or college and certainly not at school, and many literate, intelligent people can't read plays at all. But a director needs to be good at it.

Second, you need to have some conviction about why you want to stage a particular play and an ability to communicate this to a number of people. If the play is a classic, you need to understand its original context, but also know why it's worth reviving now. You may have to know how to cut it and, if it was written in a foreign language, be able to tell a good translation from a bad one. If the play is new, you'll need to champion it and argue that it should be performed. You'll have to work closely with the writer and understand what he's trying to say. You may have to help him rewrite it – sometimes drastically – so you need to develop a grasp of the way that dramatic writing works.

If you're working professionally, you'll need to convince managements that they should put their money into your production. And in the amateur as much as the professional theatre, you must understand the business side: how to budget a production, draft funding applications, understand box office estimates and so on. You need to know how to negotiate with managers and agents and how to secure rights.

Third, you have to learn how to work with a team of artists and technicians, each with his own skills and demands, but also with his own anxieties and concerns. You need to be the leader of that team, while respecting individual strengths and abilities. You need to convey your passion, while giving clear and sober guidance.

Fourth, you need to know just how important casting is and how to ask the right questions about what the play requires. If working professionally, you need to be familiar with the work of as many actors and actresses as possible, and gain some sense of what they can and can't do. You need to work with casting directors, know how to hold auditions, deal with agents, negotiate contracts and handle questions about billing. In short, you need to learn how to employ actors.

Fifth, you need to work with a designer. You have to find the right designer for you and your project, and then collaborate with him. You need to think your way through such complex issues as how to set Shakespeare and the classics, and you must be able to communicate your choices with clarity and force. You need to know how the placing of doors, furniture and other objects affects the rhythm and shape of the piece, and you must work with a production team in making your vision come to life, in budget, on time, and within particular physical constraints.

Sixth, in rehearsal, you need to give leadership, help and support to your actors, recognising that each of them has individual needs and problems. You need to give clear, practical direction to older actors who may have been on stage longer than you've been alive, but also to others of your own age, possibly from very different backgrounds. You need to be helpful and know when to intervene, but also when to leave alone. You need to demand the best without forgetting that you can't do the actors' work for them, and you must inspire, cajole, instruct and help them achieve their best.

You must develop an ear for the sound and rhythm of the play and know how to orchestrate and conduct it. You need to get actors to respond to the specific musicality of the piece, be it Shakespeare or Sheridan, Aeschylus or Ayckbourn, without cramping their own work on character and motivation. You need to learn when it doesn't matter that the action is too slow or too quiet, but also when the right thing to say is 'louder and faster'; when it needs more pace, volume and energy, but also when it should be delicate, still and quiet.

You need to develop an understanding of three-dimensional space and how to arrange actors on stage in such a way that the story is clear, the dramatic action is focused, and the audience is looking at what they should be looking at. You need to know how to create resonant images, without forgetting that the actors' innate energy and diversity paint a more dynamic picture than anything you can artificially construct with their bodies.

You must learn how to pace rehearsals, when to encourage free association, research and experimentation, but also when to insist on clearly defined objectives and tasks. You need to know when to work on tiny sections, when to run scenes, and when to run the entire play. You need to sense when to be critical and when to give praise, when to 'kick ass' and when to sit on your hands. There must be a limit to your patience, but you must discover where that limit is, and know how to express your impatience constructively.

You need to know when you should stick to your guns, but also when to abandon your most cherished ideas. You need to know where to look for help and how to find your way through the dozens of helpful suggestions that a director is offered every day. You have to be able to deal with your own exhaustion, and know how to protect yourself from being run ragged. You must remain fresh and true to your vision.

Seventh, once you get into the theatre, you'll have to work with a team of technicians and other artists on lighting, sound and music. You have to give them clear briefs, which allow them their own creativity, while also ensuring that their work is integrated with everybody else's. You have to run a technical rehearsal within restricted time, and ensure that all the work gets done. Seeing the set and costumes under lights often comes as an enormous shock, and you may have to make difficult, sometimes unpopular changes. You have to discover how to use dress rehearsals positively, how to encourage actors to take over the stage and gain the confidence that will allow them to perform in front of an audience. But you also have to give them those last-minute and sometimes stern notes that can be so important.

Finally, you have to sit in an auditorium on the first performance, surrounded by strangers, and learn from them – about clarity and dramatic logic as well as rhythm, volume, visibility and so on. You need to rehearse on stage once the production is previewing, and know how to give notes from performances. You need to cope with the response you get from the audience, from your friends and colleagues and even from the press. Letting the production find its own feet is one of the hardest things to learn; depression and a sense of loss once the play is open are all too common, even with a success. And you're going to have to be able to deal with all of that too.

But nobody ever said that directing plays was going to be easy.

Art

Becoming a theatre director requires more than simply acquiring a set of skills. Directing is an art form in its own right, and you need to accept that you're becoming that most complex and obsessive of human beings: an artist.

Directing, like any art form, is an expression of the subconscious. And like every artist you will have to learn how to draw on your own resources: your observation and experience, your knowledge and education, your obsessions and intelligence, your neurosis and vulnerability. If you want actors to work from their own emotional centre, you need to gain self-knowledge about your own. And to do this you need to be in

touch with your feelings and unembarrassed about expressing and sharing them, however private they may be. This reminds actors that good plays are about individual experience,
and it's this that will give your work that rich, rounded,
human quality which is so desirable.

A director needs to develop what the Labour politician
Denis Healey called 'a hinterland': an interest in things
beyond the narrow world of the theatre. If in the best theatre
'all human life is there', interest and knowledge of an entirely
non-theatrical subject can make a huge difference. I often
find it revealing to ask a young director what was the last film
he saw, or the last art exhibition he went to, or what novels he
reads, or how often he listens to music. A director needs to be
interested in history and society, psychology, economics and
politics, as well as fine art. Knowledge of, and interest in, the
wider world will give you a broad enough frame of reference
to do interesting work, and make you into a director who has
something to offer.

You need to develop your own approach to the theatre,
and you may find that this is in opposition to the *status
quo*. In a workshop given by Peter Brook I was asked what
my criteria for directorial decisions were. I'd just directed
A Doll's House and had been amazed by the detail and precision of Ibsen's theatrical vision. And so I said to Brook
that my 'holy grail' was feeling confident that I was following the playwright's intentions. I was told that this was
'the cult of the personality' and that such an approach led
to 'museum culture'. For Brook, the right answer seemed to
be 'theatrical immediacy', a sense of being 'in the present
moment'. The fact that I disagreed with this famous and
influential director (and still do) was useful in my own
development – it helped me understand what I was doing
and what I stood for.

Of course, there are no rules, no manual and no blueprint
to theatre directing. There's only you, the director – a living,
complex human being – working with a group of other complex human beings: actors, technicians, stage managers,
designers and so on. And you have to find your own voice,
your own way of being a director, your own vision and skill.
However many books on directing that you read, training

courses you attend, or experienced directors you assist, you need to work out who you are, what you think the theatre is for, why you want to direct, and what the values are that will inform your work. And so, slowly but surely, you can build up your own taste, your own understanding of where you stand and what your work is for.

These, then, are your artistic beliefs.

Belief

The border between skill and art is a fine one, and it's easy to lose track of where one ends and the other begins. The best productions are so rich in skill that it's easy to forget the belief and vision that went into them. Three examples: Lindsay Anderson's production of David Storey's *Home* was full of finely nuanced insights into the details of class, age and a nation in decline, caught by two of the greatest actors of the twentieth century (John Gielgud and Ralph Richardson) on a brilliantly simple set by Jocelyn Herbert. It seemed to distil to its essence England in 1970 – proud yet senile, sentimental yet cruel. Another example might be Peter Brook's breathtaking production of *A Midsummer Night's Dream*, performed by actors free of all the usual inhibitions and stuffiness so common in Shakespeare, in a brilliant white box with trapezes and spinning plates, like a dazzling Chinese circus. A third example might be Peter Stein's revelatory production of Chekhov's *The Cherry Orchard*, which caught an entire society standing on the brink of catastrophe. It was a production which had drunk deep of historical research and was free of Chekhovian cliché, performed by actors extravagant in their emotions, concrete in their characterisation, and bathed in the brilliant white light of the doomed cherry orchard.

Productions of this quality are the result of much more than simply technical skill. They derive from strongly held artistic convictions: Lindsay Anderson's lifelong fascination with Englishness and the realistic tradition in English Art, Peter Brook's spiritual belief in the possibility of a theatre free of restricting cultural contexts, or Peter Stein's commitment to realistically drawn human beings caught up in a particular historical moment. Different as these productions were, what united them was the belief that theatre could be more than show business, and that it could present the most profound truths of life.

And this should be your aim.

2

What is a Theatre Director?

Although plays have been performed for two and a half thousand years, the theatre director is a relatively recent development. This isn't the right place for a full history, but directors (as opposed to actor managers) didn't really emerge until the late nineteenth century and the naturalistic move-ment in the theatre. Men such as the Duke of Saxe-Meiningen (1826–1914), Otto Brahm (1856–1912), William Archer (1856–1924), André Antoine (1858–1943), Vladimir Nemirovich-Danchenko (1859–1943), Konstantin Stanislavski (1863–1938), Aurélian-Marie Lugné-Poë (1869–1940), Max Reinhardt (1873–1943), Vsevolod Meyerhold (1874–1940), Harley Granville Barker (1877–1946) and Louis Jouvet (1887–1951) were all in-volved in creating a new kind of theatre, which had intellectual and artistic coherence, and was based on certain key principles.

But it was not until the twentieth century, particularly in post-war Europe and America, that directing came into its own as an art form. Figures such as Erwin Piscator (1893–1966), Bertolt Brecht (1898–1956), Tyrone Guthrie (1900–71), Harold Clurman (1901–80), Lee Strasberg (1901–82), Elia Kazan (1909–2003), George Devine (1910–65), Joan Littlewood (1914–2002), Ingmar Bergman (born 1918), Giorgio Strehler (1921–1997), Lindsay Anderson (1923–94), Peter Brook (born 1925), William Gaskill (born 1930), Peter Hall (born 1930), Ariane Mnouchkine (born 1934), Peter Stein (born 1937), Peter Gill (born 1939) and Patrice Chéreau (born 1944) all produced visionary work which revolutionised the modern theatre.

Different cultures

Every culture has its own idea of the theatre director.

The British and American theatre is still predominantly commercial, and regards the emergence of intellectual and artistic theatre directors with some suspicion. Because of the changing priorities of the funding bodies, the press and the public over the last fifty years, Britain has finally developed an 'art theatre', subsidised by the state, relatively free of commercial pressures, and committed to the highest standards. But this transition was a complicated process, and British directors are still having to negotiate their way through a set of contradictory challenges and opportunities, and the last twenty years have seen the return of many of those commercial imperatives. In America, with its less generous public support for the arts, it's even harder for an artistic theatre to thrive.

In continental Europe, by contrast, the *régisseur* and the *metteur en scène* are treated as serious artists, intellectuals whose views on society are actively sought out. They are expected to express their opinions. They have an exalted role in their city, with chauffeur-driven cars, reserved restaurant tables and handsome salaries, and their appointments often have a political significance. Some develop an almost cult status, but the notion of entertainment is often forgotten. Clive James once said that directing opera is 'what Germans do now they can't invade Poland'. It's a cruel joke, but it carries a grain of truth.

Each culture has its own idea of the theatre director, and it's a role that's continuing to evolve.

Being an artistic director

Because in the past director and producer have tended to be the same person, many professional theatre directors in Britain are also artistic directors, who run companies and buildings. This can produce fine results, where a theatre is rooted in the community and where the artistic director understands not simply the work on stage, but also the town or city where the theatre is situated. The boards and funders of British theatre have usually insisted that subsidised theatres should be 'artistically led' and occasionally the artistic director has taken on the role of Chief Executive as well. I've enjoyed being an artistic director working as 'first among equals' with an executive director, but some boards prefer to have one 'boss' (so that they know who to fire when things go wrong).

It's important to stress that good stage directors are not necessarily good artistic directors, and, in a time when there's increasing pressure on theatres to perform well financially, many artistic directors have to do much more than programme, cast and direct plays. Indeed, the pressures on an artistic director can be enormous and it's often hard for him to keep his eyes on the job in hand. As a result many successful directors avoid running theatres altogether, and spend their lives working as freelancers. One of the commonly identified weaknesses of the regional theatres in Britain is the difficulty of attracting experienced and talented artistic directors.

Commercialism and subsidy

The English-speaking theatre, even the London fringe, is at heart a commercial place. The audience for new or radical work is small, and the audience for the less well-known classics is shrinking. The notion of an 'art theatre' appealing to a broad audience is on the wane, and the subsidised repertory theatres and touring companies who still uphold these ideals find themselves in an increasingly hostile climate.

The fact is that theatre is an expensive art form, appealing to a limited audience. Subsidy has kept ticket prices within the realm of possibility for middle-income audiences, but there's no denying the exclusive nature of many theatres in Britain. Furthermore, subsidy provides less and less protection from the need to achieve commercial success. As a result, some say that in recent years the British theatre has made a pact with Mammon.

Whatever the cause, there's an increasing appetite in the British theatre for sensation, celebrity and spectacle, fuelled by jaded critics, financial imperatives, and profit-seeking managements. Of course, the theatre needs high-octane celebrity events now and then. But the university graduate with a love for the great drama of the past and an appetite for exploring the modern world in dramatic form needs to look carefully at the water in which he is hoping to survive: it's a shark-infested sea.

Power

In Britain today most directors are men, nearly all of them white, and the large majority privately educated. There have been some remarkable exceptions, and the situation is gradually changing. A few impressive women directors have emerged, but still white, and still privileged. While a prerequisite for theatre directing may be an easy personal authority, which some people are fed with their mother's milk, the theatre needs to draw its artists from the widest possible social base or it will fade and die.

People who don't work in the theatre sometimes imagine that the director is incredibly powerful, and driven by a crazed appetite for power. Again, the truth is more complex. Of course, as a director, you have influence over the overall shape and feel of the production, but the idea that directing a play is like piloting a jet plane is mistaken. The fact is that any power you have – beyond the important one of casting – is contingent on the relationships you've made with the individual actors and other artists. Just telling people what to do doesn't produce creative results, and experienced directors know that actors have to give permission to direct them, if the work is to flourish.

Being a director can be confusing. It's often hard to define your role: are you an acting coach or a psychoanalyst, an academic or a journalist, a traffic policeman or a babysitter? Most actors are charming, but some are not. Their confidence is fragile, so a high level of tact is required. Some wield a great deal of power, so you need to work out how to harness that energy for the good of the production. You have to be so many different things to so many different people that it's easy to lose track of who you actually are. Directing requires the thick skin of the politician with the porous sensitivity of the artist.

Furthermore, directing can be an extremely lonely job. I once taught a group of nine young directors: I asked eight of them to stand at one end of the room looking imploringly at the ninth, and said to the ninth that this was a situation to be avoided at all costs. The things that divide actors from each other – age, technique, training and so on – are fewer than the things that unite them, and you need to deal with the different demands individual actors make, but also to respond to them as a collective.

All the people you work with – be they actors, designers, lighting designers, stage managers and so on – have their own particular role to play. But your job isn't so clearly defined and, as a result, you're sometimes left wondering what exactly you're there for. Most people moan about their job: being a director has its tremendous highs, but it does have its lows too.

A career?

And it gets worse: there's absolutely no career ladder.

Stories abound of experienced and eminent directors scraping by on tiny amounts of work, supporting themselves by teaching, writing and holding forth. At no point can you sit back and declare, 'I've made it.' You're only as good as your last show, and the belief that one production leads inevitably to another, or that if you do one thing right you'll go on to the next, is misguided. You soon discover that there's a small circle of megastar directors whom the critics love and managers employ, who get most of the work. It's often mysterious the way that some directors suddenly emerge and are lionised, while others languish in obscurity. Sometimes the difference is obvious: talent. At other times the reasons for success are imperceptible: luck, contacts, good looks and timing. There's little justice, and making a successful career as a director is as much the result of luck and determination as it is of talent or wisdom. Paranoia, bitterness and professional jealousy are the daily diet of most directors.

Furthermore, directing plays is a poor way to earn a living. I once estimated that at current rates I would need to direct ten productions a year in repertory theatres to earn enough to bring up two children and pay the mortgage. As a result many theatre directors give up when they reach forty, work abroad or move into television. Many work as artistic directors at some point in their careers, which at least guarantees a salary, even if it does saddle them with unwelcome responsibilities. A few strike it rich from musicals, or from long-running West End and Broadway hits. Some become university professors for six months of the year, in California if they're lucky. But the fact is that, despite the best efforts of the Directors Guild, theatre directing is, at least in Britain, a badly paid and exceptionally insecure profession.

Are you sure you still want to be a theatre director?

3

Starting out

Becoming a professional theatre director is a daunting challenge. Of the many young people who fancy themselves as the next Sam Mendes, shockingly few ever get to direct a single professional production.

So how do you start out?

The instinct

You shouldn't try to work as a theatre director if you lack an instinct to entertain others.

This instinct runs deep. Children play with each other and show off to adults. But soon their natural curiosity drives them to work out how to make this more entertaining – both for themselves and for others. And so they experiment with story, with sounds, with colours and with pictures. In doing this they're involved in the basic questions of theatre directing. There's no mystery to this, no special calling: it's just fun. But it's a particular kind of fun that makes grown-ups be quiet and your friends think you're funny. You're creating a show, and self-expression lies at its heart.

When adolescence arrives this becomes self-conscious. For most teenagers, 'drama' means acting. A few become intrigued by the theatre itself (how it works as a machine for storytelling) and are dazzled by the possibilities of it all. They're intelligent and want to shape and organise what's happening, and try to make it better. They hate the idea of acting themselves, or of being the centre of attention. They don't like learning lines, and are incapable of losing themselves in a 'character'. Sometimes they're the clever ones, sometimes the artistic ones, and often the bossy ones. They're the critics and the creative thinkers, the artists and the managers; they want to lead, but they also want to hide.

These are the natural directors, and it's to them that this book is addressed.

University

Theatre directors come in a whole range of shapes and sizes.

It's sometimes presumed that good directors have impeccable academic credentials, but the opposite is often the case. It's certainly true that in Britain many of the most successful ones went to university (and studied English there), but their success is as much a result of their non-academic ability as anything they learnt in the groves of academe.

It's also true that Oxbridge – 'the dreaming spires, the perspiring dreams', as the old joke has it – has produced a disproportionate number of leading directors, but again that's changing. The 'ancient universities' offer a broad range of opportunities: above all the chance to direct plays. I directed eighteen productions while I was at Cambridge, though nobody told me (as perhaps they should have done) that I was neglecting the things I was there for – whether it was studying for my degree or chasing girls.

But it's important to stress that directors don't have to have gone to Oxbridge, and there is in the profession some bitterness about its dominance. Experienced actors sometimes feel that directors enter the theatre direct from Oxbridge with neither in-depth academic knowledge nor vocational skill, but get on and do well because of contacts and a magic calling card. Of course, this can be very unfair; but it can also be true.

A degree from an illustrious university can give you a useful start, but it's not enough.

Directing courses and other backgrounds

Many would-be theatre directors go on to train elsewhere after university. Some of the drama schools offer directing courses where a graduate can receive a vocational training, and get a glimpse of young professional actors at work. These can be useful, depending on the teaching staff. There are also summer courses and other educational schemes. But the sad fact is that – in Britain, at least – there's no 'conservatoire' training for young directors.

Many directors have entered the profession through other routes. There are visual artists and choreographers who have extended their interest to include spoken theatre, often with great success. Some actors, frustrated with the directors they have worked with, have turned their hand to directing to spectacular effect. And there are writers who direct their own work (Alan Ayckbourn, Harold Pinter and Peter Gill are three of the most eminent examples), often definitively. All of these routes are legitimate.

There are many different ways of becoming a director in Britain, but none of them is cast in iron. The important thing, whatever your background, is to show that you're a serious director in your own right, anxious to learn the practical skills, modest in your claims to prior knowledge, and keen to do whatever needs doing. More than anything, it's this that will win you the opportunities and respect that you crave.

Getting to know the repertoire

Whatever your background, it's essential that you get to know a lot of plays, both classics and new writing. A director who hasn't read widely will quickly lose authority in the rehearsal room, and an artistic director who doesn't know the repertoire well will find programming decisions impossible. 'Knowing the rep' underpins everything.

When I left university, I'd read hardly any Ibsen or Chekhov, was familiar with only the most famous of the American writers and knew next to nothing about the popular modern repertoire. Although I was reasonably well read in Elizabethan and Restoration drama, as well as the obvious 'heavyweight' twentieth-century masterpieces, I read many more plays in the five years after I finished university than in the three years I was there. When I was asked to be an artistic director, I sat down and read hundreds more. Without an in-depth, almost encyclopedic knowledge, you'll be working with one hand tied behind your back.

There are, of course, some useful guides to help you through. But these can do little more than provide you with a reading list, and give you some starting points. The important thing is to read the plays yourself, from beginning to end, in some detail, and draw your own conclusions, possibly making notes on how you see the play unfolding on stage, how it might be cast, what it might look like and so on.

Getting to know new writing is harder. The essential thing is to go to those theatres which specialise in it. Most new plays that find their way on to one of the 'important' new writing stages get published, and you should read try to read all the ones you've missed seeing in the theatre. The theatres which stage new plays sometimes use 'readers': people who – for a tiny fee – read a number of new scripts every week and report on them. Sometimes an aspirant director gets taken on as a reader: a valuable opportunity to encounter new plays in script form. The 'new writing' scene is very fluid and it's hard to keep on top of it, but it's important to find out which writers you like – and which you don't – and learn to articulate your opinions and enthusiasms cogently and concisely. Some literary agents also use readers (usually unpaid) and working for them is a good way to get to know more.

Assisting

Probably the best first step of all is to work as an assistant to an experienced director.

This isn't as easy as it sounds: there are only a few training schemes around the country, funded in a variety of ways. Useful as these often are, they are intensely competitive, attracting two or three hundred applicants on average. Some repertory theatres employ assistant directors, which is where some of the best directors started out. But money spent on assistant directors is the first thing to be cut when budgets look worrying.

Both the National Theatre and the Royal Shakespeare Company employ assistant directors (and staff directors – usually older and more experienced) to work on a number of productions, and these positions can be very rewarding. Of course, these companies are so big that it's difficult to move up, but being an assistant with them does offer the opportunity to see experienced directors and actors at work, as well as gain an insight into how such large organisations operate.

Working as an assistant director is an intriguing and complex task. It can at times be extraordinarily frustrating. Even the most experienced directors can appear incompetent to the critical young eye: you sit there, feeling you know exactly how the production should develop, but having to bite your tongue. When you *do* offer an opinion, it's often dismissed. And you're reduced to being a kind of personal secretary to the director: making the coffee, going to the dry cleaners and taking the dog for a walk. Worse, you become a scapegoat for his frustration and rage.

It's sometimes hard to define what exactly an assistant director does. Of course, the job varies from company to company. One of the most crucial tasks is to keep a firm eye on the show once it's opened. I gather assistants at the National Theatre and the RSC are meant to watch every performance. At English Touring Theatre they 'put the show into' each of the theatres it visits. The point is that a production needs a director's eye to keep it fresh once it's opened, and a good assistant director has an important role to play.

Even the most rewarding assisting experiences can be difficult: watching somebody of tremendous experience and ability working with skill and panache, to achieve something wonderful which you can't quite define, but which you know is beyond your reach. He seems so confident with his actors, so at ease, that you go home wondering how you can ever do it as well. Some assistants develop an unhealthy adulation ('If only I was like that,' they think, 'all would be well'); others impersonate the mannerisms of their masters. I remember once envying an older director his grey hair: 'If only I had grey hair,' I thought, 'I could direct like that.' Now that I have grey hair too, I'm not convinced that was all that was missing.

It's sometimes presumed that directing talent will bubble up of its own right, that directing cannot be taught. But the fact is there are very few opportunities for a young person to gain an apprenticeship, and the British theatre's complacency about the training of its young directors may well come back to haunt it.

Getting a foot in the door

Since these assistantships are so competitive your application may well be turned down, perhaps repeatedly. And so many directors start out doing some entirely different job – actor, stage manager, even box office assistant. The crucial thing is to get work in the theatre doing just about anything.

When I was a fifteen-year-old 'wannabe' I got a summer job tearing tickets at the Open Air Theatre in Regent's Park. This gave me an early glimpse of the routines of the professional theatre: actors turning up *exactly* on time for their 'half', stressed by their kids but pleased by the voice-over they'd just recorded, transforming themselves into 'fairies' in moments and throwing themselves into *A Midsummer Night's Dream* regardless of rain, aircraft noises and other distractions. I only used to watch the first five minutes ('Now, fair Hippolyta, our nuptial hour draws on apace') before retiring to the bar. But it taught me something very important about the material conditions in which the 'rough magic' is expected to emerge. And when I found myself going to the pub with the late, great Esmond Knight (blinded in the Battle of the Atlantic and a definitive Chorus in *Henry V*), I learnt a respect for the best traditions in British acting that I've never forgotten.

Get your foot in the door: it's essential.

First step

Of course, as Peter Brook says in *The Empty Space*, the only way to become a director is to direct plays, and the young director should grab every opportunity available. Which is why the fringe – not just in London, but also in Manchester, Glasgow, Edinburgh, Bristol and other cities – is full of young, thrusting directors, wanting to put on a production in a room over a pub. This is a difficult thing to pull off: money must be raised, actors persuaded to work for nothing, audiences found and critics wooed. Young directors increasingly have to operate as producers, hustling their wares in a strange kind of market – in which they get paid nothing for their efforts. They dream that a good review will pull in an audience. With that will come senior members of the profession, and an invitation to direct at the RSC will be just a matter of time. It does sometimes happen like that, but the fringe is littered with broken hearts and bust bank balances.

When two or three of these young directors are gathered together the atmosphere can be murderous. Unlike actors, directors tend to be unsupportive of each other's work, ferociously critical, and gleeful when one of their competitors fail. *Schadenfreude* (pleasure in someone else's pain) is the theatre director's worst vice. But since a production can only have one director, all directors are, in theory, competing for the same job. Good theatres employ a range of directors, and we all have something to teach each other. But it's often difficult for the young director to see that.

So if after all this gloom you still want to be a theatre director, it's time to get on with the more positive challenges: working out which plays you want to direct, and how.

4

Contexts and Colleagues

The theatre is the most practical of art forms. Its economics are challenging and it can only flourish and have meaning if it finds an audience. Work in the theatre always exists within a specific context, and so one of the most important things you can do is understand the nature of the profession in which you're working.

Choice of theatre

George Devine, the founding father of the English Stage Company at the Royal Court, once told a young actor that 'you should choose your theatre as you would choose your religion'. Of course, nowadays there's often no real choice: many young directors are lucky to get any work at all and have to be prepared to direct anything, anywhere, if they want to direct at the National one day. Gaining experience is essential. And so my strong advice – at the beginning of your career – is to direct anything you can get your hands on.

One of the things that such 'promiscuity' can give you is an understanding of the context in which you're working – not just the nature of the company or its theatre, but also its audience. Without that you're in danger of creating theatre that fails to connect, and imports a particular set of ideas into an alien setting. While your audience's tastes can and should be challenged, a misunderstanding of context often leads to the values of the metropolitan avant-garde being foisted on an audience which is both baffled and bored – an audience which will then not return.

The British theatre – like so much else – is shockingly concentrated on the capital. But the best thing for a young director starting out is to get beyond the M25 (the 'beltway'), out of the narrow, often incestuous, world of London theatre. There you can see that theatre takes place in a whole range of different contexts, with diverse audiences, and artists from wildly different backgrounds. Repertory theatres, touring companies and fringe – it all connects and a good director can learn from everywhere. There can be no room for snobbery, exclusiveness or disdain: all theatre shares the same preoccupations, and the differences are superficial. I remember an experienced artistic director telling me that he hated the audiences his work was playing to. At that moment I predicted the downfall of his company, and I was right.

So my advice is to work everywhere you can, meet everybody who will meet you and direct whatever comes your way. By doing this you'll start to identify people whose attitudes you respect, who are pursuing a policy you can support, and putting on a kind of theatre that you think is valuable. This may not be the fast track to fame and fortune, and it may well take you to an unglamorous backwater: but it will give you something to believe in.

Working for free

With the theatre financially squeezed, and the ever growing number of people wanting to work in it, there's an increasing tendency for actors, directors, designers and writers to work for free: getting together, renting a small theatre above a pub, and putting on a show. The results can be remarkable. London fringe theatres such as the Gate, the Southwark Playhouse and Battersea Arts Centre usually work with unpaid professional actors and have had a significant effect on the 'mainstream' theatre. (It should be stressed that all three have actively sought out funds to pay their actors, and are making important steps towards that goal). This work should be distinguished from that of amateur groups, because the people involved are professional theatre practitioners (or hope to be). It has become so widespread (particularly in London) that the bad working conditions are sometimes worn as a badge of pride, while critics express astonishment and praise that such remarkable work should be put on for no financial reward – as if that was a guarantee of its integrity.

Of course, there's nothing intrinsically wrong with this, and many a young director would say that 'working for free' is the only way to get his first break. What is important, however, is that the theatre should be careful not to step back to the time when only the comfortably well-off could afford to work in it, and become an exclusive enclave for the educated middle classes. The theatre desperately needs to maintain its professionalism, and too much working for no money should be resisted.

Colleagues

When pressed on his plans for the Royal Court, William Gaskill, artistic director at the time, said that to him 'policy is the people you work with'. This is crucial. All the great moments in the theatre have depended on groups of like-minded people working together: the King's Men (Shakespeare, Burbage and Kemp), the Moscow Art Theatre (Stanislavski, Chekhov, Mayakovsky and Olga Knipper), the Berliner Ensemble (Brecht, Caspar Neher, Helene Weigel, Ernst Busch and Ekkehard Schall) and the Royal Court in the 1960s (George Devine, Lindsay Anderson, Jocelyn Herbert, David Storey, Peter Gill and William Gaskill).

Obviously, developing relationships with actors is essential. Most experienced directors accumulate a group of actors whom they enjoy working with and draw on from time to time (I used the same actor, Michael Cronin, in seven productions in a row). A shorthand is built up, mutual respect grows, and you can work more quickly and with less room for misunderstanding. But there's a danger in this: it can all get too cosy, and the director fails to see the actor's limitations and problems. The important thing is to balance old colleagues with new ones. I always enjoy starting a rehearsal period with a group of actors half of whom I know, and half who are new to me.

But a director has many other collaborators too. Most develop relationships with one or two designers and work with them fairly consistently (Peter Hall and John Bury, Lindsay Anderson and Jocelyn Herbert, Trevor Nunn and John Napier, Peter Gill and Alison Chitty, Michael Grandage and Christopher Oram). Sometimes these relationships last for a few productions; occasionally they last a lifetime. But, as with actors, such relationships need to be carefully monitored, and you should remember that nothing is as exhilarating as developing relationships with *new* people. Lighting designers and composers likewise become part of the director's extended family, and these long-term working relationships need looking after, but also regular review.

The people to whom directors seldom get close are other directors. But it's crucial to discover other directors you admire, who can see your work, give you honest pointers, support you when it's going badly, and bring you down to earth when you've done a hit. I once asked two director friends to go and see a production of mine which had got very bad reviews but of which I was proud. I needed them to tell me whether the critics or I had gone mad: their verdict was that we both had. This kind of advice is always worth the price of a drink.

I enjoy working with an assistant on a production. He is often my closest collaborator, supporting me in all kinds of ways – jokes, reactions, second opinions – and the person with whom I can have the most honest relationship. Once the assistant has won my trust, he becomes a sounding board for my anxieties as well as my ideas. Some directors don't know what to do with an assistant: they find him a spectre at the feast, examining the director in all his agony. I think a good assistant is the best antidote to the isolation I some-times feel.

Management

There's another group of people seldom mentioned in books and articles about the theatre: managers. Perhaps under-standably, young directors come into the business with a deep anxiety about management, the 'money people'. And indeed, there are managers who are suspicious of new ideas, cautious and conservative. Sometimes they're right to be so; at other times they're just being unimaginative. And some managers are downright incompetent. But most British theatres are well run, and behind every successful creative endeavour is a good manager.

There are two kinds of theatrical managements: commercial and subsidised. Commercial managers put on plays in order to earn a profit for themselves and their shareholders. It's unfair to say they don't care about the quality of the work on stage, but their productions are commercial propositions driven by financial imperatives. Managers in the subsidised companies, on the other hand, draw their satisfaction from running an efficient, creative business whose main job is to create productions of the highest possible standard. They too are responsible for their budgets, and are answerable to boards of management and funding bodies. But as long as the figures balance out at the end of the year, they have done their job well.

Managers are much more than men in suits. I often ask them for a candid response to a production: even if their opinion is sometimes not as artistically orientated as I would have wanted – the show is 'ten minutes too long' or 'not quite sexy enough' – it can make all the difference. Young directors should understand the realities theatre managers face, and cultivate positive and creative relationships with the best of them.

Actors

Actors are at the heart of the theatre, and you cannot succeed as a director if you don't know how you're going to work with them.

Most professional actors are genuinely co-operative, supportive of each other's efforts, optimistic and positive. They bring to their work creativity and attention to detail. They're decent people, who are dedicated to the idea of quality theatre. But actors come in all shapes and sizes, and few of them are saints. Each one wants something different from the director, and you have to work out how to give each one what they need. This diversity of need can be bewildering at first.

Many actors are very insecure. They work in an oversubscribed profession and a staggeringly high percentage of members of Equity (the actors' union) are out of work at any one time. Most earn pitifully small amounts of money, in short bursts of activity flanked by long periods of uncertainty. They depend on television and commercials for a living, and work less and less in the theatre. Many supplement their income with non-acting work: waiting in restaurants, reflexology, interior designing, script editing and building. Only a few succeed, and most are left with disappointed dreams and worried bank managers.

It's not just the environment in which actors work that's unstable, it's the nature of the job itself. Although acting requires skill and professionalism, at heart actors have nothing more to offer than themselves: their charm, their emotions, their sexuality, and their vulnerability. And so their neuroses manifest themselves in different ways: the over-assertive, talkative ones who will do anything rather than get down to work; the obedient, nervous ones, who are so pleased to get a job at all they do everything you ask and give dull performances; the senior figures who remind you of their extensive experience every five minutes and stifle freedom of expression; the aggressive young men who are impossible to direct, because they're suspicious of authority, and want to destroy the whole event (as proof of their innate superiority – or worthlessness). It's often difficult for people who don't work in the theatre to understand such neurosis, but a director has to recognise and come to terms with it.

It's this neurosis that gives rise to the image of actors as 'luvvies', spending their whole time telling each other how marvellous they are, and behaving with complete strangers as if they had known them for years. In many ways, this is a cruel caricature: some actors are taciturn to a fault. But the world of 'darling you were marvellous', 'dear boy' and double cheek kissing does exist. I've learnt that it's not quite as awful as it sounds. The sensitive director will understand why 'luvviness' occurs and find ways of supporting and understanding these most vulnerable of people.

But all the support and understanding in the world won't win some actors round. Some come labelled 'difficult', but, in my experience, they're usually the pushovers. Others are scarred by working with tyrannical directors, and see you as the enemy, or a challenge, or a problem to be overcome. Others have worked with weak directors and seem only to respond to a firm hand. All of these take every bit of your charm and skill to negotiate. And sometimes they drive you mad.

A particular challenge is working with actors who are much more experienced than you are. Older actors often bring to their work an enviable understanding of what can be achieved within the time available, and an inner confidence about what questions should be asked. But such levels of experience can also lead to a closing down of the mind, a sense that there's only one way of doing things. And unfortunately, some have a less than perfect memory for text and moves. The young director must find ways of respecting and learning from them without being intimidated. I once directed a remarkable old actor who told me over breakfast that he had fought at Dunkirk: I realised then he could probably handle anything I threw at him.

Young actors (more so than actresses) can be difficult too: they're sometimes more arrogant than they should be, often lacking in discipline, occasionally unstable and insecure, and you need to know how to guide them through their first challenging parts. The training of young actors is increasingly tailored for television and film, and you need to find ways of reminding them of the realities of the theatre. Acting training should last a lifetime, and a good director is also a good teacher.

Some actors enter the profession with no formal education at all, and from very poor backgrounds. But they are often self-taught, and are some of the most thoughtful and well-read people I know. Others have a university education and feel frustrated that it's being wasted. And yet this very intellectualism can get in the way: acting is an instinct and a trade, and an academic degree doesn't necessarily help.

The important thing about actors is that wherever they come from they're the lifeblood of the theatre, and a good director relishes the challenge of working with them, for all their vulnerability, obsessiveness and complexity.

Stars

And then there are the stars.

The British theatre needs stars for two reasons. The commercial theatre needs them in order to make money (as does the subsidised theatre to break even). And many of the great parts need to be performed by actors with 'star quality'. However much we sometimes wish that just 'good actors' were enough, stars are indispensable.

There are three different kinds of stars. The best are magnificent: household names, who can hold down a great part, fill the house, and lead a company with spirit, energy and bravura. These are the leading actors that every director dreams of, and they're the centre of most really first-class productions. The next kind are celebrities: known for something other than their theatre acting (often a part in a television soap), they usually find the technical challenges of the theatre daunting. The better ones want to learn, and can be a revelation; the bad ones are unteachable and to be avoided. And then there are the has-beens: actors who once made a mark, but whose rose is blown; they can still attract audiences – particularly older ones – but lack the energy, confidence and ability to carry the evening off.

All three can cause problems for even the most experienced directors. Perhaps surprisingly, stars are often more nervous and vulnerable than less well-known actors – they know that their reputation is on the line and that critics and audiences will enjoy pulling them down a peg. And when this vulnerability is combined with arrogance, the result can be hard to handle.

There are ways through, however. Above all, it's essential to be well prepared. Confront a star with clearly worked out reasoning and only the most objectionable won't at least try to do what you ask. And you need to approach them in the right way: above all, be accommodating, polite and flexible. If you're getting nowhere one day, break early and try again the next day. If you feel the star isn't ready to rehearse the scene you want, find another scene to do instead. But finally: never give up. Don't be intimidated. Even the most famous actor knows that he can't do it without a good director: he needs you as much as you need him.

Be strong, be clear, and be flexible – the three keys to good directing.

5

Choice of Play

Just as at first you'll have little control over the context in which you work, so you'll be lucky if you're given much choice of the material you're asked to direct. But it's essential that you direct plays for which you have some feeling and which show your strength as a director.

So how do you choose?

A free hand?

One of the defining characteristics of the really successful director is that he has the freedom to direct pretty much whatever he likes. Peter Stein, Peter Brook, Deborah Warner and Sam Mendes simply decide what they want to direct, and ways will be found for them to do it. Managements are desperate for their work, and money can always be raised.

Things are much harder, if just as interesting, for less exalted directors who run their own companies. Artistic directors have a certain amount of freedom and autonomy, but usually find their hands tied by budgetary consider-ations. They try to persuade their boards and funding bodies that after a string of commercial hits the time has come to stretch the boundaries a little. And so they programme a play by Marivaux and pray for good reviews and a reasonable audience, aware that a flop will eat into the reserves that they have so carefully built up. The realities that even the most successful artistic director has to face every day will often impose a 'safe choice'. Such programming decisions go to the heart of being an artistic director, and the challenges are considerable. And commercial success is horribly unpredict-able. English Touring Theatre's production of Peter Gill's *The York Realist* was nearly cancelled because of anxiety about its popular appeal; ironically the play cleared the company's deficit and allowed the company to go on and tour *King Lear*.

For freelance directors the situation is different again. A few of the most established ones are asked by artistic directors and managers for their suggestions. But even then, the conversation will be hedged round with restrictions: 'No, we don't want a Shakespeare because we did two last year', and 'No, you can't do *An Enemy of the People* (because it's too big, and anyway Ibsen doesn't sell) but what about *Who's Afraid of Virginia Woolf?* or *The Birthday Party?*' Often a project (perhaps another play altogether) will emerge. Sometimes the conversation fades away, and both parties go their own ways. The eventual outcome all depends on a mixture of luck and the director's status – an indefinable combination of age, experience, critical acclaim and skill.

For less established freelance directors, or those just starting out, the situation is harder still. When an artistic director has decided on a season of work he will look for directors. Often he will be contracted by his board to direct several of the productions himself. When he's looking for a guest director, he often chooses someone who has worked for the company before. It may be somebody whom he admires; occasionally it'll be somebody who has a proven affinity for a particular writer. I receive dozens of letters from young directors with a 'perfect project' for English Touring Theatre: I'm afraid I've only once taken up an unsolicited idea in ten years.

Sometimes a freelance director will be offered a play he doesn't like. This can be a difficult call: after all, what's the point in directing something you don't feel strongly about? Ultimately, my advice is that you should do it regardless, if only as a way of gaining experience.

The fact is that you need to be able to direct almost anything, and being choosy about your material is a luxury that comes later. If you can get the maid on and off in a vicarage thriller without spoiling the tension, then you've learnt something that will be useful when you come to direct Ibsen. Skills are transferable and gaining experience is all. It's instructive to look at Peter Brook's early career and see how much commercial tat he directed before he was thirty. Too many young directors develop a kind of snobbery about the plays they want to direct, which is entirely counterproductive.

Conviction

The difficult thing is you need to combine this flexibility with a deeper set of inner convictions about the kind of theatre you want to produce. You must discover what kind of material you like, so when you're asked for your opinion you have one. And you need to answer the fundamental questions: What do you think the theatre is for? What view of the world do you want to present? What do you believe in and what is your taste? If these questions are political and philosophical, it's because theatre is political and philosophical. Ultimately, you need to nail your colours to the mast and stand for something.

With a developing set of convictions and an evolving aesthetic your work can gain its own momentum, your portfolio of productions can find its own identity, and you'll start to stand for something. This is important in all kinds of ways – apart from anything it makes it clearer to management what they're buying – and will ultimately give you the power to choose the work you're going to direct.

Striking the appropriate balance between open-minded promiscuity and artistic conviction is difficult, but the most deeply held beliefs ring hollow if you have only limited experience.

Finding your writers

In developing your artistic profile you need to find out which writers you love and want to direct. Most good theatre directors develop an affinity for a particular writer. Peter Gill's career was transformed by his definitive productions of the D.H. Lawrence Trilogy at the Royal Court in the 1960s. Ingmar Bergman directed a series of remarkable productions of Ibsen and Strindberg which catapulted him into the major league. Deborah Warner made her name directing lesser-known Shakespeare texts. Richard Eyre was the ideal interpreter of David Hare's large-scale epics. Peter Stein's productions of Chekhov in the 1980s and 1990s were regarded as definitive, even in Russia.

I've managed to make a mark with my productions of Ibsen's drawing-room tragedies, whose mathematical precision, theatrical clarity, and psychological depth struck a chord in me. In modern writing, I found two plays by the German writer, actor and director Manfred Karge – *Man to Man* and *The Conquest of the South Pole* – immediately appealing for the way that they took Brecht's theatre forward into the late twentieth century. These writers have brought out the best in me and have helped me move my career forward.

This affinity is difficult to define, but important. A talented director should always be on the lookout for writers he cares about. And he will then seize every opportunity to direct their plays.

Directing classics vs. new work

You need to differentiate between directing classical work and new plays. Most theatre directors have done both (although Trevor Nunn didn't work with a living writer until he was in his late forties). A few make a career out of directing exclusively new work, but more direct mostly classical revivals.

In thinking about the value of directing the classics a whole set of questions arise. Are you working on them because you're convinced of their innate greatness, or because you've been told they're great? Do you want to direct them because the writer is safely out of the way, or because you respect and love the quality of the writing? Are you interested in the classics for what they say about the modern world, or do you regard them as museum pieces, simply part of literary culture? And if you think the classics really do speak about 'now', are you deluded? These are all big questions and you need to develop answers to them.

New work has a huge attraction. If the theatre is to speak directly to its audience, plays by living writers are essential. There's tremendous satisfaction in staging the first play of a young dramatist, and the world premiere of any play has an unbeatable sense of occasion. Some directors say that much as they would like to stage contemporary work none of it has the scope or depth of the great classics. This is worrying, since it places a false emphasis on the contemporary reson-ances of the work of the past, and attempts to judge new writers by an alien standard. But directing new writing all the time is hard to sustain.

The director of a classic text is much more likely to attract critical and artistic attention. Old plays offer the director the opportunity to make a mark, whereas in new work the director usually tries to be as invisible as possible, letting the play 'speak for itself'. Lindsay Anderson used to say that the Royal Court tried to 'do classics as if they were new plays, and new plays as if they were classics.' It's a useful motto.

Even *Hamlet* was a new play once, and it's important to remember how many theatre-goers are seeing even such famous plays for the first time. Such audiences watch the play with an open-minded interest in the drama, which more experienced theatre-goers sometimes lack. Most of my work is designed for them: they're the audience of tomorrow.

The Shakespeare challenge

The obvious problem a director faces when confronted with a Shakespeare play is that it is the product of a different time.

I sometimes remind people that four hundred years ago audiences going to see *As You Like It* at the Globe walked be-neath severed heads stuck on poles on London Bridge. And so it's hardly surprising that Shakespeare's plays feature situ-ations way beyond our own experience. Sixteenth-century England was organised in ways that we find almost incom-prehensible.

It wasn't just society that was different, it was the theatre itself. Shakespeare's audiences went to the theatre for different reasons than we do, and would have watched the plays with very different eyes. Even if we could reproduce the conditions in which they were originally produced, they would feel very odd. This was a theatre creating a new cultural and social awareness, a theatre involved in 'nation building'. The great breadth of its audience and its central position in society allowed the Elizabethan and Jacobean theatre to act as a sounding board for debate, a tool of education and literacy, like a newspaper article and a film, a public library and a fashion magazine all rolled into one. The modern theatre is none of these things.

Shakespeare's stagecraft is rich with conventions and emblems, most of which are incomprehensible to us, except in the most academic way. Although the plays have a strong sense of location, they were performed without any sets at all, in an emblematic theatre, with a painted heaven above, and a metaphorical hell below. They inherited many of the limitations of the medieval theatre. In staging such plays today we are confronted with a double problem: the conventions of nineteenth-century naturalism are clumsy, while late-twentieth-century theatricality is too technologically developed and aesthetically self-conscious.

A further challenge in working on Shakespeare is his status: Shakespeare is the man of the millennium, so whatever you do, you're bound to encounter complaints and disagreements. I'm increasingly convinced that the reason so few directors have had a success with *Macbeth* is that whatever you do, the experience of the play can never be as frightening or intense as the reader's imagination. The plays exist in the public realm, and everyone has his own idea of how they should be staged. Brecht was aware that the status of the classics inhibits us, but was equally sceptical about there being any easy answers:

> Actors and producers, many of them talented, set out to remedy this by thinking up new and hitherto unknown sensational effects which are however of a purely formalist kind ... It is as if a piece of meat had gone off and was only made palatable by saucing and spicing it up.

If you're going to direct Shakespeare, you'd better think that the meat itself is worth eating.

Jan Kott's *Shakespeare Our Contemporary* was extraordinarily influential on the way that directors conceived Shakespeare production in the last third of the twentieth century. Kott's genius was to discover a certain quality in Shakespeare that seemed to speak to a modern audience, be it the Beckettian bleakness of *King Lear*, the intellectual, revolutionary quality of *Hamlet*, or the sexual subconscious in *A Midsummer Night's Dream*. His writings found their most perfect realisation in Peter Brook's productions at the RSC.

Of course, Kott was not the first person to recognise the contemporary resonances in Shakespeare. Ever since the Restoration, Shakespeare has been appropriated by the particular world in which his plays were being staged – look at the portraits of Garrick's Shakespearean performances in the Somerset Maugham collection at the National Theatre. In the early twentieth century, Harley Granville Barker, Tyrone Guthrie and Barry Jackson all developed approaches to Shakespeare which embraced modern features, and which startled audiences by their directness.

But the fact is Shakespeare cannot be 'our contemporary' – he's a writer from an alien world, and thinking anything else is intellectually dishonest. Presenting him as if he was our contemporary has been liberating for everyone involved: I just think it's important that Shakespeare with cigarette lighters and mobile phones doesn't become as oppressive an orthodoxy as the picture-book style that preceded it.

One recent development has been the placing of Shakespeare's plays in a setting neither of his time nor of ours: *Richard III* in a Fascist Britain, *Much Ado About Nothing* in Mafia Sicily, *King Lear* in a nineteenth-century circus, *Macbeth* in a concentration camp and so on. Sometimes such productions are revelatory. At other times they cast little light either on the play or the period in which it has been relocated.

Shakespeare's great rival, Ben Jonson, generously declared that 'He was not of an age, but for all time', and a common approach is to suggest that Shakespeare is above history, society and the boring stuff of everyday life. This can be thrilling, particularly with the more abstract, fantastical comedies; but it can also result in productions which are set in a kind of 'timeless' pyjama-clad 'universalism' which has neither 'local habitation' nor a 'name', and sells Shakespeare's political, psychological and social realism short.

Of course, Shakespeare is so dynamic and protean that he can survive anything and there can be no hard and fast rules.

My only advice is to make sure that whatever decisions you make, you concentrate on bringing the characters to life in a way that is clear, drawn from the text, and makes dramatic sense. Directors of Shakespeare sometimes get so interested in the atmospherics of the particular locale they have chosen they forget to do the hard stuff: releasing the action of the play itself.

Naturalism

Directing the great naturalist dramatists of the nineteenth and twentieth centuries (above all Ibsen, Chekhov, Harley Granville Barker, Bernard Shaw, D.H. Lawrence, Sean O'Casey, Arthur Miller and Tennessee Williams) is a thrilling challenge. Each has an ability to give the domestic and the everyday a tremendous resonance (lamps being lit in Ibsen, grime being washed off faces in D.H. Lawrence, fireworks going off in Tennessee Williams). In these plays psychology is always made concrete, emotion is particular and human beings are defined by the material world in which they live. The art of directing them is to attend to the naturalism of the writing with detail and care, but also with the aim of releasing its innate poetry. This consists of much more than simply observed reality: it's carefully crafted drama, whose intricate surfaces and finely chiselled textures have their own unique beauty.

In some circles 'naturalism' is a dirty word. Many directors today talk about wanting to get 'beyond naturalism', wanting to do away with its fussy surfaces and get down to 'the real thing': emotion, poetry and the subconscious. This forgets that naturalism itself was invented as a way of describing those areas of experience that had been previously neglected: money, sex, class, poverty and so on. Emile Zola's essay *Naturalism in the Theatre* (1881) contained a famous call to arms: 'There is more poetry in the little apartment of a bourgeois than in all the empty, worm-eaten palaces of history.'

In approaching naturalistic drama, you need to remember that the original audiences found the plays immoral and shocking and it's a sad irony that naturalism is now often dismissed because it's seen as 'too comfortable'. But the fact is that after a century of restless theatrical experimentation, naturalism remains the dominant form. Sooner or later you will have to confront its disciplines.

New writing

To many people the whole point of the theatre is to put on plays by living people about the modern world. They argue that however much you try to make classic plays speak to living audiences, it's new writing that has the unmistakable feel of now. Everything else is irrelevant.

Directing new plays is hard. A brand new play comes with no blueprint, no collective memory, no agreement as to its status. This can be enthralling – you're simply directing what you see in front of you – but it requires continual vigilance. At no time can you rely on the reputation of the writing and you need to weigh up its particular strengths and weaknesses and work with them. When you're directing a new play by a first-time writer (and one of the great strengths of the British theatre is its preparedness to stage plays by new young writers) the stakes are even higher.

In preparing for a production of a new play, it's difficult to know how much you should interfere and advise on dramaturgical matters. Even the best playwrights need a critical outside eye, and the director is often the best person to provide that. But you need to be careful: some new plays feel as though they have been written by committee, and they're not the good ones. The writer's instincts are often powerful, and you need to approach them with great care. 'Dramaturgy' and 'workshopping' can be helpful; sometimes they're just ways by which theatres avoid giving a new play a full production.

One of the joys of directing new work is having a writer around whom you can approach and talk to, and ask what he means. But 'managing' a writer in rehearsals is a complex act of diplomacy. Writers are often possessive and you need to convince them that by trusting you they stand the best chance of making their work successfully available to the general public.

One of the hard things is to know just how much the writer actually understands his own play (how much is conscious and how much is accidental?). Sometimes you have to be firm; at other times you should indulge him. Writers can be oblique and complex: when a young actor (Alan Ayckbourn) pressed Harold Pinter on what a particular line meant, he apparently snapped back: 'Mind your own f***ing business.'

Practical problems

Your choice of play is going to be affected by a whole range of practical questions. It astonishes me how often I've had to postpone a production for the most mundane reasons.

Can you get the right actors to do it? Some plays are fearsomely hard to cast. You shouldn't attempt *Romeo and Juliet* if you can't find two remarkable young leads, attractive and classically trained, charismatic and talented. *John Gabriel Borkman* is impossible without two great leading actresses in their sixties. Don't try Sean O'Casey if you can't get the Irish actors. There's little point directing *Hamlet* if you haven't got an exciting young actor in the title role. These problems don't get any easier: the higher your casting standards, the harder it is to meet them.

Is the theatre an appropriate kind of venue? Context is everything. A new play by an unknown author, which requires tremendous intimacy (it deals with the sex lives of fashionable young people living in Hoxton) isn't an ideal choice for an eight-hundred-seat theatre in middle England; *King Lear* is too big for a village hall; a revival of Kleist's *The Prince of Homburg* is a bad idea in a small seaside repertory theatre. The same kinds of questions apply if you're programming for the National Theatre.

Can you or your management afford to do it? Some plays are particularly expensive, above all because of the size of their casts, and thus beyond the scope of the company's finances. Many great writers, particularly of the nineteenth and early twentieth century, are routinely sidelined for this reason: magnificent plays by Harley Granville Barker, Maxim Gorky, John Galsworthy, Arthur Wing Pinero and Eduardo De Filippo have all suffered this fate. The first question an artistic director will often ask of a project he is considering is: 'How many people are in it?'

Can it find an audience? This is always difficult to predict, but most managers will shy away from plays which they're convinced will empty their theatres. Even a revival of a sure-fire hit like *Hay Fever* can fail if the audience has seen three plays by Noël Coward already that year.

It's important that you develop an understanding of these practical limitations, particularly when you're trying to persuade managements that they should take you on.

Translation

In recent years the British theatre has become much more international in outlook, both in the classical repertoire and with contemporary writers. Some people feel that native work is being ignored as a result, but there's no doubt that this new internationalism has opened up theatrical horizons. It has also placed translators much closer to the centre.

A translator of drama faces the twin demands of producing a text that's faithful to the original, but can be spoken with confidence and credibility. Directing a good play in a bad translation (particularly if you don't speak the original language) is a horrible feeling, like skating on cracking ice. But a good translation is a joy.

The sad fact is that many of the standard translations of the great dramatists are not good enough – certainly Molière, Chekhov, Ibsen, Strindberg, Brecht and Lorca have all benefited in recent years from new translators bringing a welcome freshness to the plays, without sacrificing accuracy. The important thing is to investigate the range of translations available, and not simply choose the most readily available one.

There's a fairly recent phenomenon of what I call 'transversions', where a writer who doesn't speak the original language produces a text which should more accurately be described as 'loosely adapted by the translator from an idea by the original writer'. Of course, these can be very stimulating, and it's perhaps unfair to say that they're travesties of the dramatist's original intentions. But they do need to be recognised for what they are: borrowings from a great mind, dressed up in an intriguing way, but at a certain distance from the original.

When working on a play in translation I sometimes find it valuable to look at the original language, even if I don't understand it. When preparing *A Doll's House*, I used to read lines in Norwegian (which I don't speak) over the phone to Kenneth McLeish, trying to get him to follow Ibsen's particular rhythms in his translation. When I'm directing a play written in a language I speak, I set the original beside the translation – not simply to check on the accuracy of the translation but to get a better feel for the flavour of the original.

If you can read a foreign language well, there's value in positioning yourself as the young director who has read all the new plays in that language. Artistic directors are busy people who will be grateful to you for telling them about plays in foreign languages. With any luck, they'll let you do one. It's certainly a way of making yourself useful.

Performing rights

Any play written by a living playwright, or one who died less than seventy years ago, is the intellectual property of the writer or his estate, and is still in copyright, so a licence must be obtained to perform it. Translations are subject to the same restrictions. This is a serious matter and you shouldn't ignore it.

If you're interested in staging a play in copyright, not just professionally but also with amateurs, you need to secure the performing rights as early as possible. Most writers whose work is in copyright are represented by literary agents (whose names are usually on the reverse of the title page of the published edition, or on the front of the manuscript), and they will insist on receiving an application in writing. It's striking, particularly with professional productions (and amateur productions of recent plays), how often permission is denied. There are many possible reasons for this, but the most common is that a theatre management has bought an 'option' on the play, and has blocked anybody else doing it.

Some literary estates are tricky to deal with and, if it's a foreign play, will insist on you using a particular translation. Others may demand casting approval. Professional rights are usually granted on an exclusive basis, whereas amateur rights are non-exclusive, although you should check if another amateur production is being performed in the area at the time.

When rights are available, the agent will issue you with a licence, the basis for a contract with the writer or his agent, which will specify royalties, billing, fee schedules, exclusions and so on. It's sometimes possible to plead poverty, and the best literary agents will take into account the scale of the production and the resources available.

6

Preparation

The more plays I direct, the more I value preparation.

It's impossible to know everything about the play, the writer and his world before you start, but it's essential to find out the fundamentals. Even the most experienced theatre director finds himself under enormous pressure in rehearsals, and good actors have an uncanny ability to ask the most difficult questions at the most awkward time. A talent for busking is essential, but nothing can replace the knowledge and understanding that can be gained by thorough preparation.

Historical context

It's self-evident that plays don't emerge out of thin air and that they carry, at the very least, traces of their origins. They're the product of a particular author living in a specific place and time, and a good director needs to gain some understanding of those particular circumstances.

I try to read as much history as possible. My sense of sixteenth-century England as a land in turmoil, with powerful contradictory forces fighting each other to shape the future, derives from books by Christopher Hill, Keith Thomas and R.H. Tawney, and has underpinned all my work on Shakespeare. Orlando Figes's *A People's Tragedy*, with its vivid account of the 1905 Russian Revolution, illuminated for me the forces at work behind Chekhov's *The Cherry Orchard*. Trying to stage one of Sean O'Casey's Dublin plays without a good grasp of the Irish wars of independence would be foolish in the extreme. When I was about to direct John Osborne's *Look Back in Anger*, I found it useful to talk to people who had seen the original 1956 production. My father was one of them, and he described how, with his provincial, lower-middle-class background, and his own kind of rage, he could connect directly with Jimmy Porter's tirades. Were I to direct Caryl Churchill's *Top Girls* I would soak myself in the newspapers and novels of the late 1970s and early 1980s to refresh my memory and gain some clear, and imaginatively felt, sense of the impact of Mrs Thatcher's election on feminism and the left.

You don't need to become a historian, but you do need to understand something of the historical forces that have shaped the play.

Cultural context

But research means more than merely historical context, and you should immerse yourself in the culture of the period, the music, the poetry, the paintings and the novels.

Three things helped me understand Shakespeare's *Love's Labour's Lost.* The first was looking at those extraordinarily intricate Elizabethan woodcut patterns: here was a visual equivalent of Shakespeare's highly structured, exquisitely formal, early play. The second was re-reading Shakespeare's *Sonnets*: the play, which was written for a private audience, has all the complex and dextrous wordplay of Shakespeare's non-dramatic poetry. Berowne and his friends are aristocratic sonneteers, and only a re-reading of the *Sonnets* could give me a sense of what they were up to. The third was listening to Morley and Dowland's madrigals, which provided a perfect musical equivalent.

In approaching Chekhov, Orlando Figes's *Natasha's Dance* provided me with an essential introduction to late nineteenth-century Russian culture. John Willett's *The New Sobriety* introduced me to the cultural background to Brecht's pre-war plays: from the spindly drawings and watercolours of George Grosz to the satirical montages of John Heartfield, the cool designs of the Bauhaus, and the elegant, self-conscious decorativeness of oriental art. In the late twentieth century the paintings of Mark Rothko and Jackson Pollock provided key cultural indicators to the world of Edward Albee's *Who's Afraid of Virginia Woolf?*

Knowing the writer

You need to become as familiar as possible with the writer's other work and gain some sense of how the play you're directing fits into the rest of his oeuvre.

Reading Shakespeare's first history cycle – *Henry VI Parts One, Two* and *Three* – showed me how much more dramatic the later *Henry IV* is; it also revealed the dramatic techniques Shakespeare had mastered between the two. Understanding the pattern of 'rival brothers' that runs through Shakespeare's comedies helped me grasp the strange relationship between Edmund and Edgar in *King Lear.* And reading *Cymbeline* and *The Tempest* let me see *The Winter's Tale* as one of a group of plays concerned with social revival and rebirth, as much as individual redemption.

I read the writer's letters, poems and notebooks too. Kleist's essays and stories helped explain his difficult, beautiful masterpieces. Brecht's *Work Journal* showed me something of his voracious, satirical, provisional approach to playwriting, while his *Poems* helped me see him as a sensual poet trying to write drama in a terrifyingly unpoetic world. Chekhov's short stories and Ibsen's letters provide essential background reading to their plays.

I read as many biographies as I can. Park Honan's life of Shakespeare is probably the best account of this most elusive of literary personalities. Michael Meyer's outstanding biographies of Ibsen and Strindberg are models of the form – scholarly, readable and yielding fresh insights into the plays. Donald Rayfield's *Chekhov* gave me a fresh picture of one of my favourite authors – sexual, saturnine and modern – to be set against my previous image of him as dry, cool and fey. Richard Ellmann's *Oscar Wilde* is one of the greatest biographies to have appeared in the last fifty years. Philip Hoare's biography of Noël Coward is valuable. The two volumes of John Osborne's autobiography give an essential background to his plays. All of these insights into the writer's life help you sense something of his intentions.

The aim is more than mere literary criticism. In rehearsals you're expected to be the person who knows everything about the writer, his life and his world, and good actors will ask you hard questions. If you've read widely and thought deeply, your work is likely to have authority, style and depth. If not, you may find yourself in trouble.

Theatrical form

One of the important things to remember is that different periods in world drama used different theatrical forms.

If you're directing Shakespeare you should try to understand something of the conditions of the original performances. This was a highly dynamic theatre, with a confident and openly acknowledged relationship with its public. Contemporary accounts are revealing in many ways, particularly in how short the performances were. Like any outdoor event they required continuous activity in order to keep their audience's attention. The actors spoke quickly ('trippingly on the tongue'), and the performances were uninterrupted by elaborate scene changes. They were spectacular (the costumes and a handful of significant props were highly impressive) but without the elaborate scenery which characterises most modern productions. All of this has radical implications for how you might think about presenting Shakespeare's plays today.

Or consider the theatrical form of Restoration drama: tiny auditoriums, rudimentary scenery, candlelight everywhere, illicit trysts in darkened boxes, actors wearing the same clothes as the audience, speaking its language, communicating intimately, rich with social comment and sexual innuendo: ripe, witty and breathtaking. Trying to recreate such an atmosphere today is impossible, but an understanding of these conditions will help you understand how Restoration drama works.

The plays of the naturalistic revolution are something different again. Strindberg's 'Preface' to *Miss Julie*, with its calls for a realistic set, three-dimensional staging, minimal make-up, and the illusion of a fourth wall, is one of the most important manifestos for naturalism, even if other writers – above all Chekhov, Ibsen, Sean O'Casey, Harley Granville Barker, and D.H. Lawrence – wrote more remarkable naturalistic plays. Naturalism was a revolution in content as much as form: the naturalists said that art could and should reflect all aspects of the world, however grubby or depressing. In directing naturalism today it's important to realise that plays set in drawing rooms were not intended to be polite and un-challenging, but quite the opposite.

Twentieth-century drama has seen a constant refinement of naturalism as well as a reaction against its limitations. Brecht's desire to write plays about the complexities of society led him to develop a kind of theatre that challenged the fixity of naturalism. Tennessee Williams, Samuel Beckett, Harold Pinter, Edward Bond and dozens of others all tried to create theatre that took naturalism into a more poetically expressive mode. In preparing for productions by these writers it's essential that you grasp something of their aesthetic intentions.

Reception

It's helpful to discover how the play was received when it was written.

The deposition of an ordained English king in Shakespeare's *Richard II* (1595) must have made an extraordinary impact when first performed. Some claim (although others dispute it) that on the eve of the Earl of Essex's rebellion (1601), Shakespeare's company was asked by Essex's sympathisers to revive the play. Queen Elizabeth herself saw the parallel between Richard and her own situation: 'I am Richard II, know ye not that?' she is supposed to have said to one of her courtiers. In other words, the play crackled with contemporary political resonance.

If you direct Ibsen's *A Doll's House*, you should be aware of the enormous scandal that the play created. The idea that a wife could leave her husband, who had been nothing but kind and loving to her, who gave her every material thing she required, who looked after her and loved her, was quite astonishing to a late-nineteenth-century audience. The play led Strindberg to declare (in an otherwise grudging letter) that thanks to *A Doll's House*,

> Marriage was revealed as being a far from divine institution, people stopped regarding it as an automatic provider of

absolute bliss, and divorce between incompatible parties
came at last to be accepted as conceivably justifiable.

An understanding of this will help you direct the actress
playing Nora, because you can tell her what it used to mean.

Of course, it's impossible to recreate these conditions
now. The world has changed, and audiences interpret old
stories in new ways. But a sense of the radical energy of the
play when it first emerged will let you glimpse its original
colours.

Performance history

When you're directing a classic, it's often a good idea to find
out something about its performance history: not just the
conditions of its original production, but the way that it has
been interpreted and presented over the centuries.

You can get a sense of this through books about the
history of the theatre, production notebooks, collections of
reviews, the Internet and – perhaps most importantly –
anecdote and gossip. Thus I was intrigued to discover that
when Peggy Ashcroft played Cordelia she wore armour for
her return to England. This showed me just how courageous
and determined Cordelia is, and helped me direct Rachel
Pickup (who didn't wear armour) in Acts Four and Five. In
directing *The Cherry Orchard*, my own experience of dozens
of productions – particularly Peter Gill's and Peter Stein's –
helped me formulate my own approach: borrowing what
seemed right, rejecting what didn't. There are various books
which help you to gain insight into the way that experienced
performers have approached these difficult plays. This kind
of research allows you to work out your own view, fully
aware of the accumulation of insights and questions that
have grown over time.

But there's a danger here: too much awareness of production history can prevent you from responding to the play
in a way that is unclouded by received opinion. My advice is
to read everything you can about the production history, but
make sure that you put it to one side, long before rehearsals
begin. There's nothing more decadent in the theatre than the

tired discussion about 'How are we going to do *As You Like It* this time?' It's an obsession for critics and directors, but of little interest to audiences coming to see the play for the first time.

Site visits

When preparing *A Doll's House* I went to Oslo at Christmas (which is when the play is set). I was struck that in Norway in midwinter the sun rises at ten in the morning and sets at three. This helped me understand many things about the play: the oil lamps inside, the cold outside, the falling snow and the cosy, claustrophobic, over-heated interior. All of these informed my production. It also helped me see Ibsen's Norway as frontier territory; a place where you were judged not by your background but by your deeds; where a true life is celebrated, but a compromised one impossible. I said on the first day of rehearsals that it was useful to see it as being more like nineteenth-century Vancouver than Victorian London. A few days in modern Oslo had given me the keys to Ibsen, which I've used ever since.

When preparing a production of both parts of Shakespeare's *Henry IV*, I went to the battlefield at Shrewsbury. There isn't much to see. But a sense of the Welsh mountains over to the West, the Midlands and London stretching off to the South, and Cheshire, Staffordshire and Yorkshire to the East gave me a deeper understanding of the battle that takes place in *Part One*. The heart of England is being fought for, against an alliance of the Welsh, the Scots and the North, and a visit to this blustery, desolate, beautiful place gave me curious insights into the plays' uniquely English violence.

Site visits can be overdone, and I'm suspicious of them being undertaken for spurious reasons: going to Egypt to prepare *Antony and Cleopatra* or – worse – Lithuania for a 'Central European' production of *A Chaste Maid in Cheapside*. It's essential to remember that great dramatists often use location for emblematic, not naturalistic reasons, and too much emphasis on the site can obscure this crucial point. But a visit can give everybody involved a feel for the play's world and atmosphere: its *genius loci*.

Knowing the play

Preparation requires more than exploring the writer and his world: it means getting to know the play inside out and back to front. I wish I had a better memory and could learn the entire text before rehearsals: there are directors who do this, and can prompt a dress rehearsal from the stalls without looking at the script. It gives them remarkable authority, and I envy their skill.

But the director has to do more than know the words of the text. He needs to know the intricacies of its story. And so I often find it useful to write out an outline. I wrote the following summary when I was preparing a production of Chekhov's *The Cherry Orchard*:

> Madame Ranevskaya is coming back from Paris to her estate in the Russian country. Lopakhin, a merchant who has left his peasant roots and is now 'almost' a millionaire, meets her. He informs her that her large cherry orchard will have to be sold, so that she can pay her debts. He urges her to lease out the land and buildings so she doesn't have to lose her childhood home, but she refuses to listen. Lopakhin snaps the property up at an auction, and the cherry orchard is cut down. Ranevskaya returns to Paris, never to see her childhood home again.

This could, and should, be expanded, broken down into Chekhov's four acts, and divided into smaller 'units of action'. The essential thing is to get a clear sense of the core dramatic action and know the fundamentals of what happens. When you've done this, you'll have discovered what needs to be communicated to your audience.

Knowing the characters

You need to read and understand the play from the point of view of its characters, and work out their individual stories. Again, I wrote the following notes for *The Cherry Orchard*. Each point could be expanded, developed and contradicted:

> **Madame Ranevskaya** is convinced she has sins to answer for and that her suffering is deserved. Her husband died, her

lover abandoned her and her son drowned in the river. Now she has a vision of her dead mother dressed in white standing amongst the cherry trees. Her grief is aristocratic and comic; but so also is it human and touching.

Lopakhin is neither a lout nor a revolutionary. He's trying to do his best for Ranevskaya (whom he adores), and is proud of what he has achieved. Lopakhin is frustrated by his class, and for all his money he's still unable to write properly. But the historical process is relentless, and Lopakhin's men start chopping down the orchard even before Ranevskaya has gone.

Trofimov declares that work is the great liberator and that the land-owning class must suffer to expiate the sins of the past. But he's an intellectual and a prude who doesn't understand love. He has a vision of the whole of Russia as a garden and declares that happiness is coming soon, but Chekhov knows it will be as ephemeral as the moon reflected in the river. He looks into the future with confidence, but is in no sense rational. He declares that he's beyond love and insists that Ranevskaya face up to the truth of her life – but he's an innocent who doesn't even have a lover. He insists, ominously, that the ruling class need to atone for their sins in the past, but is merciless in teasing the peasant Lopakhin. His attempt to live without money is both touching and absurd. When he storms out in anger at Ranevskaya, he falls down the stairs. Trofimov is both a visionary and a fool.

Ranevskaya's brother **Gaev** is the perfect foil to her emotional quicksilver. He resorts to grandiloquent and sentimental speeches, which he suddenly breaks off in order to play imaginary billiards. He's a delightful, ineffectual and maddening figure whose optimism and garrulity knows no bounds – right till the end, he's convinced that his aunt in Yaroslavl will come up with the money that will save the estate, but we know that this is unlikely.

Ranevskaya's adopted daughter **Varya** looks after the house. Her love for Lopakhin is never reciprocated. She tries to hold together what can't be held together. Only the prospect of a nunnery offers her any peace. Ranevskaya tries to engineer a last-minute romantic ending but Lopakhin lacks the courage, and Varya is left weeping for her life.

Anya, Ranevskaya's seventeen-year-old daughter, who has been to Paris to fetch her mother, shows all the characteristics of youth. Her epiphanic moment with Trofimov, under the moon, beside a flowing river, is as moving as it's ephemeral. Her conviction that another orchard can be planted is touching but unfounded, as is her announcement that she's going to start a new and better life.

Charlotta, Anya's German governess, masks her loneliness under a cover of aggressive despair. When she pretends to be cradling a baby – which promptly disappears – we see closer into the heart of her misery. When considering what to do at the end she simply says 'Who cares?' The impoverished landowner **Simeonov-Pishchik** can only think about money, and eventually gets a cash windfall. **Yepihodov**, the estate clerk, is nervous and longwinded. He loves the upwardly mobile maid **Dunyasha** and has proposed to her, but is in a state of perpetual anxiety. His awkwardness expresses itself in his melodramatic and idle threat of suicide. But Dunyasha loves Ranevskaya's young servant **Yasha** and lives only for him, even though he breaks her heart. The 87-year-old footman **Firs** has been working in the house for many years. He calls the emancipation of the serfs 'the great disaster'. At the end of the play he's left alone, dying.

This is pure information: action, relationships, and events. The point is to read the play so carefully that all these points are clear in your head before you go into rehearsals. I find that writing them down sometimes helps.

One useful exercise (which actors often do for themselves) is to write down everything said about each character in the play, by the author, by the character himself, and by other characters. This can be added to the more basic information about their job, their age, what they want to achieve, where they are in life and so on. All of this is then duplicated in rehearsal. But the wise director will have done much of the work before starting.

Artistic structure

It's important to understand the artistic structure of the play: Where does the writer do his exposition? How does he integrate that exposition into dramatic life? Where are the play's climaxes? What are the key moments in its narrative development? Where are the points of sympathy and where does the author want the audience to look critically? This grasp of the play, its rhythms and its dynamics, is critical.

Once again let me quote from my production notebook for *The Cherry Orchard*:

> In **Act One** the sun is coming up, but it's only two o'clock in the morning and the cherry blossom is ghostly white in the early morning sun. When the shepherd's pipe is finally heard, everyone has gone to bed. The beauty of the open country-side by sunset in **Act Two** is contrasted with the town in the distance. Everything is put into context by the arrival of the tramp, with his song of the Russian poor: a new world is arriving in the form of an urban proletariat who will confront the landowners, and sweep them all away.

> The ball in **Act Three** brings Ranevskaya's grief and Lopakhin's triumph into the most powerful juxtaposition, heightened by the crescendos of the Jewish band and the dancers. As the house is being closed down in **Act Four**, everyone speaks of a new life, some with confidence, some terror. In the distance you can hear the cherry orchard being cut down, but nobody (except Yasha) drinks the champagne. Money is being made but Firs is locked up inside the empty house. Wherever you look, contradictions abound.

A clear grasp of the play's artistic structure will be your rock when things get difficult.

Preparing your take

When you're working on a classical play it's inevitable that historical change will mean that a modern audience will respond to it in very different ways. And so you need to work out what you're going to bring to directing the play today. You need to 'prepare your take'.

Brecht, for example, used to be considered an outsider, a left-wing refugee from Hitler, whose Marxism placed him beyond the pale. But now – particularly in France and Germany – he is seen as a classic writer, to be performed along-side Sophocles and Shakespeare. Paradoxically, the more he has been assimilated into the cultural mainstream, the more his beliefs – in communism and the inevitable collapse of capitalism – have become discredited. So how can you direct his plays now?

One way is to see them as products of their own time, and find ways to ensure that your audience sees them in the same way. Thus a 'historicised' production of *The Caucasian Chalk Circle* (1943) – which in the first scene presents the Red Army as an unquestionably good thing – would take into account the appalling destructiveness of the Nazi invasion of the Soviet Union of 1941. The director would then try to understand something about Brecht's own political and aesthetic priorities at the time, and would present a perfectly mediated historical artefact, full of energy and life, but relying on the audience's historical knowledge and imagination.

Another way (which would avoid Brecht's political naïveté about the Red Army) would be for the director to declare that the point of the play is simple: the land – like the child – should be looked after by the person best able to do so, not necessarily the owner. And so he would commission a writer to re-conceive the opening scene: set it, for example, in a London school where there's a dispute about who should run it (the parents or the local authority). The main play, a self-conscious fable, could illustrate the point, but the context in which it's set could be rendered less outdated.

Directors are coming under a lot of pressure to have 'a take'. Journalists love such an approach, as do some members of the audience: it gives them something to write and talk about. The great danger is that the dramatic action disappears under intellectual, critical analysis.

Historicism vs. contemporaneity

When you direct a classic you need to make a choice about where and when you set it. This usually comes down to a decision between a modern context and an indication of period.

A few years ago I directed Shakespeare's problematic early play, *The Taming of the Shrew*. I realised that it was driven by two key energies: money and female independence. I found what seemed like an ideal setting: 1990s Essex, where money and status were everything. We were staging it at the time of 'girl power', which provided a perfect model for Kate's teen-age rebellion: it's not Petruchio she dislikes, it's the whole idea of getting married at all. And so it was possible to show that in such a 'material world' – where spoiled teenagers rebel and hard men are after money not love – a powerful relationship could be built up between Petruchio and Kate despite it all. Theirs was a relationship which accepted their differences, while also acknowledging their connection; this was a world ignorant of feminism but alive with sexual energy, where a young girl could be attracted by an older man's outrageousness, but where a deal might be struck. At the end Kate does what Petruchio tells her ('tell these headstrong women / What duty they do owe their lords and husbands') but in return he looks after her, loves her and makes her happy. The setting made this credible.

But I also directed *As You Like It* in the purest Elizabethan style: beautiful period clothes on a glowing glass floor, with a birch forest appearing framed in black in the distance. It was informed by an understanding of Elizabethan rural society and tried to capture a concrete sense of the Elizabethan world. My favourite moment was when Rosalind, dressed as Ganymede, said to Orlando: 'Alas what shall I do with my doublet and hose?' She was able to refer to the clothes she was actually wearing: for once, the audience didn't have to pretend that a dinner suit, or pyjamas ('timeless', apparently) were Elizabethan clothes. She also looked like Hilliard's famous portrait of the young man, which gave me particular pleasure. A historical world was made luminously present.

Neither approach was 'right', but both worked well. Of course, this choice confronts the director of all old plays, and not just Shakespeare. Molière, Congreve, Ibsen, Chekhov and Brecht all pose the same question: how to respect their period, while making them alive to the modern world. It's possible that the very definition of a classic is that it survives all such directorial intervention and somehow – miracul-ously – comes through unscathed. But the important thing is to work out what you're doing, and know why.

Preparing the script

An essential part of preparing your take is preparing the script.

If you're directing a Shakespeare play you need to choose which edition you're going to work from. The best of the mainstream ones are the Oxford, the Arden and the Penguin. There are also specialist ones, such as Nick Hern Books' First Folios or the Cambridge University Press educational editions. Each of these has its different strengths and weaknesses and you need to work out which one feels right for you.

Personally, I dislike the way academic editions of Shakespeare are set out and presented. Apart from anything, I find I often disagree with many of the editorial decisions made, particularly punctuation. We don't know how Shakespeare would have punctuated his plays, and all versions are the sum of their editors' interventions. And so when I directed *King Lear* I downloaded the play from an American college website, took out all the punctuation and stage directions, edited it line by line, made my cuts, chose a font that I liked, and printed out an entirely new edition of the play. We worked from that, and we felt as if we were doing a new play.

Cutting

Many classical plays benefit from skilful cutting, and good cutting can make all the difference. With the passage of time, the way people watch plays has changed, and modern audiences are better at absorbing information 'filmically'. As a result they are much less likely to be able to follow – or want to follow – the kind of literary allusion that some classics are full of.

I've always found cutting difficult: after all, if the play is a 'masterpiece' then surely it should be performed in its entirety. I only realised the error of this when I directed *Love's Labour's Lost* – probably Shakespeare's most scholarly work. Although I'd found a setting for it, which, I felt, released its witty superficiality, as well as its darker purpose, I failed to cut enough. I realise now that if I'd cut more of the obscure verbiage, the audience would have stood a better chance of enjoying the easier passages. It's as if the original diet is too rich and if you don't thin it down a bit, your audiences will reject it altogether. I increasingly feel that clever minor cuts make all the difference: little nips and tucks which allow the meaning to emerge, without affecting the basic pattern or structure of the scene.

Edgar in *King Lear* needs some fairly severe cutting – particularly when he's in disguise as Poor Tom. The following is from my production. The words crossed out were cut:

> Who gives anything to Poor Tom, whom the foul fiend hath led through fire and through flame, through ford and whirl-pool, o'er bog and quagmire; ~~that hath laid knives under his pillow and halters in his pew, set ratsbane by his porridge, made him proud of heart to ride on a bay trotting-horse over four inched bridges, to course his own shadow for a traitor. Bless thy five wits, Tom's a cold! O, do, de, do, de, do de. Bless thee from whirlwinds, star-blasting, and taking.~~ Do Poor Tom some charity, ~~whom the foul fiend vexes. There could I have him now, and there, and there, and there again.~~

Sometimes directors make large and controversial cuts. A production of *Hamlet* at the National Theatre shocked purists by losing all reference to Fortinbras; an *Antony and Cleopatra* cut Pompey's rebellion altogether. Such cutting focuses the audience's attention on the central action, but distorts its overall meaning. At other times, directors decide to perform every word, no matter how incomprehensible. One example was Peter Hall's uncut *Hamlet*, which even included the references to the 'little eyases' – one of the least performed passages in Shakespeare. The intellectual arguments for such an approach are good, but entirely uncut productions of Shakespeare usually only succeed in trying the patience of their audiences.

You need to be careful about how you go about cutting a play, particularly a masterpiece. I've sometimes found that passages that seemed awkward and convoluted in my front room, reveal themselves to be perfect in rehearsal. You also need to be diplomatic with your actors, who may well get defensive about their parts, saying that you're cutting essential material. Sometimes they're right, and you need to take every challenge on its merits. But sometimes they're wrong, and you need to find the strength and articulacy to stick to your guns and explain why everybody would be better off without the lines in question. I usually get my cuts cleared with the leading actors before rehearsals begin – nothing takes as much time in rehearsals as discussing cuts – and present them as a *fait accompli* to the rest of the cast.

Plays in copyright can also benefit from cutting, but you should secure permission from either the author or his agent. Cutting a brand new play is even harder, but is often essential. I just advise you to persuade the writer first.

Rearranging the play

Some directors like to rearrange the play in radical ways: re-ordering scenes, re-allocating speeches, merging two plays into one and so on. The Shakespeare history plays are regularly cannibalised and restructured, to make all kinds of fascinating new dramatic shapes. The Reduced Shakespeare Company present *The Complete Works of William Shakespeare* in an hour. The Wooster Group from New York often devise work based on famous classics: *Brace Up!*, a piece loosely based on *Three Sisters*, hardly used Chekhov's play at all. I once directed a production of *Macbeth* in Germany with just three actors: the play was cut to the bone but we added commentary (both spoken and visual) and presented our audience with a dynamic deconstruction.

Such interventions can be valuable: they blow the dust off over-familiar masterpieces and allow audiences to see them in new and radical ways. But they need to be approached intelligently: the writers of these masterpieces knew what they were doing, and if your approach lacks intellectual or artistic integrity, you'll be selling them short.

7

Casting

The experienced director knows that casting is all-important, and that a production without the right actors in the right parts is bound to fail. Casting is sometimes spoken of as being 75 per cent of the director's job, and certainly if you don't understand just how important casting is, your work is bound to fail. But it's difficult to define what makes for good casting, and it is one of the things that young directors find most challenging.

What is casting?

At its simplest, casting is about finding the right actor to play the part. There are various criteria.

First, the actor must be the right age. Ibsen's *John Gabriel Borkman* includes a fifteen-year-old character – Frida Foldal – and to cast her properly you need a really young actress. Similarly, Ibsen specifies that Hedda Gabler is meant to be twenty-nine and the story best makes sense when an actress of the right age plays the part. One of the most stirring moments in *King Lear* is the meeting of the mad king and the blinded Gloucester on Dover Cliff: when both actors really are quite old, the scene carries the strongest charge. And whoever you get to play Ranevskaya's old loyal servant Firs in *The Cherry Orchard* should be as old as possible: that's the only way to make the part moving.

Second, the actor should be the right class. Of course, actors pretend to be something other than they are, and casting strictly by class would mean that the only people who could play Shakespeare's kings and queens would be royalty. But it's certainly true that a performance by an actor cast out of his class can be excruciating. Middle-class actors slumming it in working-class drama can seem deeply offensive, just as working-class actors playing aristocracy can seem false.

Third, the actor must look right. Falstaff has to look fat or the audience won't accept his single-minded devotion to 'sack' and laziness. A cadaverous forty-year-old might be perfect casting for Angelo in *Measure for Measure*, but won't raise a laugh as Falstaff when Hal asks him when he last saw his 'toe'. There's a line in *As You Like It* where Rosalind says that she's 'uncommon tall', and the part seems to work best when you have a strong, tall, almost masculine young woman playing the part.

And finally the actor must have the right 'feel' – or 'quality' – for the part. An actor playing Hamlet who isn't intellectually and emotionally 'quicksilver' will be unable to catch the extraordinary speed and pure consciousness of the part; an Othello who doesn't have a powerful sense of poetic majesty can't produce the 'Othello music.' An actor who too readily suggests a psychopath will be miscast as Nora's husband, the complacent bank manager Torvald, in *A Doll's House*.

Good and bad acting

In considering an actor for a part the other important question is 'Can he act?'

But what is good acting and how do you recognise it? It's easier to say what *bad* acting is. The audience can see the bad actor remembering his next line. When he speaks, his voice has little connection with his emotions. His body has a kind of physical self-consciousness (often called 'woodenness') that he can never cast off. His actions are either sluggish (and the audience is one step ahead of his thoughts), or else he rushes through the part so fast that his performance is little more than a feat of memory. There is a fair amount of bad acting in the British theatre, and you need to understand what its characteristic failings are.

The good actor, by contrast, has a relaxation at his core, is direct and immediate. He has an easy access to his emotions and knows how to share them with this audience. His thought processes are clear, and the audience can follow them. He immerses himself in the part he's playing, but he also enjoys being watched. He acts with a kind of playful confidence and energy that is infectious. The audience relaxes, because they know that the actor is in control.

Making judgments about acting is one of the most important skills you can acquire, if you are to help the actor perform with precision, grace and feeling.

The best actor or right for the part?

In your determination to cast a good actor, there are times when you find yourself tempted to gloss over the fact that he may be wrong for the part. This is understandable, and indeed an ideally cast actor who lacks talent is going to give you a poor performance. But the difficult thing to learn (which I had to learn the hard way) is that you can't make a badly cast actor well cast, however talented he is. There's a dangerous kind of vanity, in which the director casts an actor who isn't up to the part ('undercasts'), or even completely wrong, because he is full of confidence in his own ability to make the actor right. It's a fatal mistake.

Good casting means getting good actors who are right for the part: it's that simple, and anything else is to be avoided.

Casting friends or proper casting?

Perhaps the most searching question the young director should ask himself is this: 'Is the actor right for the part or is he right for me?' The right answer is both: putting on a play is a collaborative exercise, and the director must find people with whom he can work in a fruitful, collaborative way, where creativity, energy, pleasure and even uncertainty all have their place.

There is an understandable tendency among young directors to cast actors whom they know, and who they're confident won't challenge their authority. But one of the most important things a young director can do is overcome his fear of experienced actors. Productions full of friends from university usually fail, not because of the director's lack of skill, but because the actors lack flavour and experience. It's a difficult lesson to learn, but the world is full of extraordinary actors you don't yet know, and the small group you studied with is unlikely to contain the right actor for the part.

There's such a thing as 'professional casting', and young directors need to embrace it.

Integrated casting

Many subsidised theatre companies are trying to make their casting reflect the increasing diversity of contemporary Britain.

There are various different approaches to this issue. The first and most widespread is what could be called 'colour-blind universalism'. This argues that great drama reveals our common humanity, and proposes an approach to casting that rejects any awareness of race or ethnicity. Peter Brook has led the way with his International Centre of Theatre Research (CIRT) in Paris. One of its characteristics is that by working with actors from all over the world, Brook draws on their individual cultures and creates a complex and diverse theatrical style. Perhaps the finest example of this was his breathtaking staging of the Indian epic *The Mahabharata* (1987).

This kind of work can be revealing, but it raises issues in naturalistic theatre, where some argue race should strictly speaking be as significant a factor as age, class, look or personal qualities. It's striking how rarely Black and Asian actors appear in productions of Chekhov, Ibsen, Oscar Wilde, Noël Coward or Tennessee Williams, and when they do it's to make a particular point. Two recent examples might be Josette Simon playing Ellida Wangel in Ibsen's *The Lady of the Sea* at West Yorkshire Playhouse (1996) and Chiwetel Eijofor in Coward's *The Vortex* at the Donmar Warehouse (2002). It may be just a matter of time, but 'colour-blind' productions of nineteenth- and twentieth-century plays are a rarity.

Some argue that the way forward is to relocate the original play to another culture altogether. See, for example, Mustapha Matura's *Playboy of the West Indies*, a rewrite of Synge's masterpiece, or Tanika Gupta's adaptation of *Hobson's Choice*. Others use cultural difference to illuminate the play: in *Romeo and Juliet* the Capulets and the Montagues have often been played by distinct racial groups. A third approach is to produce classic 'white plays' with complete Black or Asian casts. There's a growing number of fine Black and Asian actors, hungry for serious work and dedicated to quality, and such casting is entirely possible.

Of course, the criteria for casting change according to the style of the play. Naturalistic work needs verisimilitude in looks and sound, while abstract work permits freer decisions. Some Shakespeare plays require a higher degree of social and political realism than others. But be careful: the fairies and spirits of *A Midsummer Night's Dream* and *The Tempest* may seem to inhabit almost entirely imaginary worlds where naturalistic casting criteria are irrelevant, but Puck, Peaseblossom and the rest can be played as courtiers to Titania's Queen Elizabeth, and Prospero's island can be seen as the classic setting for the dramatisation of early European colonialism. On the other hand, a play about the English middle class between the wars – Ben Travers's *Rookery Nook*, say – might seem eccentric if cast multi-culturally.

Young directors need to think through their own responses to these genuinely complex issues, and let neither lazy conventionalism nor the strictures of political correctness make their decisions for them.

Knowing actors

Actors are the director's raw materials, and it's impossible to cast a play if you don't know a large number of them.

The best way to find out about actors is to go to the theatre as often as possible: two or three times a week if need be. Young directors often say they can't afford to go but you can usually get cheap tickets if you try. Or why not join the interval crowd and sneak into the second half as I used to? But it's also important to watch television drama.

It's a good idea to build up your own database of actors. Keep a record of every actor you see in a play, or meet for a part, or notice on television, with a little comment next to his name, describing his essential qualities. Although I stopped doing this properly a few years ago, I've got two or three thick notebooks full of such lists, which I still refer to. You should also have a complete set of *Spotlight* at home, and it's a good idea to save old theatre programmes. And then, when you've got an evening at home and are watching TV, you should have a copy of *Radio Times* to hand with its cast lists. Slowly you can work out which actors you like, why they're good and whether or not they have been well cast.

Of course, hundreds of new actors emerge every year and keeping up to date is almost impossible. Luckily, there are people around who know more actors than you do (a director I know has an encyclopedic knowledge, and I often ring him for advice). The most important of these are casting directors. But if you don't invest time and energy getting to know actors yourself, you'll find yourself in trouble.

Casting directors

Most experienced professional directors work with casting directors. Their names and numbers are listed in *Contacts* or are available from the Casting Directors' Guild, and a quick phone call will ascertain if they're available and interested. Many casting directors give informal advice for free, but charge for their full services. How much they charge varies considerably. But remember that most of them earn their living through casting films and television, and only do theatre because they think it matters.

But what *is* a casting director, and what does she (nearly all of them are women) do? The essential thing is that however many actors you know, the casting director knows dozens more. The good ones go to the theatre three or four times a week, attend drama school showings, watch the television, and develop an extraordinary memory for names and faces. They are genuinely interested in actors, and get on well with them. In employing a casting director, it's their in-depth knowledge of actors – and familiarity with their agents – which you're paying for.

The first thing to do is to give the casting director a copy of the play to read. When she's read it you need to give her as much insight as you can into how you see the characters: age, class, look, quality and so on. When casting *King Lear,* I said to the casting director that the Duke of Albany 'should be aged fifty, with an apparent mildness, but a slow burning rage inside. He should be a bit taller than Goneril and have an air which the audience will sympathise with'.

The casting director may well challenge you on details ('Oh, I hadn't seen him like that: isn't it better if we hate him at first?') and she may be right. She may also want to know how much leeway you'll tolerate ('Does Frida Foldal [in *John Gabriel Borkman*] really have to be fifteen, or could we get away with a nineteen-year-old?'). The critical thing is to develop a free and easy dialogue.

The casting director will then draw up a list, usually by going through *Spotlight,* sometimes by referring to her own lists, and will come up with as many as a hundred names for a single part. Together, you look through this list and share your feelings. You might have worked with a couple of the actors (one was a 'terrific colleague', the other a 'nightmare'); you might have seen one of them act badly in a play the other night ('Was that just because he was badly directed, or is he always awful?'). A few of them may be wrong ('too old', 'too young', 'too quiet', 'too loud', 'too posh', 'too working-class'). You might not know some of them, and you need to take advice. Step by step, the list is whittled down.

Once the list consists only of actors whom you could imagine playing the part, the casting director (or her assistant) phones round their agents to find out if they're free – 'checking their availabilities' as it's usually called. Sometimes the agent will say frostily that the actor is 'technically available': this means that they're free but wouldn't dream of working for you, for the money you're offering and in the theatre you're working in. Other times you'll hear that although the actor is free he can't leave home because of his five-year-old twins. Sometimes, amazingly, they turn out to be both free and interested.

Blind offers

Sometimes the best way to start is to look through your list of 'free and interested' actors, decide on the one you most want, and ring up the agent and put in an offer, out of the blue. I do this more and more, particularly when I'm clear about who I want for the part. Experienced actors are flattered to be offered work without having to come in and meet, and will sometimes accept.

But you need to be careful, for two reasons. The first is that nothing can replace meeting an actor for a part with an open mind as to whether he's right, and it's rare that you can be entirely confident that your choice is appropriate. The second reason – particularly if you're working outside the dozen or so most highly regarded companies – is that meeting an experienced, even famous actor gives you a chance to convince him (subtly, of course) that you know what you're doing and that your production is going to be a hit.

You have to be particularly careful not to offer the same part to two different actors at the same time. It may seem obvious, but directors sometimes presume that their first offer has been turned down, before they get the final answer from the actor's agent; if they've moved on and offered the part to someone else, the embarrassment can be excruciating.

Auditions and meetings

People sometimes imagine that directors hold auditions sitting in a darkened auditorium, idly contemplating the usefulness of these specimens of humanity who display themselves on stage in front of them. They say things like 'Have you got anything modern?' or 'What about a bit of Shakespeare?' and shout out 'Next!' when they get bored.

In the professional theatre at least, this way of operating has almost completely vanished (although not in the world of opera and musicals). Initial meetings between actors and directors tend to be informal affairs, replete with mugs of tea, chats about the weather and gossip about what the actor has just been in – all very much on first-name terms. They sometimes seem not like job interviews at all. But of course they are, and the director and casting director are making crucial decisions that will affect the production fundamentally. They have their own intricate and sophisticated codes.

In casting a play you're not simply choosing colours from a palette. You're considering employing a human being and are making decisions that will affect his livelihood and his career. So I think it's essential that at meetings and auditions you treat actors with the utmost respect. If you've kept them waiting, apologise; if there's been confusion about what they're meant to have prepared, find out why. Actors' terror of auditions and meetings cannot be overestimated; you should do all you can to make them more comfortable.

It sometimes amazes me how little the actors' agents tell them about the job. And so the first thing you should do is say something about it ('It's an eight-week tour of *The Importance of Being Earnest*, going to Brighton, Cambridge, Richmond, Wolverhampton and Istanbul, among others. We pay a company wage and I'm seeing you for Canon Chasuble'). And you need to talk a little bit about how you see the play, why you want to do it and so on. If the actor's going to give his best, he needs to get intrigued by the project. It's in your interest to encourage that.

And then it's important – more, *essential* – to get young actors to read. Some actors find reading aloud difficult, and it's just as well to have asked the agent to warn them. I make sympathetic noises about dyslexia and say that 'this isn't a test of reading'. Sometimes, an actor will have prepared a bit of the script, and will want to read from that; at other times you need to tell him what to read. Usually, you have to read the other parts, regardless of gender, age or dialect. Once you've read a scene through, you should work with the actor a bit: 'Fine, that's good, but do you see, this character is absolutely passionate in his analysis of the world – what you're playing is too cerebral.' Or: 'Good, but don't you see just how well educated this young woman is? A Shakespearean heroine in the comedies is usually the most intelligent person on the stage, and you're making her too whimsical, too sweet.' If the actor can respond to this, you'll not just sense his native talent and appropriateness for the part, you'll also see how flexible he is, how technically and mentally agile, and how well you'll be able to work with him in rehearsal.

Middle-ranking, middle-aged actors need to be handled more carefully. You can sometimes ask them to read, but you should broach the subject with care. The established actor will assume – not unfairly – that you've seen him act before and the clever thing is to make that clear to him, and refer to his 'performance in *x*'. If I don't know the actor, I ask the casting director to brief me beforehand, and I might even pretend to have seen him when I haven't. The important thing is to talk about the play and the part in some detail, get some sense of how he sees them and work out what his approach might be. Often, an experienced actor will feel sceptical about working with young directors, and you need to gauge – without asking directly – what he thinks about the prospect.

Most senior (and by that I mean elderly) actors would be surprised to be asked to read. If anything, *you* should be trying to persuade *them* to do the part, not the other way round. They're nearly always worth it: courteous and professional, experienced and open-minded – just so long as you show appropriate respect for them and the play. If they've been acting for thirty years, before you were born, it's only fair that they might expect you to know something about them. If you don't, it might be time to do your homework.

Casting stars

There's no way round it: stars need to be taken out to lunch. The better the lunch the more likely they are to be interested. The management should pay for this, and see it as a necessary investment. If they don't, it might be worth picking up the tab yourself.

Over the brandies you need to explain how you want to direct the play, and present a convincing argument why the star should be in it. You need to remember that it's the star who has the power, and he knows he's being approached for his commercial appeal as much as his acting ability; he's interviewing you as much as you're interviewing him. Sometimes it works, and sometimes the investment doesn't pay off. But lunching the stars is an essential thing to do, however expensive, however frustrating. Sometimes it's fun too.

Sometimes lunch isn't enough. A powerful London agent once insisted that I went to see *him* in his smart office and grilled me about my plans for a play I was hoping to tour with his client, a rising young star. He wanted to know how I was going to set it, what my interpretation of the character was, who else was going to be in it, was the tour short enough, and 'was it going to come into London?' All these hoops had to be jumped through. The result was that Alan Cumming played Hamlet and made a brilliant success of it, both on tour and at the Donmar Warehouse in London.

Occasionally I take a star out to lunch and ask him what parts he dreams of playing. I then see if I can build a production around his ideas. Of course, sometimes he will want to act in a play you have no interest in directing (a leading actress once told me she wanted to do Bernard Shaw's *Captain Brassbound's Conversion*, which I went away and read, and could find no value in at all). But often a star will want to 'have a go' at a great part in a great play and if it's right for you, you should jump at the chance. Occasionally, he will have no idea and you should suggest one.

Some stars will insist on 'casting approval' – in other words their right to veto other casting. In some circles this is regarded as *prima donna* behaviour, or at least very old-fashioned, but I've increasingly come to understand that a leading actor must be made to feel secure in the actors he's playing opposite. I don't usually offer formal casting approval, but will often tell the agent that I want to 'work with' the star on the casting of the other parts, particularly the characters he's going to play opposite. Such an offer is usually seized on in theory, but evaporates once the star's commitments make it impossible to attend the meetings. But it shows the right attitude.

Ensembles

Every now and again the idea of the 'ensemble' is reinvented: a group of actors working together on a number of plays, taking it in turns to share the leading roles. This often happens in student and amateur drama and can be valuable. In the professional theatre it can be positive too: actors who know each other work better together, and the sense of a group of equals acting together can be infectious. Audiences love it: they enjoy getting to know the actors and their individual strengths and weaknesses, and respond warmly to seeing them again and again, playing three or four different parts in a season.

But ensembles have their problems. For a start, long contracts and playing a range of parts can deter leading actors, who are used to squeezing the odd lead theatre role between much better-paid parts in film and television. Then, being with the same small group of people, however excellent they may be, can lead to boredom and frustration. Most seriously, a small ensemble in a second-rate company can have disastrous consequences on the actual casting: you end up having a 25-year-old playing the 87-year-old Firs in *The Cherry Orchard* – I don't joke, it happened.

Artistic directors will point to the Berliner Ensemble of the 1950s (or the RSC in the 1960s) and say, 'Look, ensembles are fantastic,' and critics will agree. What they forget, of course, is that not only was the Berliner Ensemble enormous, it was centred round a handful of stars (Helene Weigel, Ernst Busch, Ekkehard Schall and one or two others), who played *all* the leading parts. And nowadays large ensemble companies such as the Vienna Burgtheater employ senior actors who play only four performances a year. They're on an annual salary and can't be sacked, and have very little commitment to the ensemble.

The British theatre can benefit from the ideal of the ensemble, but setting up permanent companies isn't a universal panacea for the problems of the theatre in general, and of casting in particular.

Recalls and offers

There finally comes a moment when you have to make up your mind: who are you going to offer the part to? I usually want to see a few actors again, and will ask them to read some more. (Actors say that this is much more nerve-racking than the first interview.) These 'recalls' can tell you an enormous amount – your first impression is now filtered, you can look with different eyes, and may have gained a greater insight into the part by meeting other actors for it and so on. And if after the recall you still don't know if someone is right, call them back a third time (though this is easier with young actors than older ones). Be obsessive: you need to be.

If I'm directing a play with a major leading actor, I sometimes ask him to come in and read a scene or two with the actors I've recalled. This needs to be handled with care, but can be valuable. It allows you to get a clearer sense of how they'll work together, and gives the leading actor the chance to contribute to the casting process. Apart from anything else, if you discover in rehearsals that you've made a terrible mistake, at least the responsibility is shared.

I try to gauge the opinion of as many different people as possible. Since the casting director will have brought the actor in because she thinks he may be right, she's always my first point of contact. I might say: 'x was a bit young for the part', or 'y struck me as being too affable to play the psychopath', or 'z is raw talent but I don't think she's got the skill with the language to play Rosalind just yet.' Good casting directors say: 'You're right, but I saw z in her final show at college and she could handle the language', or 'He *is* too affable, but why don't we think of him for the other part?', or even 'I don't know what you're talking about: x is perfect. For God's sake, man, explain yourself!' The dialogue is essential.

But I also ask other people for their opinion. If the actor has worked with a director I know and respect, I may ring him up. If he's worked in one particular theatre a lot, I may ask the theatre's casting director, or its artistic director, what they think. If the actor has done a lot of work on television I may ask the agent to send me a 'show reel' and watch him on video. Of course, acting in television is very different from the theatre, especially classical theatre, but it allows you to see what kind of presence the actor has, and something of his range.

I find it useful to draw up hypothetical cast lists. I imagine different people in the roles, and try to work out how the story will be affected. Do it in the abstract, and think what happens when you have Antony Sher instead of Timothy West playing King Lear – it becomes a different play, and a different story, requiring different actors in the other parts. When you do this, you realise just how interpretative casting is and how every casting decision has its consequences.

Eventually, though, you have to make up your mind, and you have to do that by yourself because (and this is important to stress) casting directors don't actually make the decisions: the responsibility has to be yours. I've twice overridden the casting director's strong advice – once disastrously, and once entirely appropriately. So take a deep breath, walk around the park, throw the dice, re-read the play and decide. The casting director will then put an offer in to the actor's agent and you have to wait patiently for a reply.

Actors and their agents sometimes take an infuriatingly long time to come back with an answer: sometimes weeks, but always as long as they can get away with. This is occasionally due to inefficiency, but more often it's because they're trying to work out whether something better is going to come their way. An actor who seemed keen in the meeting can suddenly become all jittery the next day. You occasionally have to say: 'Much as we want your client to be in the play, if we don't hear by Friday evening we're going to have to go elsewhere.' Such a guillotine concentrates the mind. But it can also mean that you lose an actor who, with a little more patience, you might have landed.

Timing is complicated: if you approach actors for theatre work too early, they may well not be interested, hoping that a better-paid television or film job will come their way. But if you approach them too late, you may discover that they're not free. As a general rule, late casting tends to be more successful, however nerve-racking it may be.

What to do when you think you can't cast it

One of the scarier moments is when you feel it's impossible to cast the play to any adequate standard. Sometimes this is your fault: you started too late or have been indecisive. And sometimes the casting director has been inefficient or been doing too many other jobs at the same time. But good casting takes a long time, and a run of bad luck (i.e. being turned down several times) can happen. So what do you do?

Occasionally a director will want to abandon a project. This happens in the biggest theatres, usually because no star is available for one of those extraordinarily demanding roles:

Hedda Gabler, Hamlet or Lear. But more often than not, the theatre is committed, money has been found, the production has been publicised and you have to keep going.

The important thing is to hold your nerve. Go back to your original lists, and scour through them for missed ideas. I've twice re-offered a part to someone who turned it down originally and discovered that his situation had changed: he then accepted it. Never imagine that the thirty actors you've seen are the only people in the world who can play the part: 'See another hundred,' as Peter Gill always says. Go back to *Spotlight* and make new lists. Making quick decisions just to get the play cast can be disastrous but 'Friday-night casting' (for a play that starts rehearsal on the Monday) does happen and isn't always bad. Whatever you do, don't despair – worse, don't make a rash decision.

If you're finding casting really hard, you may have to delay starting rehearsals, or start rehearsals without a full cast. When casting *John Gabriel Borkman* I had a run of bad luck and realised on Friday lunchtime that I might have to start rehearsing on Monday without an actor for the important part of Foldal: two hours later, a good actor accepted my offer and the result was tremendous. It's part of National Theatre legend that Peter Gill didn't cast the part of a young boy in Turgenev's *A Month In The Country* (he only had three lines to say) until the dress rehearsal. So don't worry.

The point is that casting is so important that *everything* has to bend to fit round it.

Agents

Theatrical agents are a complex group of people. Despite protestations to the contrary, they're business people who earn their living by taking ten (sometimes fifteen) per cent commission off their clients' wages. They're most interested in getting their actors lucrative work (television and film rather than theatre) and you or your manager will sometimes hit a brick wall in dealing with them. Some agents are awful: rude, inefficient and lazy. Others are brilliant: they realise that actors need to develop their skills, and that the theatre is the best place for them to do so. Try to cultivate good relations with them: they're important to you.

Actors tend to have an emotional dependence on their agents, which isn't always reciprocated. Agents often give their clients bad advice, and can sometimes dent their confidence. Actors always complain about their agents (changing agents is described as 'changing deck chairs on the *Titanic*'), but they need them not simply for their professional services, but for personal validation. The nervousness that actors exhibit when they know their agent is coming to see the show sometimes surprises me. I think an actor's agent should be like his mother: amazed and proud that his darling got through it at all, while hinting that if the production had been better directed he would have been even more remarkable. But even the most experienced actors retain a respect – almost veneration – for the people who take ten per cent of their meagre wages, sometimes for not very much work.

Billing

One of the things the agents will want to talk to you about is 'billing'.

Billing is an old-fashioned idea, but not to be underestimated. In the days when H.M. Tennent were London's leading producers, actors were known as '14- or 18-pointers', referring to the size of type in which their names would appear on publicity. There are various modern versions of this: 'above the title' ('Fred Smith in…'), 'with', or 'starring'. All these, and print size relative to title, are up for negotiation. Actors will often talk about a 'company feel', but it's surprising how often a question about 'billing' comes up and needs to be answered. A major production of a famous modern play didn't transfer to the West End because two of the three actors couldn't settle on who should be on the left-hand side of the poster. The large subsidised theatres don't usually offer billing, and prefer to make distinctions through pay differentials. Others list all the cast alphabetically, but promote the production by using a photograph of its star on the poster and print. The important thing is to be flexible: absolutist positions on billing don't make casting any easier.

Money

Actors working in the subsidised theatre are paid astonishingly badly.

I've often been told by an agent that much as an actor would like to take the part I'd offered him, and much as he 'likes and respects' the way that I work, he simply can't afford to do it. And I understand this. The average theatre wage is less than that for a junior secretary. A married man, with three children and a mortgage, simply can't afford to do the job. Every now and again the press come up with the same old story: some world-famous film star is working in a London theatre for £300 a week – 'How amazing! He must love the theatre!' What the journalists forget is that it's only the stars who can afford this kind of sacrifice. Most actors – even well-established ones – are struggling to earn a living wage.

In the subsidised theatre there's a long-running debate about pay differentials: should everybody be paid the same, or should there be a sliding scale to reflect experience, fame and size of part? The logical answer is simple. Surely the actor playing King Lear (aged 65, at the summit of his career, a famous television name, on stage all evening) should be paid more than the King of France (aged 25, just starting out, nobody's heard of him, on stage for about ten minutes)? But the difficult question is this: how big should the differential be? If King Lear is to be paid his 'commercial rate', half your wages bill will be spent on him. And then what happens to the others: are you expecting them to work for even less? And what have you lost by breaking the 'company wage' in terms of a sense of ensemble, togetherness, and unity of purpose? And, anyway, the leading actor can often afford it because of his voice-over career or repeat fees or latest film role. There's a balance to be struck, and the young director working in the subsidised theatre should support every effort to get actors better paid, while avoiding the kind of divisiveness that large pay differentials can cause.

The important thing is that if actors are to be your creative colleagues, you need to understand and face up to the financial pressures under which they work.

No money

Of course, these contractual problems often won't affect the first-time director, who is likely to be working with actors on a voluntary basis anyway. Casting in such circumstances is far more constrained, although there are many actors who will work for nothing to get exposure. In these conditions, however, you must be sensitive to the actor's need to do other work: you've got to let them go up for auditions and earn money in other ways, and only the most megalomaniac director thinks that he has 'first call' on his actors' time.

At the beginning of your career you'll almost certainly work with actors who are not paid, but you should do everything you can to move into a professional context.

'I love actors'

When I'm interviewing young directors, I sometimes spring on them a trick question: 'Do you just *love* actors?' If the answer is positive, I know that they're speaking from ignorance. Actors can be impossibly difficult people, in all kinds of ways. But a worse answer would be: 'No, I hate them.' The point is that actors are the single most important group of people in the theatre, and it is essential that you discover how to work with them.

8

Design 1: Creative

Design is important. We live in a visual culture, and audiences brought up on film and television expect a feast for their eyes as much as for their ears. The theatre is a visual art form as much as a verbal one, and directors and designers need to work closely together to ensure that everything that appears on stage looks good and is imbued with visual meaning.

Designers

The relationship between you and your designer is central. Apart from the play itself and the leading actor's performance, it's the designer's work that audiences will most remember.

Audiences (and some critics) tend to see the director and the designer as doing almost the same job. And, of course, in good productions the two roles are close. But they're also distinct. Some directors have a limited visual imagination and are dependent on their designer to interpret their understanding of the play in three-dimensional terms. Similarly, many designers find the literary element of the theatre difficult, and struggle to understand the complicated process that actors go through in rehearsal. Whatever their relative strengths, however, it's important that both director and designer understand the distinctiveness of their roles as well as knowing where they overlap.

The relationship works best when there's mutual respect and a shared set of values. Directors are often – sometimes rightly – blamed when this breaks down, and directors sometimes treat designers as people who simply decorate the setting that they've already decided on. But there are also designers who show little respect for the director, and see the production as a blank canvas on which to project their own dreams and fantasies.

The relationship is a delicate thing – sometimes a love affair, sometimes a night of hell – and there are no ways of predicting whether it will work out or not. The point is that you can't direct a play without a designer and you need to find the right one. Not many decisions will be more important to the production's fortunes.

Finding a designer

Finding the right designer is difficult. How do you go about it?

The best way of forming an opinion about a designer is to see his work in the theatre. Then, if you like what he's done, you can ring him up and arrange a meeting, where you look at his portfolio, share your thoughts about design, and strike up a relationship. You can usually get his phone number (or his agent's) from the theatre where you saw his work, or from *The Designers' Register*. Most young designers are on the lookout for work and will want to meet a director who may be able to employ him.

But there are other ways. The designer Alison Chitty and I used to run an annual 'designer dating' day at the National Theatre Studio. We would get together twelve young directors and twelve young designers. In the morning, the designers would lay their portfolios out on tables. The directors would go round, look at their portfolios, talk to them for ten minutes each, and strike up relationships. Then, after lunch, it would be all change, and it was the directors' turn to be interviewed by the designers. We would encourage the designers to ask difficult questions: 'Who's your favourite Quattrocento painter?', 'What does the colour blue mean to you?' and so on. At the end of the day we would hand round a list of everybody's name and contact details. Our aim was to help both groups meet their opposite numbers, in the hope that relationships – even long-term ones – might be struck up. We also wanted to help young designers to see themselves as equal partners with directors, and provoke the directors to see designers as colleagues with their own particular skills and talents.

Many art schools run theatre design courses, which have annual exhibitions open to the public and which you should attend. One of the best is Motley – the stand-alone graduate theatre design course run for many years by the formidable Percy Harris – which usually exhibits at the National Theatre Studio. The Linbury Biennial is a fine initiative that gives a dozen young designers the opportunity to show their work at the National Theatre and be commissioned by a theatre company, and their exhibition is always interesting. There are dozens of others.

Be bold. Meet everyone you can. You've nothing to lose.

Principles in theatre design

There's a stand-up fight raging about theatre design.

On the one side are the 'purists': 'Designers', they argue, 'are swamping the stage with their visual ideas, and leaving no room for the actors to breathe life into the play. Classical texts,' they say, 'are being swamped by superfluous ideas, many of which run contrary to the spirit of the play. Catastrophe looms!' On the other side stand the 'visual' brigade: 'We live in a visual culture,' they argue, 'and powerful imagery is the only way to save a dying art form; the text is often incomprehensible, and people are not interested in "listening" to plays any more.' Both positions are ferociously defended, but in many ways they represent a false opposition.

The theatre is, of necessity, a 'visual experience'; audiences watch with their eyes as much as they listen with their ears. The visual element is as old as the theatre itself. Epidauros, Shakespeare's Globe, Stanislavski's Moscow Art Theatre, the Berliner Ensemble and the Royal Court in the 1960s were all theatres whose work was exquisitely visual: the masks, the costumes, the white cycloramas, the realistic sets. Design is essential, and a director who denies that has failed to understand his chosen art form. It can be breathtakingly simple, or outlandishly complex: there are no rules. But the theatre has to please the eye as much as the ear: it is a visual art form as well as a verbal one.

In working with a designer I feel that certain critical questions should be constantly asked: How does this design serve the play? Does it let it be clear? Does it carry the necessary information? Is it a pleasure to look at? I think the ideal design serves the action of the play with effortless elegance, and provides the essential means for releasing its meanings. Many designers have achieved this: look at Caspar Neher's designs for Brecht, or Jocelyn Herbert's work with Lindsay Anderson, or Alison Chitty's work with Peter Gill. In such relationships the director focuses the designer on the particular demands of the play. In return, the designer provides aesthetic flair and visual verve. When both work closely together the results can be productions of grace and beauty.

A design team

Most designers are responsible for both set and costume design. Some, however, particularly in opera, concentrate on one or the other.

There are advantages in both ways of working (although managements usually prefer having just one designer, because it's cheaper). Most designers have a better feel *either* for set *or* for costume. I like to separate the two so long as both set and costume designers understand and respect each other. The show benefits from a greater degree of individual focus as a result.

Theatre design is a collaborative art form, and a wide range of different disciplines is brought to bear. Designers are visual artists of a very particular kind, whose work only exists in combination with other artists: the playwright, the actors, the lighting designer and you, the director. Furthermore, the final result is the product of an entire team of 'mini-designers': costume makers, props buyers, stage managers, builders, scenic artists, furniture makers, design assistants, model makers, specialist props makers, make-up artists and so on. Experienced designers come to a project with bulging Filofaxes full of contacts, and with specialists in tow. I value this sense of a 'design team', and I always want to find out who they are and what they do. I try to get to know them: they're *my* collaborators too, after all.

Analytical process

So how do you set about working with a designer?

Every director–designer relationship is different. Some designers study the play with an almost scholarly attention to detail and I've been embarrassed in early design meetings to find that my designer has read the play more carefully than I have. Others – including some eminent ones – argue that too much attention paid to the text limits their creativity. In any case, they argue, that analysis is the director's job. Some want to talk for hours about the play and the production. They expect you to work with them in the studio, discussing endless intricacies, even acting as a kind of inept design assistant, cutting up paper, painting pieces of card, punching holes and so on. Others want a quick design meeting, and then disappear off into their studio where they can work undisturbed by the director. Neither is 'right'; you and your designer have to find out which is best for you.

The more productive processes usually start with a careful analysis of the action of the play. I find it useful to sit down with the designer and read the play from beginning to end. When I directed Shakespeare's *Henry IV Parts One* and *Two*, the 'scenographer' Pamela Howard and I went away to a hotel for a weekend and spent three days reading aloud every word, asking ourselves all those questions you hear in the rehearsal room: 'Who are these people?', 'What do they want?', 'What is the condition of their lives?', 'Where does each scene take place? and so on. This analytical work was deliberately pre-visual, and we carefully avoided coming to any design decisions at all. Each designer will have a different way of recording this analysis – some in words, some in pictures, often in a combination of both. Pamela had a huge sketchpad, which she slowly filled with a mixture of doodles, sketches, diagrams and plans. This provided the basis for all our subsequent work.

Such analysis lets you and the designer understand more carefully those few scenic elements that the play absolutely requires. This may be something very ordinary – the door through which Nora leaves in *A Doll's House* – or something much more complex – the offstage presence of an extraordinarily mysterious and beautiful cherry orchard which Madame Ranevskaya looks at longingly through a window.

The same principles apply when you're working on Shakespeare. Peter Brook and Sally Jacobs must have undertaken such an analysis of the practical demands of *Antony and Cleopatra* – extraordinarily fast shifts of locations, from Egypt to Rome and back again in moments – in preparation for their light-footed production of the play. In *As You Like It*, the action needs to move from the cold repression of Duke Frederick's court to the freedom and warmth of the Forest of Arden. Peter Stein solved this brilliantly by staging the first section in the foyer of the theatre. He then ushered the audience into the auditorium where an entire forest world was presented. When I directed the same play, the designer Bunny Christie came up with an underlit floor which could change from steel blue to warm white, with black screens behind which slid open and revealed silver birch trees in the distance.

Design research

Designers often come to an early meeting with a pile of picture books and visual reference material. These will include paintings and photographs from the period, shots of other productions of the play which broke new ground, free and tangentially related sketches and drawings, cuttings from magazines, photographs of modern art installations and so on. It's important to look at this work with an open mind. Much of it may seem irrelevant at first, and some of it will remain irrelevant. But one or two things will jump out and give you and the designer the key to the production's visual language. Apart from anything, looking at such material is a good way of exploring your shared tastes.

Paintings from the period can be very useful. When I went to Oslo in preparation for *A Doll's House* I bought a book about the great Danish painter Vilhelm Hammershøj, which Bunny Christie and I used as the basis for our setting. Here was a direct contemporary of Ibsen's, painting the interiors of middle-class apartments in Copenhagen with lonely women sitting on chairs as the light fades. It struck us as a perfect model for Ibsen's 'symbolic realism', and much more appropriate than the paintings of Edvard Munch, whose expressionist work is so often evoked in productions of Ibsen, but which is much more useful for Strindberg. Similarly, the Russian painter Ilya Repin provides a perfect visual source for Chekhov, just as the paintings of John Singer Sargent capture the elegant society of Oscar Wilde's London. The bleak beauty of Masaccio, with his red angels flying above the desert, inspired my production of Shakespeare's *Henry IV*, and Piero della Francesca's *The Baptism Of Christ* gave me a powerful image for Poor Tom in the wilderness of *King Lear*. In opera, Stanley Spencer's paintings of biblical events taking place in an English village gave Jackie Brooks a visual fix for Benjamin Britten's comic *Albert Herring*, while Goya gave the costume designer, Mark Bouman, a perfect reference for the highly sexual, class-ridden, Catholic world of Mozart's *Don Giovanni*. Of course, paintings can take directors and designers down blind alleys. Productions of classical plays shouldn't be simply animated fine art (*pace* Jonathan Miller) – the live theatre is too messy and impromptu, too dynamic a form to be placed in the highly restrictive frame of the oil painting – but establishing a visual language is often helped by reference to a painter.

Many plays (especially by Shakespeare and the Greeks) don't require realistic rooms; they need abstract, visually exciting, dynamic 'spaces'. And this is where looking at books of photographs of contemporary installations and art galleries is useful: a sheet of glowing frosted glass which kept changing colour gave Bunny Christie and me an idea for *Hamlet*. I once wanted to use a particularly beautiful, tough, industrial rubber flooring for a production of *Macbeth*, but couldn't afford it. After leafing through a glossy catalogue on modern kitchen design, a friend of mine had a set made out of galvanised tin. It's striking just how often such lateral thinking provides the basis for inspirational design.

When plays are set in particular rooms or places, the designer will need to find books which give details of appropriate architecture and decoration. Neil Warmington has a book on Norwegian houses, which we scoured when working on *Ghosts* and *John Gabriel Borkman* ('that stove', 'that window', 'that way of treating the walls'). A book of Elizabethan interiors inspired my production of Verdi's *Falstaff.* A monograph about Chopin's house in Poland inspired Pamela Howard's 'scenography' for *The Cherry Orchard.* And so on.

Books of period photographs can be especially useful. Chloe Obolensky's collection of photographs of Russian country houses is an essential reference for Chekhov. The lost worlds of Clifford Odets' Chicago, D.H. Lawrence's Nottinghamshire coalfields, Tennessee Williams' Deep South, Arthur Miller's New York and Harold Pinter's London can all be recovered from photographs. This kind of material is essential if your production is to have historical verisimilitude and individual visual texture.

Imagination

Once this analysis is done and the reference books are set aside, the freeing of the imagination is the essential next step.

I often write down 'a stream of consciousness' with the designer: things that we would like to see in the production. Such a list for Sam Shepard's *Fool for Love* might read: 'chicken wire, telephone poles, a tatty copy of the Yellow Pages, a child eating corn on the cob, broken old EPs from the fifties, car headlights, a drive-in movie, etc.' Or in preparing a modern dress production of Shakespeare's *Pericles* I might list colours and textures: 'steel, indigo blue, glowing paper lanterns, orange T-shirts.' These are, of course, entirely subjective, but they often bring up some intriguing and beautiful visual images and connections. It's interesting to look back on them months later and see what survived into the production.

With these lists, the designer's scrapbook, the pictures, photographs and references you've assembled, you can together slowly build up a feel for the production. It's sometimes important for the director to provide a few aesthetic principles at the outset: 'It must be nineteenth-century naturalism', or 'It needs to be abstract and simple', or 'I want it all made out of industrial junk'. At other times, though, you may decide to leave it entirely open and see what happens. The eventual result will provide the dominant feel of the production. Then, step by step, the designer can explore and develop the details.

'Konzept'

Directors and designers are increasingly under pressure to 'have something to say' when they produce a play, particularly a classic: an overarching intellectual and aesthetic concept in which the action can be presented. Some people argue that it is not enough for a production to be a clear reading of the piece, careful and elegant, unobtrusive and true. 'Transparent' productions, they say, are an illusion: after all, isn't everything you do interpretative, and isn't 'avoiding interpretation' simply imposing another, more conservative interpretation?

This emphasis on interpretation first emerged in Germany. Its progenitor was Brecht, whose relationship to the classics was always complex. The results can be revelatory. Old plays are 'deconstructed' and the 'barbarism' latent in them is laid bare. The hidden and often suppressed narratives lurking beneath the text are brought to light and change the way that we think about them. Designers create extraordinary visions, which make audiences rethink their relationship to the play and to the world. Art should make us uncomfortable in our complacency and challenge the way we think about life. Conceptual theatre productions have been very successful in doing just this.

But this way of working has produced many imitators, particularly in European theatre, some of whom are quite terrible. Thus, in many German theatres today the director is meant to spend the first day, the *Konzeptprobe* ('concept rehearsal'), addressing the entire theatre – secretaries, finance managers and all – as well as local politicians, journalists and other interested parties. He will be expected to speak about his ideas, his understanding of the play in the light of philosophical and aesthetic tradition, and his argument for its lasting significance in the modern world. It's the director's *Konzept* that's wanted; not his skill at staging, nor his ability to bring the best out of his actors, nor his profound knowledge of the play and its period, nor even his sense of playful mischief.

I call this kind of work *Konzept Theater*, and the sad fact is that for every brilliant *Konzept*, ten are distinctly third-rate: cheap design ideas disguising themselves as intellectual analyses. Peter Gill and I used to play a satirical game in which we would look at a production photograph in *Theater Heute* (the leading German theatre magazine), put our hand over the caption and quiz each other as to which Shakespeare play was being staged. A frogman, a concentration camp guard and an old man sitting on the toilet usually indicated *Twelfth Night*; a basketball team, a blind blues singer and a photo of the Battle of Britain was a dead giveaway for *King Lear*.

*Konzept*s can be brilliant. But bad ones replace free-flowing dramatic debate with single-minded pedagogy.

Costumes vs. clothes

A good production is focused, above all, on the human beings who people the play and their stories. And here costumes play a crucial part. Many plays can be performed with no set at all, but costumes are essential.

There's a useful distinction to be drawn between 'costumes' and 'clothes'. 'Costumes' are often gaudy things, bearing little relationship to what people wear in real life. They're the product of the costume designer's imagination, powerful and theatrical in their own right. As such, they can be extraordinarily expressive. A woman dressed in white, walking onto a stage crowded with men in dark heavy clothes, made a huge impact in my production of Donizetti's *Lucia di Lammermoor*. The notary Curzio is a cameo part in Mozart's *Le Nozze di Figaro*: when I encouraged Bunny Christie to dress him in brilliant letter-box red, his corrupt complicity with the Count became especially vivid. Grotesque, imaginative, highly theatrical costumes can bring the witches in *Macbeth* to life. Amazingly distorted, highly imaginative costumes can take audiences into new and thrilling worlds: what will Ariel wear in *The Tempest* if you don't have a costume designer with a sharp eye for the theatrical and the supernatural? Such costume design is an expressive art in its own right, which comes into its own in highly theatrical productions.

Clothes, by contrast, tend to be subtler, less immediately noticeable, reflecting the nuances and details of the character's life. They bear all the marks of everyday use, fit the actors in the natural, unfussy way real clothes do, and carry useful information about class, age and attitude. In productions of modern plays they are usually specifically bought – and then treated, if necessary, to look old or lived in. A leather jacket says a great deal about a character's image and sexuality. Shellsuits, cardigans, T-shirts, trainers: everything indicates something different. Such distinctions are subliminal but arise from acute observations of modern mores: 'Oh, he wouldn't wear deck shoes, much too American academic', or 'She's the wrong class for twin-set and pearls'. Such decisions are linked to interpretation of character and the world of the play.

Such an approach isn't limited to modern plays. Characters in Chekhov, Molière and Shakespeare all wear clothes of a particular kind, full of revealing details about class, status, and character, and a good production of a classic play reflects the distinctions of its world through clothes as much as anything else. Your costume designer needs to have researched the period so carefully, and to have understood these nuances so precisely, that he knows how to express them in the chosen period.

The best costume designers – and their essential assistants, the costume supervisors – work closely with the actors in the 'fittings'. They try things out, talk with them carefully, and build up the appropriate costume step by step: 'That dress doesn't hang quite right: can we change its line?', 'Do you think she'd wear a brightly coloured blouse to the office? Shall we try a white one?', 'Don't you think Doctor Dorn [in *The Seagull*] should have a flamboyant scarf?' and so on. Clothes have to be developed alongside the actor's work on character; if they don't express his notion of the character, the

experienced actor will tell the costume designer – and you –
in no uncertain terms.

Good costume designers have a sophisticated understanding of actors' psychology. All actors want to look good
on stage, but their vanity can be alarming. This needs to be
understood: good theatre requires a degree of sex appeal and
an actress may well be right when she says green isn't her
colour. Occasionally, though, this desire to look good needs
to be overruled; or at least the actor should be encouraged
to think differently. The best costume designers know how to
do this with consummate tact. But you may be asked to lend
your support.

I sometimes find it difficult to say much of value to costume designers. My eyes glaze over when they describe the
difference between the cut of French clothes in the 1770s and
the Empire style of the early nineteenth century. I used to be
impatient with their meticulous attention to period, but
have come to understand its importance. Good costume
designers understand something more profound about the
world than I at first imagined.

Wigs

There are three reasons why wigs are required.

First, in certain periods in the past, men and women –
particularly in the upper and professional classes in the late
seventeenth and eighteenth centuries – wore highly artificial,
'powdered' wigs. These are an essential part of their costume
and characters dressed in clothes of the period, but without
wigs, look naked. Second, modern actors' hair is inevitably
different from the customs and fashions of the past. Actors
wearing Elizabethan clothes nearly always seem too close-
cropped: wigs can give them the long flowing locks and facial
hair that was so much a part of the period. Actresses often
have short hair, or hair that's cut in such a way that it's
inappropriate to the play, and wigs can change all that too.
Third, wigs can be expressive: a too-young King Lear might
benefit from a flowing white beard; Mother Courage might
look best in a close-cropped grey bob. Moustaches and side-
boards, bald wigs and hair extensions: all of these carry a

particular expressive energy, and need careful monitoring and prompting.

A wig can be liberating for an actor: it's part of the 'mask' that he needs to feel that he *is* the part. But I've sometimes thought that a wig is a hindrance to the performer, and can even be a distraction to the audience. Older actors will often want to talk to you about their wig long before rehearsals begin. Listen to what they're saying, but be careful not to get too caught up in it. Whatever you do, don't let too much energy go on the wig: you may have to be brutal and insist on a different one.

Wigs need to be carefully looked after, dressed and re-dressed. This is usually the job of the wig mistress. They must be well fitted and the actors must learn how to fasten them so that they look right and are secure. Hiring or making them is expensive and is easily overlooked when budgeting. The best designers bring a sophisticated understanding to this delicate task.

Wigs are an essential part of the box of tricks that you and the designer have been given.

Make-up

Attitudes to make-up have changed radically in recent years. This is partly because theatre casting is increasingly like television, where actors are cast for what they *are*, not for what they can be transformed into. It's also because of a more scrupulous kind of realism that can't see the value in applying make-up to obscure the real stuff beneath: the lines, wrinkles and blemishes of the real actor. Better, subtler lighting has changed attitudes too.

Most actors in a modern production apply only a very small amount of make-up, just enough to ensure that their features are not bleached out by the lights. Occasionally an actor will appear on stage at the technical rehearsal with too much make-up (you can see it easily from the front row of the stalls). This places a fixed mask over the character's face, which stops the audience engaging with the idiosyncratic, vulnerable human being beneath. I tend not to raise this directly with the actor (it's a strangely personal issue), but ask the wig designer or the costume designer to deal with it. But it does need to be addressed.

Of course, there's still a demand for specialist theatrical make-up, whether it's Gloucester's gouged eyes in *King Lear*, Bosola's scarred face in *The Changeling*, the statue of the Commendatore in *Don Giovanni*, the fairies in *A Midsummer Night's Dream*, or the trolls in *Peer Gynt*. In my production of Manfred Karge's *Man to Man*, Tilda Swinton wore a thick white cake of make-up, with a yellow splodge under one eye: a Brechtian effect which brilliantly expressed the violence that has been done to the character.

Specialist make-up is extravagant and brilliant, and usually takes hours to apply, but is a long way from the kind of sober realism that's central to the theatrical repertoire. Make-up specialists are eager for the challenge of this kind of work.

Furniture

I sometimes feel that I could direct plays without sets, but never without props and furniture. People live in a world shaped by the chairs they sit on, the tables they eat at, the paper they write on, the glasses they drink from. Most of the time the theatre tries to reflect this.

A piece of furniture is a physical object, whose dimensions and shape carry powerful meaning and affect the performances in subtle, intriguing ways: the tiny, constricting sofa which forces intimacy when a couple sit on it; the way the conversation changes when the two characters go from the soft, feminine *chaise longue* to the rectangular, wooden kitchen table; the long hard bench which makes the characters feel at school when they sit on it; and so on. Such furniture is rich with character and implication, and good designers take these subtle differences into account.

In a good production, the relationship of the people to the furniture can be poetic and moving: Torvald and Nora sitting opposite each other at a table with only a wedding ring between them; King Lear on his throne, ignorant of the catastrophe that's about to strike; Mrs Holroyd washing the coal dust off her husband's dead body on the kitchen table. Each of these has its own unique stage poetry: as powerful and meaningful as language or music or anything else.

Positioning the furniture

Positioning the furniture well is essential.

Sometimes you will find that a scene doesn't work because the furniture is in the wrong place: in relationship to the audience, to the entrances onto the stage, or to the other pieces of furniture. This can be as simple a matter as sight-lines. I was shocked at the technical rehearsal for *Look Back in Anger*, when I found Jimmy and Cliff's armchairs were so far downstage that about fifty people (at the far ends of the first four or five rows) couldn't see Alison standing at her ironing board. Or the problem can be about distance. In *Hedda Gabler*, Tesman and Brack retire into an inner recess to drink punch, while Løvborg and Hedda sit on a nearby sofa pretending to look at pictures of her honeymoon, while actually speaking about their past love affair. I endlessly readjusted the distance between the two: too close and it was unbelievable, too far away and there was no danger.

Or it can be about making the scene more expressive: I kept rearranging the chairs in Act One of *The Cherry Orchard* to discover the right physical relationship between them and the window out of which Madame Ranevskaya looked long-ingly. At the technical rehearsal of *The Taming of the Shrew* I found a way of releasing the sexual tension in a scene by turning the sofa around and placing it with its back to the audience, thus allowing the seduction of Bianca to be glimpsed, not exposed.

These are matters that can make or break a production. You should work them out in the model of the set. Or you can sort them out in the first weeks of rehearsal. And, as my examples show, sometimes you don't see them until you get on the stage. But whenever you see the problem, it's essential that you grasp the nettle, however disturbing the actors may find it. They'll thank you for it later.

Props

Even the sparest of productions require a few 'props' (properties), and the fewer that are used, the more important the care and attention to detail. Brecht led the way in insisting on the specific, material, almost sensual reality of the props – Mother Courage should pluck a real capon, Galileo's scientific equipment must be entirely functional. It's extraordinary how much information such things can carry.

Letters are particularly hard to get right, and are needed in nearly every classical play in the repertoire. I find myself saying things like: 'The paper doesn't feel right. It's too white. We don't believe in the seal either: it looks like an ASM botch job. Why don't you go to the Victoria and Albert Museum and find out?' One of the problems is that letters, particularly in period productions of Shakespeare, can feel so old-fashioned. Even the best stage managers tend to resort to the standard cream paper, coloured ribbon and blob of red sealing wax, and I've yet to find a designer who will focus on letters with the attention to detail they deserve.

The great plays of the naturalistic theatre sometimes require props to have a dual function, both realistic and symbolic: Konstantin's dead seagull, Osvald's pipe in *Ghosts*, the glass menagerie in Tennessee Williams, the drinks cupboard in *Who's Afraid of Virginia Woolf?* or Pozzo's atomiser in *Waiting for Godot* – each has to have its own uniquely realistic *raison d'être*. To ask for an abstract seagull is to miss the point – it must look like a real seagull before the audience will grant it the symbolic role the author intends.

Sometimes, a naturalistic play will require dozens of props. Many of these will not actually be used in the production, but will give an atmosphere that the constructed set lacks. For example, the glasses, bottles, cigarettes, peanut dispensers, beer-mats and so on that populate a bar; the saucepans, cookbooks, bottles of wine, dustpans and spice racks which litter the average modern kitchen. This array of props is usually called 'dressing', and I'm often struck by the way that an empty naturalistic set can be transformed by it.

In contemporary plays, in the world of brand recognition, the details of the props can be very telling about character:

'What's she reading – Jackie Collins or Jane Austen?'; 'What brand of cigarettes does he smoke – Marlboro Lights or Camel?'; 'Should he drink Tennant's Export or Carlsberg?'; 'What newspapers do they get delivered?' These are all tiny details, but the accumulation of such details reinforces the dramatic action.

Sometimes you have to be contrary about props. When I was directing *Henry IV*, it struck me that the audience would only appreciate the amount of 'sack' that Falstaff drank at the Boar's Head if it was served in glasses, so you could see the liquid going down his throat. I was told that this was wrong for the period, and we used handsome opaque pewter tankards instead. But when, a couple of years later, I directed Verdi's *Falstaff* (based on *Henry IV* and *The Merry Wives of Windsor*), I insisted on glasses (however anachronistic) and I realised I'd been right all along.

Props matter more than you might think.

Less is more

The essential thing is to be original and creative in your work with the designer, but to be wary of having too many brilliant ideas. If you overload the stage with imagery, you may find you've closed down your options. Worse, you may mystify your audience. The best design often consists of the simplest elements: a perfectly placed chair, a beautifully proportioned door; a chalked circle on a wooden floor. Less really is more.

I sometimes remind designers of Brecht's beautiful poem in homage to Caspar Neher:

> The war separated
> Me, the writer of plays, from my friend the stage designer.
> The cities where we worked are no longer there.
> When I walk through the cities that still are
> At times I say: that blue piece of washing
> My friend would have placed it better.

9

Design 2: Practical

Theatre design is a practical business and an understanding of this will allow you to work with greater flexibility, and earn you the respect and co-operation of the production team.

The model

I regard a carefully built scale-model of the set as the only reliable language that I share with the designer.

I once worked with a designer who didn't 'believe in' models, and it felt like trying to discuss poetry written in a language I didn't speak. The model is the central point of reference: instead of talking about abstract ideas it allows you to look at real objects in a real space, in much the same way that your audience will.

Designers sometimes start with a model of the theatre in which the production is going to take place. When I was assistant director at the Almeida, the artistic director's most prized possession was a scale-model of the entire theatre, with every brick in that famous back wall carefully modelled, textured and painted. Such a model defines the physical framework within which you'll be working. It's a good idea to sit for a while with the designer, trying to understand how it works. Look at the way the stage relates to the auditorium, where the focal points are, what the dynamics of the space are – tall and shallow, wide but low – and so on.

When you start working with the designer using the model, it's essential you work provisionally and sketchily. Most designers start with pieces of white card, as a way of investigating their ideas in purely spatial terms, free of colour or texture. Placing two bits of white card on either side of the stage creates a different dynamic from one piece of white card upstage centre. A curved card wall has a different impact than a flat one. You need to think 'laterally' and avoid settling on anything too early.

Then the designer might spray some colour onto one of the pieces, or get a bit of textured 'brick', or even just a scrap of material from another model. I've often placed a bit of 'floor' from another model onto a couple of match boxes, if only as a way of seeing whether a wooden raked stage might be a good idea. Each of these little experiments reveals new strengths and new problems. But all the time you're trying to discover an appropriate space and an interesting visual language for the play.

Once these ideas have started to gel, the designer can model them up in more detail, settling on the colours, textures and so on. And then you will suddenly find that a different coloured floor changes the whole atmosphere; a window set into a blank wall suggests a house; the branch of a tree in the distance suggests a forest. Step by step, the designer will develop the model.

Sometimes your designer will present you with a beautifully built completed model, which looks deceptively finished. But you need to be wary: just because it looks like a set doesn't mean it's the right one, and you may need to stick your heels in and explain why it's not going to work. In an early model for *Hedda Gabler*, Pamela Howard had flowers growing out of an earth floor, in an intriguing and expressionistic fashion. I knew as soon as I saw it that it didn't sit right with Ibsen's sober naturalism, and said as much. But when, in Act One, we had real flowers in real vases littering the floor, we were quite properly following Ibsen's stage directions: 'All round the main room are vases and glass containers full of cut flowers; other bouquets lie on the tables.' Working on *King Lear*, Neil Warmington came up with a cracked marble floor. Beautiful as this was, it was inappropriate for the great outdoor scenes in the second half, and we quickly came to understand that a tough, worn, oak platform floating in a sea of white dance-floor seemed a much better idea for Lear's 'great stage of fools'. The crucial thing is to see each element as flexible and provisional and to keep asking questions.

It's sometimes difficult to know exactly how to interpret even the best-made model, and I will often say to my designer: 'What in the model is different from what it will look like in real life?' If the answer is vague, I insist that it be more finished before I can give it full justice. And I insist on a scale-model of a figure or two – dressed, if possible, in the clothes of the relevant period – and maybe some furniture, so I can see the way the set is going to feel when it's inhabited.

The model needs to be approached with a mixture of experimentation, daring and respect. It's your most important tool. It can take you to the right answer.

Drawings

Designers usually supplement their work in the model with drawings and other two-dimensional visual material, which are often exquisite: photographs, sketches, montages and so on. I pin these up in the rehearsal room and am inspired by them. In addition, some designers (inspired by Brecht's designer Caspar Neher) work up 'storyboards', which catch the key actions in the drama, and provide some sense of how the scenes could look on stage, when they're inhabited by the actors. These can be exceptionally useful. A word of warning, however: beautiful artwork doesn't always translate into good design, and you should remember they are the means to an end, and not the sum of the production itself.

The technical aspect

Theatre design is a skilled and technically challenging job, which requires much more than vision. Like the director, the designer's job is intensely practical, and he needs to work with a host of different people on deciding how his ideas can best be realised.

And so, in addition to the model and the drawings, the designer will need to provide technical drawings: reliable blue-prints which a production manager and set builder can take away and work from. It's essential that these are precise architectural drawings, detailed in every way. If your designer fails to do this, you mustn't be surprised if your set doesn't fit, falls down or comes in over budget.

In fact, the best designers have a sharp eye for detail – from the cut of seventeenth-century wigs to the shape of 1920s door handles – as well as technical knowledge of materials, paint and engineering. I'm sometimes surprised by how detailed so many design issues are – the quality of the paint, the weight of the fabric, the hang of the curtains, the angle of the side wall, the luminosity of a particular colour and so on – and you need to understand and respect this. Designers should provide reference material to the set builders and painters for all of these details.

The fact is that there's a direct connection between a design's practicality and its aesthetic merits: if a set is technically awkward, it's likely to be inelegant too. Form and function are intimately linked. And, as so often, necessity can be the mother of invention.

Production managers

One of the key relationships you must cultivate is with the production manager. But what is a production manager and what does he do?

The production manager is in charge of all aspects of the physical, technical and budgetary delivery of the show. He answers to the company's senior management but is usually granted quite a lot of autonomous power. Most repertory theatres have resident production managers, while commercial managers and touring companies, who tend to do fewer new productions, employ them on a freelance, show-by-show basis.

Production managers come in all shapes and sizes. Traditionally, they're arrogant blokes with a big set of keys, an abusive tongue and a condescending manner to anybody who belongs to the 'artistic' side of the theatre: actors are 'turns', designers are 'girls' and directors are 'trouble'. This caricature is slowly dying out, but isn't completely dead. There is, however, a new kind of production manager appearing – all computers, mobile phones and suits. Having worked with both, I sometimes find it difficult to know which is better – or worse.

Being a production manager is a difficult job, and carries real responsibility. It's the production manager's job to get the physical aspects of the production built on time and on budget. He needs to ensure that the set and its environment are safe for the actors to work in, and in compliance with health and safety stipulations. He also needs to deliver a set that is in accordance with the director's and the designer's vision. Production managers are under constant pressure, but the intelligent director will discover how to work with them.

The most important thing to communicate to the production manager is that you and your designer know what you want. You need to meet him well before rehearsals, so he can cost your model and give you some indication of its practical possibility. It's useful to have a conversation with him right at the beginning of the design process. I might ring him up and say: 'Tell me what size of show we can afford, and do you think a revolve is out of the question?' This sets the practical parameters.

It's crucial that you and your designer are seen to be united in your decisions, and speak as one in production meetings. If you don't, you'll lose the confidence of your production team and waste valuable time. Inevitably, though, you'll be faced with an issue that you hadn't anticipated. The clever thing is to work through the answer together, away from everyone else, and come back when you're agreed.

Productions always develop during rehearsal, and it's sometimes difficult to answer all the questions that you're asked. The best thing is to prioritise your decisions, so you can say to the production manager: 'We know that the walls need to be seven feet high, but we haven't yet quite worked out where we want the power socket to be.' It sometimes feels like you're feeding a tiger bits of raw meat so that he doesn't eat you up whole, but it's a sensible way of working with busy people.

Production managers need to stick to the budget. It's impossible to exaggerate just how tight money in the theatre tends to be, and you need to understand that these constraints are genuine. A good production manager won't use this as a get-out clause, but will find constructive solutions that save money and preserve your aesthetic decisions. But you need to be flexible too: tight budgets are not always a bad thing, and it's better to have a little on stage, but for it to be perfect, than a great deal that looks shabby.

The production manager is going to confront you with physical limitations: 'That graceful arch won't carry the weight of an actor unless it's made of super strong steel, which we can't afford.' Or: 'That door piece is so big, we're not going to be able to get it through the dock door in three of the theatres we're touring to.' Of course, such physical problems are his responsibility, but you need to understand and respect them.

It's important that the production manager has scheduled the production properly: from setting design deadlines, through to working out the details of the tea breaks in the technical rehearsal. Good companies need schedules, and they need to be respected. Otherwise, people end up working too many hours, everybody gets exhausted, and quality is affected.

Stage managers

It was only when I started to work abroad that I came to realise just how good British stage management is. I remember a distinguished Belgian artistic director explaining to me that this was because Britain was a maritime nation and that good stage management was like good seamanship. It would have been undiplomatic to point out that the Belgians have their own maritime tradition, but I did say that the next time I worked in his theatre I wanted to bring my own team.

The fact is that one of the best things about the British theatre is the quality of its stage managers: professional, good-humoured, reasonable and helpful. There are various reasons for this, the most important being that, with its roots in commercial theatre, the British theatre values practical abilities, as much as intellectual or artistic ones. Stage managers work long hours for not very good money, and their commitment and goodwill is too often taken for granted.

But who is the stage management team, and what do they do? On most professional productions, the team consists of three people: the Company Stage Manager (CSM), the Deputy

Stage Manager (DSM) and the Assistant Stage Manager (ASM) (on some big shows you'll have two ASMs). Their roles are much more diverse than their titles would suggest. They're usually appointed by the Production Manager.

The CSM has a managerial role, and acts as the management's representative in the theatre (especially on tour, or in the West End). Thus it's the CSM to whom actors first turn when they've been taxed too much on their payslip, or when they want to know about parking, or even when they feel the show isn't working artistically. During performances, the CSM's role is to oversee the safe and efficient running of the production as a whole.

The DSM has a more technical role. He comes to every rehearsal, and draws up the 'book' (sometimes called the 'Bible'), the definitive record of all the staging decisions made. A good book records every cut, every textual change, every move, and every stage direction. It should also record every lighting and sound cue and other technical information. It should have enough detailed information to allow an assistant director to remount a production ten years later. The DSM uses the book to 'call the show' when it's on stage: flying the production like a jet aeroplane from his little 'prompt box' in the wings, with a whole system of 'calls': 'Mr Smith, Miss Jones, Mrs Zanzibar and Master Antelope to the stage please. Stand by LX. Stand by sound. LX 127, Fly 33. Sound 212, GO . . . ' And so on. The DSM is also meant to 'prompt' if an actor forgets his lines.

The ASM works harder than anyone else. In the rehearsal period he's the 'gopher', endlessly running small missions, picking up the dining-room chairs from the hire store, spraying down the gilt on the table, fixing the fan and checking the 'mark-out' against the plans. During the performance, he's constantly running around backstage with a whole set of different jobs: giving the leading actress her handbag, carrying on the sofa in the Act One scene change, splashing water on the window when Falstaff is thrown into the river and so on.

ASMs used to appear on stage in non-speaking parts (as 'acting ASMs'), and many of Britain's older actors started out as ASMs in their youth. It sometimes still happens: I once persuaded one of my favourite ASMs to dress up as a peasant in *The Seagull* to be given a tip by Madame Arkadina. I think she came to enjoy her ten seconds in the limelight, but I know she wouldn't be offended if I told her that she should think carefully before considering a career change. Be wary when managers start talking about 'acting ASMs': things can get badly compromised.

There are a number of other technical people involved in the production. Shows often have a technical stage manager, who is responsible for all the purely technical elements: the slide projector, the wind machine, the flying pieces and so on. They also need a wardrobe mistress responsible for making sure that the costumes are washed, ironed, repaired and generally looked after. On a big theatre production, this might be two or three people; West End musicals have six or seven. You also need a sound operator and a lighting operator. Sometimes productions have other specialists: animal handlers, children's chaperones and so on.

This is the technical team, and you can't do without them.

The director and the technical team

It's essential that you get on well with your technical team. You'll sometimes sense a latent suspicion of you and your designer (as the people who are responsible for making everybody's lives so difficult). But in my experience, that's usually accompanied by an astonishing commitment to getting things right, and you soon discover that the cynical joshing is simply a form of self-protection against the charlatan directors that technicians sometimes have to suffer.

Chat to them, buy them a drink, take them out for dinner; they're on your side if you want them to be!

10

Rehearsals 1: Starting out

The main aims of the first week of rehearsals are twofold: to give the actors an overall knowledge and understanding of the play and their part in it; and to set the pace and tone of subsequent rehearsals. Starting is always difficult, but both objectives need to be met.

The first day

Many directors say that the first day of rehearsals is the most difficult. I sleep only fitfully the night before, and am plagued by anxiety dreams. I wake at six, drink too much coffee, forget to eat breakfast, and head off to rehearsals, usually arriving an hour early. I pace around, chat to the stage management (who are always so calm), stare out of the window, drink more coffee, try to read the paper, glance at the play gloomily, and wait for the actors to arrive. The anxiety is all-consuming: 'Have I done my homework?', 'Have I cast it well?', 'Is the design going to work?' and 'What about that very difficult sound effect at the end of Act Two – will I ever know what it should be like?'

So what's the best way to start? Obviously, you need to ensure that everybody knows each other. The first day of rehearsals sometimes feels like hosting a cocktail party for a group of total strangers, all of whom you're meant to know well – and no one has bothered to mix the gin and tonics. I usually get everybody to introduce themselves, and say clearly what their role is. In a big production, you find there are fifty people in the room: the actors, the designer, the stage management team, the marketing team, the theatre's management and so on. Of course, people never really listen to these introductions and so you have to do it again later in the day (I've often resorted to the tired joke that there will be a 'test at the end of the day'. I once tried to name everybody myself, but when I forgot the name of my own marketing manager

I learnt that such showing off was best avoided). And then everybody needs to be welcomed. Jokes need to be cracked. And you must be seen to be smiling.

The strange thing is that this doesn't get any easier. Although experience can give you confidence in your ability to spot dangers, it also means that you know just how badly it can all go wrong. The fact is that by the first day of rehearsal it's already too late to repair some things.

So what do you do next?

A read-through?

I believe in the value of a read-through, when everybody sits down together, and the actors read the play aloud, uninterrupted from beginning to end.

Some directors dispense with a read-through altogether, or postpone it for a few days until the actors have got to know each other better. Instead, they get the actors to do warm-ups, exercises and games as a way of freeing their bodies and spirits. In doing this they aim to create an atmosphere of artistic endeavour, and are breaking down the inhibitions that actors often bring to the work. I've even heard of one young director starting his rehearsals with a run-through – actors stumbling around the rehearsal room, holding their scripts and trying to make some sense of what they're doing. But I'm convinced that it's important to put the main subject of the work – the play itself – firmly in everybody's minds, and I regard my colleagues who dispense with a read-through with a mixture of jealousy and incredulity.

Many actors hate the read-through. This is the moment of truth, they think, when their unsuitability for the part will become clear to the world at large. They have dreamed up entire performances in the privacy of their own bedrooms, only to be shocked that the other actors and the director have entirely different ideas. Even the most experienced actors will confess to read-through terror.

I always ask the actors to read as straightforwardly as possible, not to try to make it 'too wonderful', but to speak loudly and clearly and let everyone in the room hear the play as if for the first time. If you've decided on cuts it's a good idea to give those out now – although I tend to circulate them a couple of weeks before rehearsals begin. Some plays have extensive stage directions, and I usually ask the DSM to read aloud the few which matter, omitting things like 'pause' or 'nervously' or 'with a heart-rending sigh'. I encourage the actors to close their scripts during the scenes in which they don't feature and listen to the others. A well-managed read-through can be a positive experience for all, although it's probably best to think of it as a necessary evil: I'm not quite sure how else you can get a disparate group of people to focus on the same play.

I admit that I find the read-through valuable in a way that I wouldn't want the actors to know about – it allows me to rehearse in my mind all the hundreds of decisions I've already made, about casting, design and so on. It also gives me an opportunity to watch the actors I'm about to spend weeks with, and glimpse their strengths and weaknesses, their needs and ways of working, the level of their preparation and so on. I regard a read-through as a sneak preview into what I'm going to spend the next five weeks of my life living and breathing. But I keep it to myself: if the actors thought I was coming to any conclusions they would get up and go.

Showing the model

When the read-through is finished there is an odd sensation: what next? The greater the play, the stronger the sensation: what can you say when a group of good actors have just finished reading a masterpiece like *King Lear*? This is why I sometimes schedule the read-through for the afternoon, so the actors can go home afterwards, or retire to the pub, or just sit around drinking tea. Some directors ask the designer to show the actors a model of the set, which – along with the introductions and the read-through – gives the actors the most complete introduction to the production.

In recent years, however, I've not always shown the model on the first day. This is because I want the actors to think about the play and their role in it, and not worry till later about the colour of their costume or the demands of the design. Actors are usually too preoccupied on the first day of rehearsal to take in a model properly, and if you're doing something slightly 'different', you want the actors to have got used to you and your way of thinking before they're exposed to your *Konzept*. And so, these days, I tend to show the model at the end of the first week.

When I assemble the company for the model showing, I usually start with the actual set obscured (with a bit of card or something). I think it's useful for the actors – who are not always the most visually literate people – to hear something of the process that you and the designer have been involved in *before* they look at the model itself. When the designer Pamela Howard and I presented the model for Ibsen's *The Master Builder*, I said something like this:

> In thinking about the play, Pamela and I scoured through a lot of documentary material about large middle-class houses in Christiania (Oslo) in the 1890s. We wanted to make sure that the 'home without sunlight' that Solness speaks of – and into which the young Hilde Wangel wants to let in the light – is made visible. We also researched Norwegian architects' offices in the 1890s, because we wanted to capture the particular atmosphere of Solness' workroom in Act One.
>
> Because it's a three-act play with three locations (and we want to do it with only one interval), we've had to find a way of sharing certain elements (the floor and the sidewalls) in all three sets. We've looked at Ibsen's stage directions, and tried to come up with sets that allow the most important ones to take place. Thus in Act Two, when Hilde Wangel enters from the garden, Solness' dark sitting room will be flooded with light. In confronting Ibsen's notoriously difficult Act Three, however, in which Solness has to climb up the steeple of the tower he's built and then fall off, we've decided to reverse Ibsen's intentions and will be asking the audience to imagine Solness climbing his tower in their midst.

I try to share our thinking with the actors as clearly and as openly as possible, without getting too caught up in the kind of detailed – and somewhat arcane – aesthetic discussions that I've enjoyed with the designer.

Even the best actors get bored quickly, and they will let you know soon enough that it's time to show them the model itself. Once you do, they are usually positive and drily complimentary ('It'll be fine'). It's important to encourage them to ask questions, some of which will be valuable, and some of which will need simple clarification ('How steep is the rake?' 'Will I have to climb that ladder?' 'That door looks awfully narrow'): remember that they have to spend weeks walking around on a set that you and your designer will look at from the comfort of the stalls. Occasionally, however, an actor will object more forcefully, sometimes with good reason. If you find yourself in this situation, and you're dealing with a strong personality, then I'm afraid you're in deep trouble. It's almost certainly too late to re-design the production, and you'll have to find ways of persuading him that, between you, you can overcome the problem. I try to avoid this situation arising in the first place by showing an early plan to the leading actors before finalising it with the designer.

By the beginning of rehearsals most costume designers will have assembled reference material and done some costume drawings, which I ask them to present after the model showing, more to give a flavour of the production and its period than precise descriptions of what the actors will be wearing. Good costume designers know that costumes must be specifically designed for individual actors, and that the way a performance evolves in rehearsal is going to affect the clothes that should be worn. I always emphasise that these are initial drawings and that the main work gets done in the fittings. But never underestimate how important costumes are to your actors and to their performance, and try to understand just how sensitive they may be about them: you need to keep as many options open as you can.

A good atmosphere, but who's in charge?

One of the key things to establish in the first few days is a good atmosphere. Jokes and laughter are important in that they defuse the tension and help create a sense that the actors are doing something pleasurable. Laughter loosens the brain and frees the spirit, and you should ensure that pleasure and joy inform everything you do in the theatre.

Alongside the jokes, however, you need to establish something more serious, namely a sense that all questions are allowed ('stupid questions are particularly valuable') and that it's a shared understanding that's being looked for. You need to show you're aware that your preparations will take rehearsals only so far, that all problems in the theatre are practical, and that your actors are not attending a university seminar. Actors speak approvingly of an atmosphere some directors create in which failure is never mentioned, where the actors' creativity is celebrated and their energy and goodwill are harnessed. This is something you should aim for.

Some actors are good at talking, while others prefer to say nothing. And so one of your roles in early rehearsals is to lead and shape the conversation, encourage the quiet ones, and rein in the chatterboxes, bring the group forward to understandings and agreements, know when to kick a discussion into touch, and when to allow it to ramble. You're the chairman: actors will address most of their comments directly to you and expect you to listen and respond. This can be difficult, particularly when you're conscious of the limited rehearsal time you have, and want to give everybody the space they need. But it's an essential task.

You need to give your actors clear leadership. The emphasis in recent years on the collaborative nature of the theatre is positive, but certain decisions need to be made – often under a great deal of pressure – and ultimately you are the person who has to make them. If you can't do this, then someone else will (often the leading actor), and your production will have lost its sense of purpose. Thus in the first week, as well as establishing a creative, pleasurable atmosphere, you need to establish – often in ways that are subliminal – that you're in charge. Peter Gill once said you have to make that clear in the first five minutes of the first rehearsal. When you've done that, all manner of collaboration and investigation is possible.

Schedule

One of the essential things you have to do is draw up a rehearsal schedule.

Rehearsal hours in the professional theatre are usually 10.00 till 6.00, with an hour's lunch break at 1.00. You must take a tea break in the morning and in the afternoon, and if you don't the stage manager – or sometimes the actors – will tell you that you should. Occasionally, depending on Equity regulations, you can call an evening rehearsal (7.00 till 10.00), and sometimes, particularly towards the end of rehearsals, you can rehearse on a Saturday morning. In Britain, the rehearsal period for a professional production is usually four weeks, which often shocks theatre people from other countries, who sometimes conclude that our work is superficial as a result. It's longer in the 'flagship' companies, but shorter in the smaller reps and commercial companies.

I think it's a good idea to call the whole cast for the first few days, perhaps the whole of the first week, when you're reading through the play and talking about it. This gives them the chance to familiarise themselves with the play and get to know each other. And here the tea breaks are as useful as anything that happens in work time.

Once you start to work in more detail, calling the whole company can become counterproductive. Some directors insist on having everyone in rehearsal all the time so as to create an 'ensemble', and this can produce wonderful results. But the fact is that actors sitting around not working on their scenes become frustrated and bored, and it's wise to limit calls to when you reasonably think you're going to need them. Then you can expect the actors to come to rehearsals prepared, having studied the scene in detail by themselves, and with their lines learnt. When you move into the last week of rehearsal and want to run the play, you'll need everybody together again. And it's often then, in that exciting and stretching time, that the real 'ensemble' is created.

Scheduling isn't always easy. You may find that an actor isn't available every day, and that one of the conditions of accepting the part was that he had to go to a wedding, or do a day's filming, or evening performances (and matinées) in another show. The rest of the production team will need to make calls on your actors too. The costume designer and the wardrobe supervisor will need them for fittings; the sound designer will want to record the chatter of a party and need all the younger members of the company to go to a recording studio. And then, of course, your actors are ill, forget to read the 'call sheet', or simply fail to set the alarm clock.

I tend to delegate these complicated (if slightly dull) scheduling negotiations to my assistant. And so I say that I need to work through Acts Two and Three on Wednesday and Thursday, and hope that he'll schedule all the other extra calls accordingly. In the past I've tried to schedule a whole week ahead, but have learned from experience that it's wiser to plan no more than two or three days in advance.

A four week rehearsal period on my production of *Hedda Gabler* (a four-act play, in one location, that lasted about two and a quarter hours) looked something like this:

Week One: Establishing Facts

MONDAY 'Meet and greet' and read-through
TUESDAY Reading at the table
WEDNESDAY Reading at the table
THURSDAY Starting to stand up Act One and Two
FRIDAY Starting to stand up Act Two and Three

Week Two: Sketching

MONDAY Sketching Act One
TUESDAY Sketching Act Two
WEDNESDAY Sketching Act Three
THURSDAY Sketching Act Four
FRIDAY Revisiting missed sections

Week Three: Detail

MONDAY Detailed work on Act One
TUESDAY Detailed work on Act Two
WEDNESDAY Detailed work on Act Three
THURSDAY Detailed work on Act Four
FRIDAY Revisiting missed work

Week Four: Running

MONDAY Detailed work on Acts One and Two
TUESDAY Detailed work on Acts Three and Four
WEDNESDAY Run first half in the morning.
    Run the second half in the afternoon, with notes
THURSDAY Detailed work in the morning from Wednesday
    Run play in the afternoon
FRIDAY Detailed work demanded by the run
SATURDAY Final run-through in rehearsal room and notes

The following chapters describe this work in more detail.

The important thing to remember is that while you are doing the 'sketching work' and the 'detailed work' – much of which is organisational – you are constantly developing the more interesting work on language, blocking and character, and helping the actors create their performances.

11

Rehearsals 2: Establishing Facts

The main aim of the first week of rehearsal should be to ensure that everyone involved becomes familiar with the play as a whole.

'Boring things matter'

I often say that 'boring things matter', and encourage a way of reading the play which forbids opinion and is concerned simply to establish what can be proven. I might say something like: 'Don't tell me what you think about the characters. Just tell me what you know and can prove. This is a foreign land that you're exploring for the first time, and before you can understand its culture you need to know its history and geography.' Such an approach allows you to establish a consensus early on, before divergent opinions have time to emerge. Agreeing on important factual matters provides the best possible springboard for the imagination.

What happens in the story?

Timothy West has an analysis of the story of *The Cherry Orchard*: 'In Act One the cherry orchard is going to be sold; in Act Two the cherry orchard is about to be sold; in Act Three the cherry orchard is being sold; and in Act Four the cherry orchard has been sold.' Of course, his point is to show that Chekhov's masterpiece doesn't have much of a story to it. Nevertheless, establishing what happens in the story is essential work.

It's sometimes a good idea to get your actors to write a synopsis, particularly if the play is complicated. This should be factually based and uncoloured by opinion. The first draft can be very simple and overarching, and each subsequent draft can get more and more detailed, but all the time resisting a judgment or having an opinion about the character. A synopsis of *Hamlet* could go through the following three drafts:

DRAFT ONE Hamlet revenges his father's death.

DRAFT TWO Hamlet meets his father's ghost, who tells him that his brother, now Hamlet's mother's husband, murdered him. Hamlet revenges his father's death.

DRAFT THREE Hamlet's friend Horatio alerts him to the fact that his father's ghost has been seen. Hamlet meets his father's ghost, who tells him that his brother, now Hamlet's mother's husband, murdered him. Hamlet is upset by this and pretends to be mad. He stages a play that he thinks will catch the conscience of the king, and kills his girlfriend's father by accident. Eventually, after much prevarication, Hamlet revenges his father's death.

Of course, in *Hamlet*, the action is often delayed, talked about and planned for, but it is nevertheless the dramatic heart of the play. Each new draft contains the words of the previous draft, but can be expanded at will, until the only possible further expansion would be to adopt Shakespeare's text *in toto*. By concentrating on 'pure action', you're focusing on what needs to be communicated and what the audience needs to see.

Who are the people in the play?

Actors need to ask simple, commonsense questions about the characters in the play.

Again, the important thing is to establish the facts. 'Hamlet is a Prince, he goes to university in Wittenberg, and his mother has married his uncle following his father's death.' 'Goneril is the eldest of Lear's daughters. Regan comes next and Cordelia is the youngest. He has no sons.' 'Torvald [in *A Doll's House*] has just been appointed manager at the bank. He suffered from bad health, and was cured when his wife secretly borrowed a sum of money and took him to Italy.' 'Davies [in *The Caretaker*] is a homeless tramp who is given somewhere to live by Mick; he says his papers are in Sidcup.' And so on.

Facts about class, age and role in society underpin any realistic portrayal of character, and once again it's essential to discover what can be proven: what, for example, is an 'ancient', which is how Iago is described in Othello? Why doesn't Hamlet inherit the throne automatically after his father's death? What is 'a master builder' (as opposed to an engineer or an architect) in nineteenth-century Norway? How has Lopakhin made his money and how did Madame Ranevskaya lose hers? The answers to these questions can be found in the text of the play, or are easily resolved by research. But they need to be asked.

What do the people in the play do?

In some ways this is the most important question of all, and it's only by answering it, and making that answer compre-hensible to your audience, that your production will tell a series of human stories.

A useful exercise is to ask the actors to write out a detailed synopsis of their character's part in the play: scene by scene, section by section. Again, this should concentrate on what can be proven from a close reading of the text and must be factual and precise. And here it's important to be pedantic: 'What happened to Rosencrantz and Guildernstern on the journey from England?', 'What did Nora do which allows Krogstad to have such control over her?', 'What support does the King of France give Cordelia when she returns?' The best plays deserve the closest possible attention and the more particular your grasp of the characters' individual actions, the more interesting your production will be to watch.

This analytical work provides the foundation on which the production is built. It also provides the basis for the more wide-ranging and imaginative work on character and psychology.

Charts, diagrams and maps

I find it useful to have charts, timelines and maps pinned on the rehearsal room wall.

When I directed Shakespeare's *Henry IV*, we had a map of England so we could trace the movements and locations of armies and princes, carriers and rogues, justices of the peace and poor conscripts. When preparing *The Cherry Orchard*, Pamela Howard drew a map of the house and the estate (all textually supported), with clear locations for the river, the railway, the ballroom, the orchard, Simeonov-Pischchik's estate and so on.

With Ibsen's *Ghosts*, I asked my assistant to draw up a timeline. This clarified when Mrs Alving married Captain Alving, when she left him to stay with Pastor Manders and when she returned, when Osvald was born and when he was sent away, when he went to Paris and when he returned to his mother in Norway. It led right up to the moment when the action of the play starts.

Units of action

I like to have a 'scenario' pinned on the wall of the rehearsal room as well: a graphic analysis of who is in which scene (which is particularly useful for scheduling).

In addition to the acts and scenes that most authors provide, you can divide the action up further, with each new entrance into the play marking a new mini-scene (the standard scene breaks in eighteenth-century French and German drama, relating to the *scenae* of classical drama). But then you can go further, and discover smaller units, when there's a clear change in atmosphere or subject. In Italian theatre, and in French plays which derive from *commedia dell'arte*, the action can be broken down into a series of *lazzi*: small, flexible units of self-contained action. Modern plays often have such 'riffs', or runs of action, and it's useful to work out where one ends and another begins.

Identifying such units ('unit-ing') helps actors see the logical, step-by-step progression of the play. These 'units of action' become the basic map of the play. But you need to be careful: adhering to such unit-ing too rigorously can block the flow of action, and make the production feel jerky when you try to run it. As with so much in these early days, you're simply gathering the tools required to move rehearsals onto the more creative phase in the second and third weeks.

12

Rehearsals 3: Warm-ups, Improvisation, Games and Exercises

When directing a play, the most important thing you can do is realise the writer's intentions. But for rehearsals to be creative they often need more than detailed attention to the text, and this chapter summarises some of the non-textual work that directors employ to stimulate creativity, receptivity and the imagination. It also outlines some of the exercises that have been developed to help actors perform in a way that is detailed and specific, alive and varied.

Warm-ups

Just as you should stretch your thigh muscles before you go running, so it's valuable for actors to warm up their bodies before they start rehearsals. This can consist of simple physical stretching – calves, thighs, tummy and neck – as well as vocal warm-ups and mouth exercises which increase oral dexterity. For some actors, this takes the form of physical jerks – sit-ups, splits, running on the spot, aerobics and so on. For others it consists of wandering around the rehearsal room, vaguely stretching their limbs and occasionally saying 'ah'. Some actors will do this for themselves, but some directors start rehearsals with mandatory group warm-ups, which can give a focused, physically-aware start to the day's rehearsals.

You need to decide what you feel about warm-ups. My feeling – which is shared by most experienced directors – is they are the actors' responsibility.

Theatre games

In the 1960s and 1970s the theatre was transformed by the development of theatre games.

Games are useful for building up a sense of physical connectedness between actors, as well as engaging parts of the imagination not readily available just through talking. They can free an actor's intuitive responses, and encourage spontaneity and receptivity. Peter Brook is a genius at devising games that stretch the actor's mental and physical versatility, and the result can be a kind of acting which is astonishingly free and open to whatever happens on stage. Others have followed, often with startling success. The great guru of theatre games is Viola Spolin whose two books are a treasure trove of ideas which you should plunder liberally.

I don't use theatre games any more, and only a few professional directors use them extensively. But they can be invaluable and some actors love them. If you're keen on them, just make sure you share your enthusiasm with your actors, particularly the sceptical ones. Insisting on theatre games can get rehearsals off to the worst possible start if you're not careful.

Improvisation

Improvisation (acting without a script and making up the words and actions as you go along) helps performers explore their parts and the world of the play imaginatively. It also encourages them to be spontaneous and receptive to whatever they're confronted with.

Improvisation is essential when a company is creating an adaptation of a novel or film, or devising a drama where the story line is already determined. Companies like Joint Stock and its successor, Out of Joint, use improvisation to help new writers develop scripts. The actors take scenes from the original source material and set up lengthy improvisations as a way of exploring an appropriate theatrical form. Other companies – Shared Experience, Complicite and Trestle – use improvisation to create compelling and original, physically expressive work. Much of this work is based on the European traditions of physical theatre, especially clowning and *commedia dell'arte*.

I used to love devising improvisation exercises. I remember setting up an improvisation 'space' into which two actors would enter and simply start an improvisation. The only rules were that each actor had to accept the other's suggestion: if one actor said, 'Lovely day today isn't it?', the other actor shouldn't say, 'No it's pissing down with rain.' I became obsessed with what I called 'pure story' and used to insist that each moment should take the story further: no going back, no hesitation, no character development. And I had a little drum that I would beat if I wanted the actors to abandon what they were doing, step back into the square, and start something entirely fresh. The point was that imagination was infinite, and each new idea could produce something marvellous.

When I use improvisation nowadays it tends to be much more limited in scope and consist almost entirely of paraphrasing, particularly when working on an old play in difficult language. There it can help actors crack open a scene, clarify thought lines, and unlock emotions. Rehearsing *King Lear* I asked the actors playing Edmund and Gloucester to work through the 'duping scene' (1.2) in their own words (which turned out to be full of 'effing and blinding'). This two-minute exercise helped them to find the energy of the scene free of the constraints of the text. Some actors are very afraid of improvisation and I cannot imagine insisting on an improvisation in the face of such terror: it would be counterproductive.

The best book on improvisation is Keith Johnstone's *Impro*.

Theory

Drama theory has blossomed in recent years. Some of the key notions are Antonin Artaud's 'Theatre of Cruelty', Jerzy Grotowski's 'Poor Theatre' and Peter Brook's 'Total Theatre', and in the higher reaches of academia you encounter notions about 'the semiotics of performance', a 'post-structuralist approach to spoken drama' or 'reception theory in early modern drama'. All this has absolutely no bearing on professional theatre practice. Most actors will have read the key texts by Stanislavski at drama school, and it's important to be familiar with the basic terminology of 'naturalistic' acting.

A few will have read Brecht, and it's useful to have a grasp of what he was driving at. But it cannot be said loudly enough: drama theory is for colleges and universities, but irrelevant in the pragmatic world of contemporary theatre.

Actioning

The director Max Stafford-Clark has perfected his own, highly analytical approach to acting, called 'actioning'. In this, every moment in a play is given a particular 'action', a verb which describes precisely what is done by one character to another. Thus, an actor saying a word as simple as 'hello' is asked to discover the appropriate transitive verb: is he 'seducing' or 'greeting' or 'challenging' or 'provoking' or 'enticing' the other one? This can be expanded to encompass entire speeches, and even whole scenes.

The great value of actioning is that the process of finding exactly the right verb helps produce a precision and focus in the acting: it makes 'the truth concrete'. The results can be remarkable and although I don't use Max's system extensively, I will often ask an actor what 'action' he is playing. But it has two problems. One is that the endless search for a transitive verb replaces intuition with analysis: acting becomes a kind of thesaurus game. A bigger problem is that it's of little use in helping an actor feel at home in great verse drama. For example (*Macbeth*, 3.2):

> Come, seeling night,
> Scarf up the tender eye of pitiful day
> And with thy bloody and invisible hand
> Cancel and tear to pieces that great bond
> Which keeps me pale. Light thickens
> And the crow makes wing to th'rooky wood.

You could say that Macbeth's 'action' is to 'invoke the night to descend'; but this won't help your actor feel at home in such terrifying poetic virtuosity.

'He said, she said'

Brecht devised an exercise (as part of his 'alienation effect') in which the actor was encouraged to preface each of his utterances with 'he said' or 'she said'. Thus, the actress playing Cordelia would reply to Lear's challenge ('what can you say to draw / A third more opulent than your sisters?') by saying: 'In answer, Cordelia said "Nothing, my lord".' What this does is to place the actor's decision to speak in a particular light, open to criticism as much as approval. Like actioning, it focuses the actor's mind on the specificity of what the character is saying and doing. But again, like actioning, it can quickly become banal: of course 'he said' whatever he says – you're just repeating what the text indicates.

Beats, or 'finger-clicking'

This is an intriguing exercise, in which the actor clicks his fingers every time there's a new 'beat' in the language. In verse it usually occurs on the end of the line or at the caesura:

> Now is the winter **click** of our discontent **click**
> Made glorious summer **click** by this son of York **click**.

In prose, the *click* is more difficult to pin down. Here's how a passage from *The Importance of Being Earnest* might be articulated:

> The line is immaterial. **Click** Mr Worthing, I confess I feel somewhat bewildered by what you have just told me. **Click** To be born, **click** or at any rate bred, **click** in a hand-bag whether it had handles or not, **click** seems to me to display a contempt for the ordinary decencies of family life that reminds one of the worst excesses of the French Revolution. **Click** And I presume you know what that unfortunate movement led to?

The value of 'finger-clicking' is that each new action is a new beat, marked by a new click. This helps give the pause clarity and precision (particularly important in comedy). The acting has a decisive energy as a result, which sharpens up the thought, the wit and the attitudes. The fact is, however, that this exercise only uses what is already indicated by the rhythm and punctuation of the original.

A word of warning

Improvisation, games, exercises and theory are the stuff of gossip and jokes in the professional theatre, and it's important to realise why most experienced actors are resistant to them.

The fact is that this kind of work – in the professional theatre at least – has almost completely fallen out of fashion. Few professional directors use games, and most experienced actors find the whole idea faintly embarrassing. The exercises I've described are the hallmarks of particular directors and are not to be superficially imitated. There are stories about directors doing three-hour warm-ups every morning and failing to get down to the play itself. The important thing is to show the connection between whatever exercises you want your actors to do and the work on the production itself; nothing infuriates experienced actors more than feeling that valuable rehearsal time is being wasted.

Improvisation has come in and out of fashion, but is – quite rightly – *de rigueur* in actor training. In the professional theatre, however, it's best used in an informal, practical way, and you should be aware of the depth of resistance you may encounter if you impose too much improvisation on experienced, 'text-based' British actors. Since acting and directing are unquantifiable, drama theory is a way of creating an academic subject that can be taught and examined. As a result, many young graduates enter the profession convinced of the value of theory, but with very little sense of what impact it will have in practice. Most actors harbour deep suspicions of theatrical theory. The young director who goes into rehearsal with his head full of this kind of work is liable to hurt himself badly when he hits the brick wall of the working actor's innate empiricism.

Let me give you an example: I was talking with a couple of actors recently, who were working on different productions in two important London theatres with highly regarded directors. Both had started rehearsals on the same day and were exchanging incredulous tales about 'bean bags' and games and improvisation. 'With four weeks rehearsal on a difficult play, he wants us to do the kind of rubbish we did at drama school!' one of them said. They just wanted to concentrate on the details of the play and their characters as soon as possible and felt they were wasting rehearsal time. They typified a growing mood amongst many experienced actors today.

There are many irreverent stories about even the gurus of games and exercises. While rehearsing *Oedipus* at the Old Vic the actors were asked by Peter Brook to express in improvisation the thing that they were most frightened of. John Gielgud walked onto the middle of stage and said in his plummiest tones: 'Peter, we open in one week.' When the same director asked his actors to share the extremes of isolation by sitting on the floor with paper bags on their heads – and was persuaded to do the same – he found himself left alone with a bag over his head while the cast sneaked out to the pub.

Be bold, be adventurous, stretch your actors. But know their limits.

13

Rehearsals 4: Language

The words in which the play is written are the key to everything.

One of the qualities of a great play is that you can find almost everything you need in the text itself: story, character, ideas and so on. The theatre has acute technical limitations. However powerful the visual images, however brilliant the lighting and the sound effects may be, the spoken word is central, and if the actors are not speaking the words intelligibly, musically and audibly, the play will go for nothing.

There's a growing worry that some actors are so caught up in their desire to create a three-dimensional character that they have little interest in the spoken word. Writers and directors like David Mamet, Harold Pinter, Peter Gill and Peter Hall have all talked of an approach to character that is centred on the speaking of the text. They express frustration with a kind of acting that is so psychological that it fails to respond to the play itself. David Mamet declares that

> The actor does not need to 'become' the character. The phrase, in fact, has no meaning. There *is* no character. They are lines of dialogue meant to be said by the actor. When he or she says them simply, in an attempt to achieve an object more or less like that suggested by the author, the audience sees an illusion of a character upon the stage.

Similarly, I've heard Peter Gill joke that he'd prefer actors to say the line in the 'right way without knowing why' than in the 'wrong way, but cleverly'.

You need to develop your own views on these questions. I tend to side with the language obsessives, but am aware that it can hinder the actor's individual creativity. But I do know that ignoring the language of the play is a big mistake.

Re-reading

And so I think that the main substance of the first week's rehearsal should be getting to grips with the text. Depending on the difficulty of the language, I will usually spend the first few days getting the actors to read the play through three or four times. I stop the reading frequently, drawing the actors' attention to things in the script they might not have noticed, asking questions, provoking thought, and sharing opinions.

But this mustn't become a free-for-all. Once you allow and encourage discussion it can be difficult to know how to maintain momentum. I sometimes deliberately leave questions unanswered, knowing that time will reveal all. It can be a good idea to get the actors to read the text through again, with hardly a comment. It's astonishing how often the point of the scene will emerge, your insights will be confirmed or challenged, and the actors' questions answered.

What is being said?

Despite Peter Gill's joke, if your actors really don't understand what they're saying, it's unlikely your audience will.

And so one of the first things they need to do is gain an exact understanding of everything that's being said: not intellectual interpretation so much as simple comprehension. This is sometimes trickier than you might think. Each play is written in its own way, in its own particular language, and it's crucial you build a shared understanding of how that language works.

With Shakespeare this is essential. I conduct the first week of rehearsals with the whole cast sitting around a table littered with every available edition of the play, as well as half a dozen reference books (dictionaries, guides, glossaries, encyclopaedias, websites, etc., but no critical works). I encourage an atmosphere in which questions can be asked about the exact meaning of everything that's said, and not just the most obscure lines. I then get the actors, or my assistant, to look up almost every other word in a decent dictionary or a Shakespeare glossary. The footnotes in academic editions are sometimes useful in making meanings clearer, but occasionally hide them beneath a cloud of interpretation. You need to do the work yourself.

Because language is always evolving, you need to be on the lookout for defunct uses of familiar words. This can be startling. An apparently ordinary phrase like 'what's the matter?' has a different meaning today ('what's wrong?') than it did in 1600 ('what's the substance of the complaint?'). In Act Four, Scene Two of *King Lear* Albany's messenger says that Edmund

> Informed against him
> And quit the house on purpose that their punishment
> Might have the freer course.

'On purpose' doesn't mean 'deliberately' but rather 'with the intention of'. Try saying the line out loud with the two different meanings and you'll see how a close understanding of the nuances of the language is essential if the acting is to be clear.

And then, of course, there are the *double entendres*. Eric Partridge's *Shakespeare's Bawdy* is an amazingly useful little book, which can shock you into seeing obscene wordplay in even the most apparently innocent line. Restoration comedy is similarly full of innuendo: the very title of Wycherley's *The Country Wife* has a sexual connotation, as does much of the dialogue. And when producing *The Importance of Being Earnest*, I was astonished to be told – perhaps incorrectly – that 'Bunbury' was contemporary gay slang for buggery, and 'earnest' was code for homosexual.

Even twentieth-century plays benefit from this kind of textual attention, particularly when they're written in an unfamiliar dialect. Look at this speech from Ena Lamont Stewart's extraordinary *Men Should Weep* and work out exactly what is being said (perhaps with the help of a native Glaswegian):

> Lily, money disnae stretch. Ye pit oot yer haun for yer change, and whit dae ye get? A coupla coppers. A ten shillingy note's no a ten shillingy note ony langer. I dinna ken whit they dirty rotten buggers in Parliament are daein' wi ma money, but they're daein somethin.

Or the first speech of David Mamet's *Glengarry Glen Ross*:

> John . . . John . . . John. Okay. John. John. Look: (*pause*) The
> Glengarry Highland's leads, you're sending Roma out. Fine.
> He's a good man. We know that he is. He's fine. All I'm saying,
> you look at the *board*, he's throwing . . . wait, wait, wait, he's
> throwing them away, he's throwing the leads away. All that
> I'm saying, that you're wasting leads. I don't want to tell you
> your *job*. All that I'm saying, things get *set*, I know they do,
> you get a certain *mindset* . . . a guy gets a reputation.

What exactly is being said?

The fact is that nothing can substitute for careful, detailed reading of the text, and your actors must understand everything they're saying before they can begin to act it.

Paraphrasing

One way of ensuring such understanding is to ask your actors to go through their part, line by line, putting everything they say into their own words. This is particularly useful when you're working on Shakespeare. An example might be:

> Of government the properties to unfold
> Would seem in me t'affect speech and discourse
> Since I am put to know that your own science
> Exceeds in that the lists of all advice
> My strength can give you. Then no more remains
> But to your sufficiency as your worth is able
> And let them work.

A rough paraphrase of the Duke's extraordinarily dense speech which opens *Measure for Measure* might go like this:

> If I was to explain to you the nature of ruling, it would appear
> pretentious and pompous, because I've been told that you
> already know much more than I am capable of telling you.
> So there's nothing left to do but let you get on with it, as well
> as you possibly can.

Paraphrasing encourages actors to concentrate on the meaning of what is said. It's a way of releasing the everyday quality of the dramatic action and helps the actors discover its vernacular energy. And when they return to the original text they embrace the words with alacrity, and an increased appreciation of its particular qualities: 'Shakespeare says it so much better than I do, and in less words' is the reaction to this exercise that I've most enjoyed hearing.

'Speak the speech, I pray you, as I pronounced it to you'

Once you and your actors have established a basic understanding of the text, it's necessary to attend to its intricacies: its inflections, cadences, rhythm and punctuation. Text work should extend way beyond the first week of analytical rehearsals and I regard my views on the text as central to what I can offer the actors. I return to it all the time, right until the opening night, and beyond.

You may face a problem when an actor finds it difficult to speak the line properly, with the right stress, or intonation. This may sound simple, but it astonishes me how frequently even the most experienced actors miss the point. The best thing to do is to explain the precise meaning of the line, without using the author's text, in the hope that something logical will fall into place and your actor will work out how to speak it.

But there sometimes comes a point when the best thing is to give 'a line reading' – that is, to say the line in such a way that the meaning you know is there is made clear to the actor. Some actors hate this – they feel you're interfering with their own private work, and that they will never be able to say the line right again; they want to discover the meaning and intonation for themselves, and bitterly resent having it imposed by the director. Others, some very experienced, are grateful for such help – particularly when working with a director who has a good ear for such things. They say it gives them a shorthand to the structure of the thought. I think it can be extremely useful, but I've learnt the hard way that it needs to be handled carefully.

Hamlet tells his actors to: 'Speak the speech, I pray you, as I pronounced it to you, trippingly on the tongue.' No greater authority for line readings need be cited.

Shakespearean verse

Perhaps the greatest challenge for modern actors in Shakespeare is the speaking of the verse.

In Shakespeare everything is said, and there's no such thing as a 'subtext'. His language has an extraordinary ability to express both the inner workings of the human heart and the outer form of social intercourse. It's highly structured and tremendously natural, entirely artificial while also having a direct connection with everyday speech. This makes it difficult to speak convincingly. The five-beat line (the iambic pentameter) may be the natural rhythm of the English language (and of the human heart), but plays are not written in verse any more (*pace* Tony Harrison), and very few actors are instinctively at ease with its disciplines. You need to help them discover a way of speaking the verse which is true to its rhythms, musicality and poise, without sacrificing its meaning and psychological reality. And here the form of the writing is the best indication of its content.

Have a look at Romeo's speech at the opening of Act Five of *Romeo and Juliet*:

If **I** may **trust** the | **flatt**'ring **truth** of <u>sleep</u>
My **dreams** presage some | **joyful news** at <u>hand</u>.
My **bosom**'s **lord** sits | **lightly** in his <u>**throne**</u>
And **all** this **day** an | **unaccustom**'d <u>spirit</u>
<u>**Lifts**</u> me **above** the **ground** | with **cheerful thoughts**.
I **dreamt** my **lady came** | and **found** me <u>**dead**</u>
<u>**Strange**</u> dream that **gives** | a **dead** man **leave** to **think**
And **breathed** such **life** | with **kisses** in my <u>**lips**</u>
That **I** revived and | **was** an <u>**emp**</u>eror. +
Ah **me** how **sweet** is | **love** itself poss<u>**essed**</u>
When **but** love's **shadows** | **are** so **rich** in <u>joy.</u>

The syllables marked **bold** are the five beats in the line, those <u>**underlined**</u> are the major stresses (which are usually at the end of the line). The | indicates a 'caesura'. The + marks a 'run-over' of the vowel-sound. The metre – in all its complexity – is ignored at its peril.

Most of the lines are in a regular iambic metre ('ti-tum ti-tum ti-tum ti-tum ti-tum'). But the fourth line has eleven syllables and thus ends with a 'feminine ending'. This piles the pressure onto the first syllable of '**spir**it', followed by a stress on '**Lifts**' at the beginning of the next line (the result of this 'trochee' – 'tum-ti' – is a physical sensation of being lifted).

The last line is especially interesting. At first sight, you might think that it should be 'When but **love's** shadows'. But this forgets that love has already been referred to, and so the meaning is simpler: 'When **even** the shadows of love are so rich in joy'. The individual thought is more particular.

The best way of regarding the caesura is to see it as a halfway mark in the middle of the line, dividing it into two distinct clusters of meaning. So for example: 'If I may **trust** the' *what*? 'The **flatt**'ring **truth** of **sleep**'. 'And **breathed** such life', *how*? 'With **kisses in** my **lips**'.

The 'run-over' occurs where one line ends with a vowel ('**emp**eror') – and an open mouth – and the next one starts with a vowel, in this case the sighing sound 'Ah me'.

This kind of close scrutiny can be revealing for your actors. It helps them speak a difficult text, with a confidence that makes it easier to understand. The danger occurs when the actors count beats, hunt out caesuras, and fail to speak like real human beings. The opposition between 'beautiful speaking' and 'meaning' is an outdated one. The glorious noise that used to be so prevalent in Shakespearean acting is superfluous. An actor who can speak Shakespeare with fluid, confident grace will be able to command the attention of your audience.

Verse-speaking has attracted theories of all kinds. Sir Peter Hall is proud of having been called an 'iambic fundamentalist' for his notions of a single, rigorously defined way of speaking the verse. In this, the end of the line is all important, the fifth beat is the key, the caesura must always be marked, end-stopping is obligatory and so on. This is important stuff, but all that Peter is really doing – I'm not criticising him for it and I don't think he'd deny it – is spelling out to a younger generation of actors, the basic shape, pulse and quality of the ten-syllable verse line.

The crucial point is that the iambic pentameter is the most natural verse form in the English language, in existence from Chaucer to Tennyson. Actors need to be helped to understand its simple, and flexible, power.

'The what?'

Directors who want the language of the play to be powerfully expressed often face the challenge of persuading modern psychologically-trained actors to 'commit' to the words.

One technique I've seen used by Peter Gill goes like this. The actor playing Richard III, for instance, starts the opening speech 'Now is the winter of our discontent'. The director provokes him: 'Now is the *what* of your discontent?' 'The **winter** of our discontent', 'The winter of your *what*?' 'The winter of our **discontent**', '*When* was the winter of your discontent?' '**Now** is the winter of our discontent', '*whose* discontent?' '**Our** discontent' and so on.

Some actors hate 'the what?' and say that it freezes up their instinct. Others, including some very experienced ones, love it. The point is much more than simply to get actors to speak louder (though that's needed too); it's a way of getting them to feel the economy and force of the writing, in which every word counts, is packed full of meaning, and demands commitment.

Prose

The best actors have an intuitive understanding of the musicality of spoken language, and an essential part of your job is to help and encourage this. Even the most experienced actor will sometimes say 'I just don't know how to say this line', and it's important that you develop an 'ear' for the cadences and flow of prose as much as verse.

Prunella Scales has drawn up a set of 'principles of stress in spoken English'. Characteristically, she prefaces them by emphasising that they should be ignored – *often* – for the sake of sense and character:

1. Assume there is only one main stress in every grammatical sentence.
2. Stress nouns before adjectives and verbs before adverbs. When in doubt, go for the noun.
3. Don't colour 'colour' words, e.g. 'red', 'brilliant', 'rolling', 'pomp', etc – they should work for themselves.
4. Don't stress negatives – they should work for themselves.
5. Don't stress personal pronouns and possessive adjectives – they're strong and don't usually need help.
6. Let subordinate clauses ride without stress or emphasis. Also phrases in brackets or any form of parenthesis. Also look at the possibility of saying them all on one note. This will allow you to take them as slowly or as quickly as you like.
7. Don't stress prepositions, conjunctions or particles (unless playing news readers, sports reporters, or any other users of Mediaspeak).
8. In compound verbs, go for the main verb, not the auxiliary. E.g. don't say 'Much **have** I travelled in the realms of gold' or 'I **will** arise and go now...'
9. Don't make heavy weather of titles, formal phrases of introduction, vocative phrases such as 'Good my lord', 'Nay, I protest Madam', etc. or casual oaths such as 'Pox on't', 'for Christ's sake' etc: often they're there only as courtesies, rhythmic aids or to draw attention to the speaker.
10. In Restoration Comedy particularly, it's often useful to take whole phrases on the 'upbeat'.

These commonsense principles are particularly valuable when you're directing prose comedy.

Listening carefully to your actors will give you all the insights you need. If the phrasing isn't right, your production won't get the response the writer is expecting. When it's spot on, the play will be released.

The 'understood'

It's important to make your actors aware of what their character has already mentioned – what is 'understood'. Thus at one point in *John Gabriel Borkman*, Mrs Borkman says, 'We have a long road to travel together.' Her son, Erhart, replies,

'It's a very short road we'll be travelling together.' In early rehearsals the actor insisted on stressing both 'road' and 'together', until I pointed out that travelling a *road together* was understood: it was the *shortness* of the road which was his new thought. It's a tiny detail but it makes a difference.

Similarly, Theseus's first speech in *A Midsummer Night's Dream* includes the lines:

> But **oh** me**thinks** how **slow**
> This **old** moon **wanes**.

The beats are on 'oh', 'thinks', and, above all, 'slow'; the moon has already been mentioned ('Four **happy days** bring **in** / An**other moon**') and is an 'understood': it's the slowness of the old moon that matters. The thought is less particular if the actor stresses the obviously attractive – but unstressed – word 'moon' instead.

Of course, 'the understood' extends beyond a repeated word in a speech or interchange. It can stretch right across a scene, when a character refers back to something that was said ten minutes earlier. You need to be 'tuned' to this and point it out when you notice it ('You've already referred to the money you owe, you're now talking about how you're going to pay it back: move the story on!'); clarifying the 'understood' helps an actor be clearer.

Modern texts

The best modern drama has its own verbal brilliance. Three examples:

PAM (*off*) In there.
> *Len comes in. He goes down to the sofa. He stares at it.*
> All right?
> *Pause. Pam comes in.*
LEN This ain' the bedroom.
PAM Bed ain' made.
LEN Oo's bothered?
PAM It's awful. 'Ere's nice.
LEN Suit yourself. Yer don't mind if I take me shoes off? (*He kicks them off.*) No one 'ome?

Or:

> You need a friend. You have a long hike, my lad, up which,
> presently, you slog unfriended. Let me perhaps be your boat-
> man. For if and when we talk of a river we talk of a deep and
> dank architecture. In other words, never disdain a helping
> hand, especially one of such rare quality.

Or:

> Birth was the death of him. Again. Words are few. Dying
> too. Birth was the death of him. Ghastly grinning ever since.
> Up at the lid to come. In cradle and crib. At suck first fiasco.
> With the first totters. From mammy to nanny and back.
> All the way. Bandied back and forth. So ghastly grinning on.
> To now. To this night.

Edward Bond's beautifully economical South London dialect;
Harold Pinter's deliberately ornate, slangy artifice; Samuel
Beckett's luminous, punning, resonant poetry: each is unique
and demands absolute precision in the way your actors speak
the language. Your approach should include detailed textual
insight, literary appreciation of echo and resonance, 'con-
ducting' of pitch, rhythm and melody and so on. This is
crucial stuff that must not be ignored.

The actor's psychological work on 'character' (explored in
the next chapter) will only take him so far; once it is rooted
in the details of the language, the result will feel integrated
and purposeful.

14

Rehearsals 5: Character

Once the analysis of the play and its language has begun, you can turn your attention to the important question of 'character'.

There are many different ways of helping your actors develop their characters, but by far the most valuable is to share your psychological insights in a clear, easily understandable, textually supported way. I try to make all my work on character an organic part of the whole, difficult to distinguish from textual analysis, physical expression, blocking, costumes and so on. In fact, almost everything that I say or do in rehearsals is related to the question of character, and I see my role here as, above all, a guide to the play itself.

Many systems and exercises have been devised to help actors discover and create their characters, some of which I summarise below. I've tried them all at different times, with different degrees of success. But nothing can replace your own obsessive interest in the psychological truths of the characters, and your sympathetic engagement with the actors' struggle to realise them. Some directors dismiss discussions about character as being the actor's job. To an extent they're right. But if you're not interested in the actor's approach to his character you're not going to be able to help him very much.

Psychological qualities

It's impossible to direct a play without some feeling for the fundamentals of human psychology.

In a good play the characters are sharply differentiated: one has a melancholic disposition, a second gets angry quickly, a third has a romantic sensibility, a fourth is an intellectual and so on. To simplify ridiculously: in *Hamlet*, Fortinbras is strong, Ophelia febrile, Horatio loyal, Gertrude womanly, Claudius greedy and Hamlet is – well – all kinds of things.

Similarly, in *A Doll's House*, Torvald is conventional, Rank melancholic, Krogstad threatening and Nora apparently eager to please. These are all basic characteristics, which are fairly easy to define and share with your actors.

But it's not enough to note such psychological manifestations; you need to understand their causes. Richard III's murderous actions have motivations – as, surely, do Iago's – and you need to help your actors work out what they might be: jealousy, a sense of being an outsider, an inferiority complex, sexual anger and so on. Human beings are driven by psychological forces – some inherited, others learnt – and it's crucial that you're intrigued enough to explore what these are, and committed to helping your actors realise them. Of course, you need to be careful: motives are often mixed – even apparently altruistic ones – and actors shouldn't be asked to play a simplification. Nor should your audiences be expected to submit themselves to an extended psychoanalytic workshop. But in a good play, characters do things for a reason and your actors need to discover those reasons if they're to play them convincingly.

In the greatest plays, as in life, characters are driven by their subconscious, as well as their conscious, mind. Hamlet's disgust at his mother's sexual relationship with his uncle is both irrational and entirely true to life. Her first husband has died and she has married Claudius quite properly. And yet to Hamlet, this produces the most profound crisis (Oedipal, some argue): his father's place in his mother's bed has been usurped and he nurses a deep hatred for his replacement. Similarly, Ranevskaya's longing for her cherry orchard is more than simply the materialism of the Russian landowner: seen from the nursery where she played as a child, the white blossom of the cherry orchard releases in her a melancholic reminder of her youth and her lost innocence.

You need to share these insights with your actors. Such observations are more than psychological case studies or literary criticism: actors can't play an essay. But the intelligent actor will find them useful: they will give him a glimpse of just how deep his character's feelings and motivations go.

Character and contradiction

Character is a difficult thing to define.

Actors talk about 'finding their character', 'building a character', 'getting to the heart of their character' and so on. But when you try to describe a real person's character, you find that it's full of complexities and contradictions. Crucially, you realise that people change according to whom they're with, or what they're doing: I can be all sweetness and light with people I'm trying to impress and foul to my children; intellectually arrogant one moment and struck dumb with my own stupidity the next.

Such contradictions lie at the heart of any credible dramatic character. Lear, who is such a bad father at the beginning, discovers by the end an entirely different relationship with his youngest daughter. Ranevskaya is profound and shallow, generous and greedy in equal measure. Nora loves her husband but leaves him in order to be true to herself. Jimmy Porter is capable of the extremes of savagery and tenderness, wit and obtuseness. In all of these great characters, contradiction is central.

Brecht made a political point of emphasising such contradictions. He showed, for example, that the contradiction at the heart of Mother Courage – that she thrives off the war that kills her children – is the product of a contradictory world. Similarly, Shen-Te (the 'good woman') in *The Good Person of Szechwan* has to become Shui-Ta (the 'wicked man') in order to survive.

The crucial point is that such contradiction is the very stuff of human life and you need to encourage your actors to find their character in contradiction as much as in consistency. Anything else will be two-dimensional and shallow.

Human nature

In discussing character, actors often talk about 'human nature'.

While there are, of course, certain universal needs and fears that are found in every age and place – food, sex and warmth, death, danger and hunger – most human behaviour is specific to a particular place and circumstance. What actors usually mean by human nature is their own nature, and they interpret everything from their own standpoint. But any analysis of behaviour needs to take into account the particular circumstances in which it takes place.

And so an actress playing Ophelia is more likely to grasp the reality of her descent into madness if she understands the narrow limits of her experience, as well as her elevated, aristocratic position in society. Her relationship with Hamlet is much more than simply romantic; it's driven by her father's ambition and her brother's protective concern. It's a love affair that's played out under the public gaze, and her 'madness' is a highly realistic expression of her repressed feelings and sexuality.

I tried to help an actor playing Molière's Don Juan to see his character as more than simply a portrait of timeless male heterosexuality: not only is he an aristocrat, he's a product of eighteenth-century rationalism, which was in the process of undermining the authority of the family, society and religion. The moment when he tries to bribe a religious beggar into denouncing the existence of God gains radical potency when the actor understands Juan's philosophical and social circumstances.

It's only when your actor grasps the particular environment in which his character lives that he can understand the full weight of his actions. It's part of your job to show that 'human nature' changes according to the circumstances in which it finds itself.

Traditional character types

When directing the classics, it's important to be alert to characters that are refinements of stock figures, whether from popular theatre, fairy tales, the Bible or whatever. An example might be the Earl of Gloucester in *King Lear*. It's evident, particularly in the early scenes, that Shakespeare has drawn Gloucester from the *Pantalone* figure in the Italian *commedia dell'arte*: old, short-sighted, lusty, powerful and full of his own importance, yet deeply foolish at the same time. In trying to help Michael Cronin discover the particular qualities of this part, I found it useful to give some sense of this. Michael was rightly resistant to taking this too far, but I think it helped him see Gloucester's petty-mindedness at the beginning of the play – his metaphorical blindness before his literal blinding – as an archetypal image of bumbling old age.

Trofimov in *The Cherry Orchard* offers another example. Nineteenth-century Russian drama and novels often feature an idealistic student, full of speeches and passion, but utterly ineffective and foolish. If the actor is given some understanding of this tradition, he's likely to catch the delicate irony in a speech such as this:

> Just think, Anya, your father and grandfather, and all your ancestors were serf-owners, they owned living souls. And can't you see, looking out at you from every tree in that orchard, every leaf, every trunk, those human beings? Can't you hear their voices? Owning people – I mean, it's corrupted all of you, those who came before and now yourselves, so that neither you nor your mother, nor your uncle, are actually aware that you're living on credit, at the expense of people you wouldn't even let over your front door.

Chekhov shows that Trofimov's idealism and concern for his fellow man is no more brave and original than his mother's greed and sentimentality.

Great writers transform raw material into sophisticated art, by imbuing it with particularity, pathos and tragedy. The stock character is refined, but you should help your actor understand the stock on which it has been based.

Class

In helping an actor develop his character, it's essential that he understand the particular nature of his class. Class affects everything. It's partly because Hamlet is a prince that he has such a highly developed level of self-consciousness. Brutus and Cassius in *Julius Caesar* are from the very best Roman families: their assassination of Caesar is a palace coup rather than a popular revolt. Sganarelle (in Molière's *Don Juan*) is a servant: his conservative religiosity – as well as his final shout for his 'wages' – is a manifestation of that. Engstrand (in Ibsen's *Ghosts*) is a poor carpenter: his 'morality' is compromised by his need for money, and his attempt to prostitute his own daughter is driven by financial necessity as much as greed. Judge Brack (in *Hedda Gabler*) is an important man in a very small city: hence his mixture of outward propriety and inner corruption.

Of course, you have to be careful in talking about class. Human behaviour shouldn't be seen as narrowly deterministic. Just because someone is an aristocrat doesn't mean that he swans around being 'aristocratic': class attitudes and behaviour are the aggregates of a whole range of individuals of that class. Brecht insisted that 'if you're playing a peasant, you must play an individual peasant'. And certainly, getting convincing performances of working-class and peasant characters is especially difficult. This is sometimes the fault of the writing (Noël Coward's portraits of working-class characters are particularly condescending, while some people argue that Shakespeare's poor people are little more than 'comic relief'). But it's sometimes because of a particular kind of sentimentality that actors bring to working-class roles, all heroic posturing, aggressive toughness and romantic struggles. Casting genuinely working-class actors in these roles goes a long way to addressing this problem.

I often remind actors of the particular nature of their character's economic and social position. Take Mrs Borkman in *John Gabriel Borkman*. In rehearsal, Gillian Barge had discovered a powerful, self-dramatising streak in the character, which released its power and allowed her 'back-story' to become evident. But I soon started to feel that the particular tone she was taking was too 'bourgeois', too self-pitying and insufficiently austere. When I pointed out that Gunhild was from one of the best families in the capital, Gillian found a way of balancing this tendency for self-dramatisation with the right kind of haughty, aristocratic pride ('I mean, how could it happen? How could such a terrible thing happen to just one family? To *our* family, of all people! With our reputation! To think that it should all fall on *us*!').

Or take the Earls of Kent and Gloucester in *King Lear*. The play starts with both Earls deep in conversation about the

King's imminent division of the kingdom. It was only when I said to the actors that they should think of the scene as two senior cabinet ministers worrying about their Prime Minister's decisions, that the scene gained the appropriate *gravitas* and illusion of power:

KENT I thought the King had more affected the Duke of Albany than Cornwall.
GLOUCESTER It did always seem so to us. But now, in the division of the kingdom, it appears not which of the Dukes he values most, for equalities are so weighed, that curiosity in neither can make choice of either's moiety.

Some young directors dismiss discussions of class as dull and old-fashioned ('Stalinist' was one term of abuse I've heard). I've seen Peter Gill assemble a group of twenty actors and line them up by 'class', and it taught me an unforgettable lesson. Class is one of the essential elements in defining characters, and is ignored at your peril.

The character's journey

It's important to help your actors chart a clear sense of their characters' 'journeys' through the play. This is more than simply an analysis of story: it's an appreciation of the individual lines of energy that drive the play. Two of my favourite female characters are Isabella (in *Measure for Measure*) and Nora (in Ibsen's *A Doll's House*), and both are remarkable for the changes they undergo.

Isabella starts as an over-enthusiastic novice ('have you nuns no further privileges?'). When Lucio asks her to intervene on behalf of her brother Claudio (who has been condemned to death for getting his girlfriend pregnant), her first response is that she should do nothing ('Alas, what poor ability's in me / To do him good?'). When she goes to see Angelo she becomes increasingly eloquent, and it's this very eloquence that makes Angelo desire her. When she says that she will denounce him, his 'Who will believe thee, Isabel?' plunges her into her first crisis. The second crisis occurs when she goes to see Claudio, who tries to be noble but simply wants to live. She's about to storm out of the prison in rage ('Tis best that thou diest quickly'), when she's confronted with a Friar who tells her about Angelo's fiancée Mariana, who will sleep with Angelo in her place. Then, she is astonished to hear that Angelo has not only slept with Mariana, but executed Claudio too. This spurs her to seek justice. But when Angelo is condemned to death, she's persuaded by Mariana to beg for his life. Her reward is to find out that Claudio is alive, that the Friar is the Duke, that he's in love with her, and that her nightmare is over. Thus, Isabella's 'journey' is a learning curve from the cold chastity of the nunnery to the possibility of marriage, by way of a confrontation with death, loneliness and humiliation.

In *A Doll's House*, Nora is the wife of the newly appointed bank manager, Torvald Helmer, and the mother of his three young children. At the beginning she pretends to be birdbrained. But in fact Nora is shrewd and proves quite capable of paying off her secret debt to Krogstad (Nora used the money to take her husband on a successful health-cure to Italy) while letting Torvald think she's extravagant. For much of the play her outward behaviour is conventional: she's done everything for her husband's sake and is content to play games for him, flirt with Rank, and dance the tarantella for both of them. But Krogstad's threats take her to the brink of suicide. It's only at the very end, when she's changed out of her Neapolitan peasant costume, packed her case, and reconceived of herself as an independent woman, that the Nora of feminist legend starts to emerge. The journey she takes in the three days covered by the play – from childish obedience to articulate defiance – is much more interesting than the famous door slam with which it ends.

You should talk about such journeys (or 'through-lines') with your actors – or draw up a synopsis or 'timeline' if you prefer. The important thing is that communicating a vivid sense of through-line encourages your actors to see their characters in terms of development, not stasis: it allows them to get a sense of ebb and flow, of energy and dynamic. A clear journey makes the difference between 'epic' storytelling ('this happens, and then that happens') and 'dramatic' storytelling ('this happens, *because* that happens') and it brings a play to life.

Back-story

Good writers construct their characters with a 'back-story': a sense of what they did before the action of the play begins.

Ibsen's plays demand a particularly detailed understanding of this. In rehearsing *Ghosts* I wanted to help Diana Quick grasp the complexity of what had happened to Mrs Alving.

> Mrs Alving had originally been attracted to her dashing and well known husband. His secret alcoholism and bad behaviour culminated in his affair with their maid. She confided in the sympathetic Pastor Manders who insisted that she return to her husband. She accepted this advice and stifled the truth, while also developing an interest in alternative thinking and radical writing.

All of this informed the way that Mrs Alving greeted Manders, defended the radical books that are on her table and treated her son, Osvald, on his return from Paris. If you haven't shared a clear understanding of every phase of this back-story your actress's performance will inevitably lack the depth of feeling that's required.

But grasping the back-story is important not just in Ibsen and other nineteenth-century naturalistic writers. It's necessary in Shakespeare too, even if the clues are sketchier. Two examples: in the first scene of *A Midsummer Night's Dream*, Theseus says to Hippolyta:

> Hippolyta, I wooed thee with my sword
> And won thy love doing thee injuries.

When you understand that in the legend Hippolyta is an Amazon – one of those mythical, matriarchal fighters from the *Iliad* who fought against men as their equals – you can begin to build up an image of her as an independent-minded woman, capable of fighting a hero, but also of loving him.

A second example is at the end of the first scene of *King Lear.*

GONERIL   You see how full of changes his age is ... He always
   loved our sister most and with what poor judgment he hath
   now cast her off appears too grossly.
REGAN   Tis the infirmity of his age. Yet he hath ever but slenderly
   known himself.

According to Goneril, Lear made the biggest mistake in parenting – loving one child more than the other – and, according
to Regan, has always been foolish in his dealings. This psychological information is revealing about the entire family
dynamic and can subtly affect the way all three characters
interact.

Significant details

In working on character it's important to develop an eye for
significant detail.

There's a tiny moment at the end of a beautiful, if often
neglected scene (3.4) in *Much Ado About Nothing.* It's the
morning of Hero's wedding, and she's nervous. The young
maidservant Margaret is making obscene comments ('Is
there any harm in "the heavier for a husband?" None I think,
an it be the right husband and the right wife – otherwise 'tis
light and not heavy') when suddenly Ursula returns and
announces:

> Madam, withdraw. The Prince, the Count, Signor Benedick,
> Don John and all the gallants of the town are come to fetch
> you to church.

The contrast between the romantic dignity of this and
Margaret's wisecracks made me realise that Ursula could be
an older woman who had known Hero since she was a child,
and was almost a replacement mother in her life. This
informed my casting, and the actress's performance.

Another example is Edgar's vulnerability in his first encounter with his brother Edmund in *King Lear.* Before Edgar

has said anything, Edmund has introduced him to us as 'the catastrophe of the old comedy'. And Edgar's gullibility is such that he can fall for Edmund's deceit in seconds. After all, Edmund has been away for nine years and Edgar doesn't know him well. Immediately after their first encounter Edmund describes him as:

> a brother noble
> Whose nature is so far from doing harms
> That he suspects none. On whose foolish honesty
> My practices ride easy.

Thus, Edgar's narrative can be presented as a kind of *éducation sentimentale*, from naïveté to fully-fledged experience, by way of gullibility, rejection, exile and humiliation. If the actor starts right, with an eye for the significant detail, his subsequent journey will be possible.

A third example is where Hedda Gabler deliberately mistakes Miss Tesman's extravagant hat:

HEDDA We're going to have problems with that maid.
MISS TESMAN With Berta? Problems?
TESMAN What d'you mean, darling?
HEDDA (*pointing*) Look. Here on this chair. She's left her old hat.
TESMAN Hedda . . .
HEDDA Suppose someone came, and saw?
TESMAN Hedda, that's Aunt Julia's hat.
HEDDA Really?
MISS TESMAN Yes, Hedda, mine. And it's certainly not old.
HEDDA I didn't look closely.
MISS TESMAN (*pinning on the hat*) As it happens this is the
    first time I've worn it. The very first time.
TESMAN It's a wonderful hat. Magnificent.
MISS TESMAN Now, Jørgen, it's nothing of the kind.

A woman capable of such destructive wit is capable of a great deal more, as the rest of the play is to reveal. Drawing the actress's attention to an apparently insignificant moment can illuminate the rest of the part.

What's at stake?

Any dramatic situation worth playing contains within it elements of danger, and you need to help your actors discover what's 'at stake' for their characters.

Thus, when directing the first scene of *A Midsummer Night's Dream*, I teased the actress playing Hermia that it looked as if it was her Ford Fiesta that was at stake, not her heart. By not engaging with the historical conditions in which Hermia lived (primarily Elizabethan England, despite Athens), her disobedience towards her father lacked the enormity that Shakespeare surely intended. Similarly, when directing *King Lear*, I reminded the actor playing the Earl of Kent just how extraordinary his decision to become a labouring man was. This was a senior aristocrat disguising himself as a bricklayer, in a very hierarchical society: he had sacrificed everything because of his beliefs.

Similarly, when directing Ibsen's *A Doll's House*, I spoke to Kelly Hunter about the courage – perhaps folly – it took for Nora to leave her husband at the end of the play. We agreed that she would be regarded as a moral deviant, without any support of any kind, with few financial resources, nowhere to live, and no access to her children. Reading the play from the perspective of modern feminism can ruin its explosive power.

And so you should always ask 'what's at stake?' By defining the danger you realise the courage that's needed to overcome it: and thus it becomes dramatic.

Tone of voice

In the best-written plays a huge amount of information can be drawn from the particular nuances of how a character speaks.

Look, for example, at the extraordinarily compact speech with which Philo opens Shakespeare's *Antony and Cleopatra*:

> Nay but this dotage of our general's
> O'erflows the measure. Those his goodly eyes
> That o'er the files and musters of the war
> Have glowed like plated Mars, now bend, now turn

The office and devotion of their view
Upon a tawny front. His captain's heart
Which in the scuffles of great fights hath burst
The buckles on his breast, reneges all temper
And is become the bellows and the fan
To cool a gypsy's lust.

This is a minor character, but the intellectual control, the sarcasm, the disapproval of Cleopatra and the admiration of Antony's military prowess, all give a strong sense of an establishment insider, suspicious of the foreign and the new, devoted to the status quo and anxious about the changes that his boss is bringing about.

Or look at Mick in Harold Pinter's *The Caretaker*:

You're stinking the place out. You're an old robber, there's no getting away from it. You're an old skate. You don't belong in a nice place like this. You're an old barbarian, honest. You got no business wandering around in an unfurnished flat. I could charge seven quid a week for this if I wanted to. Get a taker tomorrow. Three hundred and fifty a year exclusive. No argument. I mean if that sort of money's in your range don't be afraid to say so.

A careful reading of this – with its mixture of cockney menace, estate agent jargon and petty superiority – will give you a range of insights into the character of Mick: brutal and extravagant, edgy and stubborn, conservative and prejudiced, defiant and difficult for Davies to deal with.

Share your feelings about the character's tone of voice: the actor will thank you for it.

Stanislavski

The Russian actor and director Konstantin Stanislavski (1863–1938) was the first person to attempt a 'science of acting'. Together with Vladimir Nemirovich-Danchenko (1859–1943) he set up the Moscow Art Theatre (MAT) in 1887 with the aim of forging a new kind of theatre, largely in reaction to the kind of melodramatic, bombastic acting that characterised mid-nineteenth-century Russian theatre.

Stanislavski's various books are among the key theoretical texts of modern theatre. Perhaps his greatest achievement was that he analysed the basic components of naturalistic acting and broke it down into a series of relatively simple questions. These are, above all: 'What does the character want?' (his super-objective), 'How does he go about achieving them?' (his objectives), and 'What stops him from achieving them?' (his obstacles).

Stanislavski is the father of modern acting and you need to familiarise yourself with the most useful of his terms.

Super-objective

A character's super-objective is the overarching desire that drives him through the play.

Lopakhin's super-objective in *The Cherry Orchard* is to get away from his peasant roots and become someone in society. Lear's super-objective is to go into retirement without losing his power or status. Hamlet's super-objective is to avenge his father's murder, and Mrs Alving's is to be reunited with her son and live by 'truth'. The super-objective is the engine that drives the character forward.

But defining the super-objective can be difficult: each of the examples above is questionable, and changes through the action of the play. They also depend on individual interpretation and the extent to which you allow for sub-conscious motivation. Thus, you could argue that Hamlet's super-objective is to live in a way that uses his brain to the fullest or that Lear's real super-objective is to be rid of his two elder daughters and die with his youngest daughter in his arms. Lopakhin's super-objective might be to become loved and accepted, and Mrs Alving's to lay the ghost of her dead husband.

It's perhaps best to regard the defining of the super-objective as a kind of speculative game that can be revealing, but is hardly scientific.

Objectives

Easier to define – and much more useful – are individual objectives. Look at Act One of *King Lear*. I'm convinced that Lear has divided the kingdom before the scene starts: he gives his eldest daughters their shares before he offers Cordelia the chance of winning 'a third more opulent than your sisters'. In other words, he starts the scene knowing how he wants it to end: his youngest daughter will be given the most desirable part (no doubt London and the South East) because she will deserve it most by loving him most. If the actor playing Lear carries that objective through the scene, he will know how to react to Goneril and Regan's formulaic declarations. He will also bring the drama to a high point of expectation when he turns to Cordelia – 'our joy' – and asks her what she can 'say to draw / A third more opulent than your sisters'. Without that sense of objective the acting of the scene will lose energy and purpose.

Another example is the great scene in *Ghosts* (Act Two) when Osvald's objective is to tell his mother about his illness. Osvald is off-stage in the dining room after lunch, where he's smoking a cigar and finishing off the liqueurs. When his mother asks him to come in to see her, he talks about everything but his objective. There's a telling stage direction in which we sense this objective, without knowing exactly what he's going to say: '*A silence. Dusk slowly begins to fall. Osvald paces up and down the room.*' And then he sits down on the sofa next to his mother, and slowly, but with great difficulty, tells her the painful, embarrassing truth, that he will become

> an incurable cripple for the rest of my life, and all because
> of my own stupidity . . . It's so shameful. So carelessly, without
> a thought – to have thrown away health, happiness, every-
> thing – my future, my very life!

Thus, his objective here is to tell his mother that he's suffering from an incurable illness (a code for syphilis), and that it's all his own fault. An actor who didn't understand this would find it hard to play the scene convincingly.

The clarification of such objectives makes the acting purposeful, focused and enjoyable. I remind actors of their objectives constantly, not just in rehearsal, but when the production has opened as well. If all you do for your actors is clarify what their characters want, you've given them a great deal.

Obstacles

The third element in the Stanislavskian system is the obstacle: the problems the character hits in trying to achieve his objectives. The way he responds to his obstacle is critical, and the particular choices he then makes are the key to any understanding of character.

In *Ghosts* the obstacle to Osvald's objective is dual: his own sense of shame and his mother's rising anxiety:

OSVALD I've got something to tell you, mother.

MRS ALVING (*strained*) Yes?

OSVALD (*staring straight in front of him*) Because I can't stand it any longer.

MRS ALVING Can't stand what? What is it?

OSVALD (*as before*) I couldn't bring myself to write to you about it – and since I've come home . . .

MRS ALVING (*grips his arm*) Osvald, what is it?

OSVALD Yesterday and today I've tried to put these thoughts out of my mind – to break free of them. But it's no use.

MRS ALVING (*stands up*) Osvald, you must tell me what's wrong!

OSVALD (*pulls her back down onto the sofa*) Sit down, mother, and I'll try and tell you.

Eventually, he overcomes this obstacle and manages to tell her everything he knows.

In Act One of *King Lear*, Lear's first obstacle arises when Cordelia says 'nothing'. Difficult as it is, her commitment to the truth is the absolute opposite of what he was expecting. He takes deep offence, and feels rejected. Once Cordelia has clarified her position, Lear disclaims 'all my paternal care / Propinquity and property of blood' and tells her suitors

(France and Burgundy) that 'now her price is fallen'. He is used to being obeyed and getting his own way and ruling by an act of emotional will. Now he's made a fool of himself and can't climb down, and his great rhetorical curses ('For by the sacred radiance of the sun / The mysteries of Hecate and the night') are his pathetic last resort. The way that Lear struggles with this obstacle and tries to drive Cordelia out of his sight defines his character at the beginning of the play.

Isabella in *Measure for Measure* comes up against her first major obstacle when Angelo says that he will release her brother if she will sleep with him (2.4). She overcomes this by assuring herself that her brother wouldn't allow her to do what Angelo wanted:

> I'll to my brother.
> Though he hath fallen by prompture of the blood
> Yet hath he in him such a mind of honour
> That had he twenty heads to tender down
> On twenty bloody blocks, he'd yield them up
> Before his sister should her body stoop
> To such abhorred pollution.

But when Isabella visits him in prison to tell him this (3.1), she meets her second major obstacle: Claudio's overpowering desire to live ('Sweet sister, let me live'), whatever the consequences. This obstacle seems insuperable, and she runs off helplessly cursing her brother: ''Tis best that thou diest quickly.'

This pattern of objectives and obstacles, of struggle and conflict, lies at the heart of any good drama. Showing the actors how strong their objectives are – and how challenging are the obstacles they face – is essential to good directing.

Actions and reactions

I sometimes remind actors of the biblical phrase, 'by their deeds shall you know them'. In other words 'character' isn't a fixed entity; it's defined by the particular decisions that the individual makes and the actions that spring from those decisions.

Take *Othello*. The fact that Othello ('the Moor') wooed and won Desdemona, a young daughter of the rich, white 'ruling class', says a great deal, both about Othello's status in Venice and about his courage in the face of the kind of casual racism that Desdemona's father represents. Then, when the call comes, he's prepared to give everything for a state that both needs and rejects him. When Desdemona comes up with the novel idea of going with her husband to Cyprus, he supports her. When Michael Cassio is caught drunk and brawling, Othello acts forcefully in stripping him of his rank. When Desdemona pleads his case, he quickly accepts Iago's suggestion that they may be having an affair. And so Othello comes to believe what he's always been told – that he doesn't deserve Desdemona. This is a man caught between being an insider and an outsider, and his actions and reactions are dictated by that fundamental insecurity.

Such insights are more than mere literary criticism: if you can help your actor understand the particular nature of his character's actions and reactions – his 'choices' – he will be able to make them visible to the audience. A useful exercise is to ask him to summarise his character's story (as above), and to draw attention to the choices that are made, by prefacing each choice with 'instead of'. Thus, the sentence above ('then, when the call comes, Othello is prepared to give everything for a state which both needs and rejects him') could be elaborated as follows: 'then, when the call comes, and the state needs him, *instead of turning his back on them for their racism and ingratitude,* Othello is prepared to give everything for a state which both needs and rejects him.'

By having his attention drawn to the choices his character makes, your actor will bring his individuality to life.

The Method

The American director and actor Lee Strasberg (1901–82) expanded and extended the Stanislavskian approach and created at the New York Actors Studio what is known as 'the Method'. This is an analytical approach to acting which is exceptionally psychological, and dependent on the actor subjecting himself to the most grilling self-analysis. It has been particularly influential on film acting, where the minutiae of emotional response are most visible.

The key concept in Method acting is 'emotional recall'. This is a technique that an actor can use to help him stimulate the emotion that's required at a particular moment. And so, if an actress has to express grief when she hears that her brother is dead (Isabella in *Measure for Measure*), she can use her own memory of bereavement – or heartache if she's never been bereaved – to trigger the emotion that the moment requires. An actor who needs to express the excitement of having won a battle (in *Coriolanus*) might use the memory of winning a sports match to help release some of those sensations. The memory of being in a very cold climate can help the actor produce the sensation of being cold (on a hot stage).

This fairly simple idea (nothing less than rooting the actor's imagination in his own experience) has been mystified in all sorts of ways, and there are stories of American film actors going to extraordinary lengths to discover the emotion they're trying to express. But the fact is emotional recall is a *sine qua non* of any good acting, and a good director encourages emotional memory all the time: 'I think it's a bit like when you first went to secondary school', or 'Remember when you desperately fancied that guy at a party' or 'I remember when I first became a dad, I felt this same mixture of exhaustion and exhilaration.' British actors don't talk about 'emotional recall' much, but it's important to recognise the term if it emerges in rehearsal.

Lee Strasberg's thoughts on acting can be found in *Strasberg at The Actors Studio*. One of his most exceptional pupils was the actress and teacher Uta Hagen, whose books are among the most useful things ever written about acting.

Who says what about whom?

When helping an actor develop his character, one useful exercise is to ask him to assemble a 'character collage', consisting of three different sets of quotations:

Everything the writer says about the character
Everything the character says about himself
Everything other characters say about him

Take Hedda Gabler. In his preliminary notes, Ibsen describes her as a 'pale, apparently cold beauty'. He also says that 'The title of the play is *Hedda Gabler*. I intended to indicate thereby that as a personality she is to be regarded rather as her father's daughter than as her husband's wife'. Then, on her first entry, Ibsen writes:

> *She is 29, a woman of style and character. Her complexion*
> *is smooth and pale; her grey eyes are cold, clear and calm.*
> *Attractive, light-brown hair, not particularly full. A modish,*
> *loose-fitting morning dress.*

Ibsen's image is precise and deserves careful study, not so much as a guide to casting but as a clue to Ibsen's conception of the character.

And what do the other characters in the play say about Hedda? Before she has even appeared, Miss Tesman talks of her in tones of awe, mixed with disapproval:

> General Gabler's daughter. The style she had, when her father
> was alive! D'you remember her riding beside him, down the
> road? In that long black skirt? With the feather in her hat?

Hedda's husband, Tesman, tells his aunt that 'some of my friends must be quite green-eyed' about this marriage, but soon adds, 'Before we were married, she often said she'd never be happy unless she could live in the old [and expensive] Falk villa.' When she does appear, Tesman says to his aunt: 'But don't you think she looks well? Don't you think she's filled out on our travels, rounded out?' Miss Tesman's final line is even more telling: 'Special. That's what Hedda is.' Mrs Elvsted speaks about Hedda's schooldays: 'You were in a higher class. You terrified me . . . When we met on the stairs you pulled my hair.'

And finally what does Hedda say about herself? Not much: she's too busy fending off unwanted attentions and fighting for her own independent way of life, despite the claustrophobia of her marriage. But early in Act Two she says the most revealing thing of all: 'I've only one talent. For boring myself to death.' The wit, the self-destruction and the self-awareness all make for a fatal cocktail.

This collage of information and opinion can be brought together to create a powerful sense of a character in three dimensions. One of the most striking things is just how contradictory these statements can be: Hedda is both vicious and kind, is spoken of with awe and condescension, has no sense of her own uniqueness and yet is outrageously arrogant. All of this is true, and the actress needs to embrace these apparently contradictory characteristics, and show each of them in turn, in specific, concrete moments.

This exercise isn't just for actors; it can be useful for directors too. Reminding yourself of these opinions can sometimes solve a problem. When directing *King Lear* I found it difficult to find the appropriate image for Lear's penultimate entrance – with Cordelia on the way to prison – until I noticed Edmund's description of him as the 'old and miserable King': this made me realise just how frail he should be at this point and helped me stage the moment with conviction and pathos.

It should be stressed this exercise is no more than reading the play carefully and intelligently. So long as you and your actors do that, all at least stands a chance of being well.

Hot-seating

I occasionally use a rehearsal technique called 'hot-seating': getting an actor to answer questions about his life strictly 'in character', using the first person only. This is valuable because it allows the actor to clarify his objectives. It also lets him explore the limitations of his character's knowledge or understanding. But it's important that you're precise about what moment in the character's life you're looking at – otherwise the character becomes omniscient ('on the day I end up shooting myself' and so on). This is Hamlet before he's met his father's ghost:

DIRECTOR So you're a student?
ACTOR And a prince.
DIRECTOR Which is more important?
ACTOR Both.
DIRECTOR Do you want to become King one day?
ACTOR That depends.
DIRECTOR Do you like the other students?
ACTOR Some of them. I like Horatio.
DIRECTOR What do you do at University?
ACTOR Put on plays.
DIRECTOR And now you're back here in Elsinore, what do you
feel?
ACTOR It's a shit heap.
DIRECTOR So, what happened to your dad?
ACTOR Dead.
DIRECTOR How?
ACTOR Just died. Asleep in his orchard.
DIRECTOR Natural causes?
ACTOR Seems so.
   Pause
DIRECTOR What's that over there?
ACTOR Looks like my father's ghost.
DIRECTOR Any questions for him?

Or Hedda Gabler just before she commits suicide:

DIRECTOR How do you feel?
ACTRESS Trapped.
DIRECTOR Why?
ACTRESS Brack's got me. Every which way. The bastard.
DIRECTOR So why don't you talk to your husband?
ACTRESS Don't be stupid. He doesn't know about me and
Løvborg.
DIRECTOR So?
ACTRESS Better death. That's the only way out. Shoot myself.
That'll shock the bastard. That's the only way to be free.

The value of this exercise is it helps your actor see just how
limited his character's knowledge and choices are at any
particular moment. Good performances show a character's
blindness as well as his insights.

Imaginative speculation

With all this analysis it's crucial you don't neglect perhaps the most important element of all in constructing character: the free play of the imagination. The actor needs to be encouraged to think speculatively about the material basis of his character's life.

Some of the key things are:

What kind of house does he live in?
What is his working day like?
What is his diet?
What does he earn?
What did his father do for a living?

Some of this will require research. Much of it is purely speculative. But it allows your actor to get some sense of his character's everyday life, before the drama begins.

Similarly, the actor should be encouraged to think about the more personal elements of his character's life:

His childhood
His relationship with his parents
His sex life
His emotional stability
His tendency to depression

Again, this is largely speculative, but can be useful.

With *King Lear* we found it valuable to talk about what Christmas at the Lears might have been like. We imagined Goneril as a surrogate mother, all organising and proper, if rather cold, Regan giving out presents, very much the soul of the party, but not to be trusted after a few glasses of wine, and Cordelia not joining in, but being loved and doted on by her irascible, domineering, over-emotional father. Some of this became evident in the way the three sisters interacted with each other and with their father on stage.

Rehearsing Ibsen's *Ghosts* we speculated about Osvald's life in Paris: where he lived, what his paintings were like, whom he knew there (this was the time of the great Impressionist exhibitions), what his love life was like and so on. This helped give his obsessive commitment to light and the 'joy of life' some imaginatively felt, concrete detail. Similarly, we wondered what the radical books on Mrs Alving's table were and made many wild (and bawdy) guesses about Engstrand's 'sailor's hostel'. None of this could be proved, but all of it helped.

Speculation can sometimes run away with itself. I remember wondering what would happen to the characters in *The Cherry Orchard* after the 1917 Russian Revolution. We came up with all sorts of fanciful scenarios about the maidservant Dunyasha having seven children and dying in the siege of Leningrad during the Second World War. But the biggest shock was when we realised that Lopakhin – sometimes presented as a hero of the revolution – would be one of the first to be shot as a rich peasant, or 'kulak'. Chekhov, of course, wouldn't have known this, but it allowed us to find many points of sympathy with Lopakhin without resorting to crude Marxist hero-worship.

It's important to let this speculative approach to character be as playful as possible. If you take it too seriously, you start to think that you can communicate it to the audience through the text itself.

'My character wouldn't do this'

One of the objections you occasionally have to confront is when an actor says: 'My character wouldn't do this.'

When this is in reaction to something his character says or does in the play, it usually implies that the actor hasn't understood the author's intentions. That should be easy to fix: the best thing is to return to the details of the play, and come to a closer agreement about why the character *does* say or do it. But when it's in reaction to something extraneous to the script, the discussion can become more complex: you may have to go back to first principles (language, class, circumstances, what's at stake, objectives, obstacles and so on).

I'm surprised how often I need to return to such fundamentals. Even the best actors find their ways to the truth in a crab-like fashion: through experience and excess, trial and error. You need to be prepared to answer even the crassest questions.

Character improvisation

Improvisation can be useful in helping actors develop their character. It is particularly helpful when an actor is creating a small part, which has to make a big impact.

Take Oswald in *King Lear*. Shakespeare gives very few indications as to who he is meant to be, other than Goneril's faithful servant. And so I gave Grant Gillespie just a few guidelines – above all, that money mattered more to Oswald than anything else, and that he couldn't be from the ruling class. Grant worked away at this endlessly in rehearsal, improvising a vast range of different characteristics (for a while it was southern Irish, at other times explicitly camp). The eventual result was untrustworthy and disloyal, ignorant and dangerous, eager to please and immoral. My only real contribution was to encourage Grant to try out as many different ideas as he could, until a couple of them started to stick.

Improvisation can also be useful when you're trying to catch a sense of the character's everyday life before the drama begins, a feeling of the characters in repose, going about their daily life. Thus, when directing *Look Back in Anger*, I set up an improvisation of Jimmy and Cliff reading the newspapers while Alison did the ironing – no words, no jokes, no communication, just the Sunday morning routine: the rustle of the papers, the pipe smoke, the noise of the iron. When, finally, I allowed the actor playing Jimmy to start the play ('Why do I do this every Sunday? Even the book reviews seem to be the same as last week's. Different books – same reviews'), the rituals and routines had a 'lived-in' feeling.

William Gaskill's landmark production of Stephen Lowe's *The Ragged Trousered Philanthropists* started with a ten-minute, entirely unscripted sequence in which the men came in, set up their painting equipment and started stripping, scrubbing, and redecorating the building. This was created through lengthy and detailed improvisation, in which the rhythms, sound and routines of hard physical labour became the substance – and meaning – of the scene, and of the play itself. The result was mesmerising and laid a vital foundation for the action to come.

Some directors use improvisation a great deal. Their actors improvise for hours, sometimes walking through town in character, sometimes meeting each other for the first time in character. The great strength of such an approach is that it helps an actor build up his character's 'mask'. The danger is that characterisation becomes a set of physical tics, funny voices or stock reactions, rather than a human being capable of change and development.

Brecht

The poet, playwright and director Bertolt Brecht (1898–1956) had a particular approach to the notion of character. At the heart of everything he stood for was a critical attitude to the modern world: following Marx, he felt that it was not enough to 'describe the world, the point is to change it', and this attitude informs his complex and often contradictory theories about acting.

Brecht is his own worst enemy. His essays have led generations of actors and directors into a theoretical jungle, in which superficial aesthetic ideas have been mistaken for substance – above all, the much disputed 'alienation effect' – and crude, demonstrative acting is excused on the grounds that it's 'Brechtian'. But Brecht's writings on the theatre need to be seen as provocations at a particular time and place, a reaction against the headlong embrace by half of Europe's theatre-goers of the ghastly stupidity of fascism. And they can be exceptionally useful.

Acting in a 'Brechtian' way (or in a play by Brecht) requires, above all, an attitude towards 'what is being shown'. And so an actress playing Mother Courage needs not simply to act out the emotions of a woman who loses her three children in war. She must also show that it's her own fault, that her dependence on war to keep her business going leads inevitably to her losing the people she loves most. This doesn't mean that the acting should be cold, passionless or lacking in feeling. Indeed, the film of Helene Weigel playing Courage shows a performance of quite exceptional emotion and power. But it does mean that the acting must be channelled through a real critical intelligence.

A Brechtian approach to plays by other writers can be revealing. An actor playing Hamlet can demonstrate that his intellectual meandering is an example of the typical ineffect- iveness of the ruling class misfit, just as an actor playing Lear can point up the king's journey from regal untouchability to shock at how little he's done for the 'poor naked wretches' that live in his kingdom. Similarly, an actress playing Madame Ranevskaya can be more than simply an object of pity, once she and the director have read Chekhov's plays with some understanding of the behaviour of the Russian landowners of the period.

Indeed I would argue that Brechtian acting is nothing more than 'realistic' acting: seeing a character in a particular world at a particular time, making decisions which have an impact on the way other people live their lives, and not desperately seeking the affection and approval that Brecht said was such a factor in the sentimental, bourgeois theatre of his time.

Interpretation

One of the unintended consequences of the Brechtian revo- lution is that in approaching a part – particularly a major classical role – an actor is expected to bring more than simply close reading, motivational analysis and playful speculation. This is the whole area of decisive 'interpretation': the determined creation of a character who exists beyond and above the play that has been written. Many actors – especially experienced ones – come to rehearsals with very strong interpretations worked out in advance, and you will need to listen carefully to their proposals. You need to work out whether they are appropriate and see how they can be integrated into the rest of the production. Sometimes they will strike you as brilliant, at other times absurd.

Certain leading actors have a reputation for shaping the entire production around their own particular interpreta- tion. This can be very exciting, especially for those members of the audience who know the play well and enjoy seeing it being reconceived. Indeed, many would argue that interpre- tation is inevitable and that any pretence at not interpreting is simply evasive. My own feeling is that it's perhaps *because* it's inevitable that it should be resisted, and that playing an interpretation is less interesting than playing a real, three-dimensional figure. Interpretation is perhaps more appealing to the critic who has seen the play dozens of times, than to the ordinary theatre-goer encountering the play for the first time.

Whatever view you take of the interpretative approach, you need to ensure that such performances derive from the text, and exist within the production's overall conception.

A limit to what can be shown

It's important that you remind your actors that there's a limit to what can be shown: their work on character will only communicate to an audience if it's made particular through action. An actor playing Cornwall in *King Lear* might suggest that his character's propensity for brutality derived from dysfunctional parenting, or from very low self-esteem. Intriguing as such insights are, it's almost impossible to show them on stage.

It's essential to make a distinction between real life and a play. When a character in a play is subjected to psychoanalysis some things are revealed, but others are imposed, and the result betrays the analyst's own obsessions as much as it reveals the truth of the character. Intriguing as such psychological insights can be, they're limited if they're not tied to the details of the text. Psychological insights need to be made concrete. If they can't be understood, they're not worth attempting.

Truth is concrete

The best service you can give your actors is to make the drama specific and detailed.

One of Brecht's wisest aphorisms was that 'the truth is concrete' and I believe it should be tattooed onto the forehead of every young person wanting to make a career as a theatre director. Of course, as a materialist, Brecht was writing about the world as much as about the theatre, but it's an essential precept for good directing too. What it means is that everything must be expressed specifically, in detail, in relationship to concrete particularities.

As a student directing a production of *All's Well That Ends Well*, I discovered that you could only believe in the arrival of Helena on her pilgrimage when she came on stage carrying a suitcase. Suddenly so much became clear: the truth had been made concrete. Lear's mock trial of Goneril and Regan only started to work when the actors were given a real 'joint stool' to play with. In *Hedda Gabler* we only sensed the reality of her suicide when the stage management provided a loud pistol that left a whiff of blue smoke, and an entirely realistic (plastic) pool of blood on the floor beside her head when the curtain was drawn aside. One of the most memorable things about Peter Gill's production of his own play *The York Realist* was the loving attention to the rituals and rhythms of pouring tea. This was more than mere realism; with its commitment to the concrete and the particular, it embodied a whole approach to art – and life.

The phrase 'the truth is concrete' applies to much more than props: it's about your entire approach. Thus, we only get a sense of Macbeth's 'evil' when we see his hands covered in Duncan's blood. We will only believe in Romeo's protestations of love when we see what it drives him to do. When Timothy West as Lear touched Cordelia's cheek with his finger and tasted her salt tears to answer his rhetorical question 'Be your tears wet?' we understood the full extent of his journey.

The most important thing you can do in rehearsals is to search for the specific details of the dramatic moment. It's this, more than anything else, which will make your production memorable.

15

Rehearsals 6: Blocking and Movement

Traditionally, the single most important thing the director does is to work out where the actors should stand. This is called blocking – for reasons I've never understood. Older actors will joke 'Where do you want me to stand?' on the second day of rehearsals, harking back to a time when blocking was all. In the modern theatre the director's role is much more complex. But the fact is that by the end of the second week, you need to have made serious headway in realising the physical form of the production on stage.

The point of blocking

The point of blocking is to find a physical form for the dramatic action. Blocking is a complex business, but there are certain criteria for good blocking:

> The characters should motivate the moves
> The moves should help tell the story
> The positioning of the actors should guide the audience to look at what matters
> The blocking should enable the audience to see everything it needs to see

Everything you do should fulfil these criteria.

Blocking and design

Blocking starts long before rehearsals begin, in your work with the designer. There are several decisions that you make in the designer's studio that will drastically affect it. These provide the fixed elements in the scene's physical dynamic, and need to be carefully considered.

First, it's important to work out where to place the entrances and exits. This comes from an analysis of the actions required by the play: 'The Inspector has to come in from the front door, because if he comes in from the kitchen the story won't work'; or 'Firs has to use a different door from the one through which the rest of the family leave, because otherwise the audience won't believe that he's been left behind.' And you need to see the way that these entrances will affect the action on stage. Thus, if you put an entrance upstage centre – which can be very striking – it will be impossible for a character to come on surreptitiously. If the actors already on stage have to notice him, they'll have to turn their backs to the audience. Entrances far down stage pose a different challenge: if the actor enters in sharp profile it's difficult to work out how to make his features 'available' to the audience without cheating.

Secondly, you need to be careful about where you place the furniture. This is partly about atmosphere, but it's a practical matter too. If the sofa is placed at too sharp an angle, and you need a long scene with two people sitting talking to one another, the actor on the downstage end will be continually upstaged, having to speak most of his lines away from the audience. Similarly, if the stove is in the upstage right corner, intimate gatherings around it will be difficult. Such things are best worked out in advance: actors don't take kindly to the furniture being rearranged after they have been rehearsing with it in one position for two and half weeks.

Designers will sometimes provide drawings of how they think the blocking of individual scenes should look. Caspar Neher used to draw scenes in Brecht's plays in some detail, and it's interesting to compare photographs of the final result with his original drawings. Pamela Howard did the same when we were working on *The Cherry Orchard*. However, as Peter Brook points out in *The Empty Space*, it's important to recognise the limitations of such an approach: living actors will always create a richer set of images than a pen and ink drawing – or figures in a model box – can. More importantly, good actors don't like to have their moves and postures tied down by the designer before they start.

Distance and obstacles

It's often a good idea to design the set and position the furniture in such a way that the distances a character must cross in order to achieve his objectives are dramatically interesting, and the physical obstacles imposing.

Thus, in *King Lear* you should make sure Lear's last entrance – carrying Cordelia – is as far away from the centre of the stage as possible (without being *too* far: he's got to carry her): this will give it additional impact ('Howl, howl, howl, howl'). In *The Cherry Orchard* you need to have distance in Act Two between the entrance and the 'shrine', so the entrance of Ranevskaya, Gaev and Lopakhin can feel as if they are ambling across open countryside. If a new play is set in the Managing Director's office, it might be a good idea to place the desk some distance away from the door, but facing it, so other characters need to cross the room before they can sit down for an interview with their boss.

How do you get them to do it?

Moving actors around the stage isn't always easy and requires diplomacy and skill.

It's essential that when you start blocking, you approach it in the most provisional way possible. If you get hooked on certain moves too early, you'll spend a great deal of time unpicking them later. I try to avoid this by keeping blocking decisions open for as long as I can. I once fixed the moves of a scene on the second day of rehearsal: two weeks later I realised that I'd done it all wrong and had to start again.

I try to ensure that the gear-changes that take a production from its first read-through to the first night are as smooth as possible, and don't come as a series of shocks. I've devised the following system that works well for me. It allows the blocking to be organic and derive from the actors' own impulses, leaving room to shape the physical action gradually.

Once we've finished the read-through and the textual analysis with the whole company sitting around a table, there comes a moment – usually after three or four days – when I take the table away, but leave the chairs arranged in a circle.

I then encourage the actors to start making eye contact with each other as they read. I tell them they're free to get up, walk around the room, stand on a chair, kneel in front of each other, or stay glued to their chair if that's what they prefer.

Then, after a few days of this, I set up my own and the stage manager's desks at one end of the room, and put three or four wooden chairs or a bench in the middle of the room, and ask the actors to use them as they want. I then ask that only the people who are in the scene should be on the rehearsal 'floor'. Slowly, bit by bit, the actors start discovering physical relationships amongst themselves, wandering about, occasionally making contact, sometimes striding across the room, sometimes taking another actor by the hand, but all the time exploring the play in three dimensions.

After two or three days of this, I ask the stage management to tape a 'mark-out' on the floor. I then show the actors where the entrances are, and where the furniture will be in each scene. But again, I won't start with anything other than a few obvious, strictly logical instructions: 'You need to come through that door because that's the way in from outside', or 'The drinks cabinet is over there and you should keep going over to that every time your character pours herself another drink', or whatever. The actors can go wherever they like, within the physical constraints of the mark-out.

It's only when we've been through all this that I start to settle on specific moves: moment by moment, motivation by motivation. But even then I try to keep everything as provisional as possible. The important thing is to keep sketching, and leave the fine detail as late as you can get away with.

If you start by giving actors physical freedom, appropriate physical relationships will naturally start to emerge. If you block too early, you restrict their impulses. The trick is to observe your actors' physical suggestions carefully and start to develop the blocking from them.

Physical motivation

If the actors are to move round the stage they need to know why. If I get up from this computer and go to the kitchen, I do so because I want to make a cup of coffee. And so it's not

enough simply to tell the actor to move across to the cupboard, you need to tell him why he might do so: to get his
coat, close the cupboard door, or hide from the sinister
woman who has just entered the room. In other words, the
moves must derive from a series of impulses that the
characters feel. And if you don't construct the moves out of
the details of the characters' impulses you'll get into trouble.

But physical motivation is complicated and it's sometimes
difficult to define what exactly a character's physical objectives are. I might leap up from my chair and pace around the
room because I find this book difficult to write, don't like sitting still for very long and need to express my inner anxiety
and turmoil. To an observer the moves might seem contradictory: if I set off towards the kitchen to make some coffee,
I might have a little insight into how the next section should
work, turn the kettle on, return to my desk and forget all
about the coffee. Such is the strange inconsequentiality of
real life, which the theatre often needs to express. But even
inconsequentiality is driven by motivation.

'Why?'

As soon as you start moving actors around the stage you'll be
asked the question 'Why?'

The old joke answer – 'Because I told you to', or 'Because
you're being paid to' – won't really wash. Actors have very
different attitudes to blocking. Some are desperate to get the
scene blocked before they've worked out what's going on or
understand what their motivations are. Their instinct is to
fill the scene out with frenetic energy and constant movement. Others stand around like lumps of clay, refusing to move
anywhere at all until they have worked out their physical motivation in detail. Occasionally an actor will be eager to 'find a
reason' for a move you want him to do. This can seem helpful
at the time, but its very helpfulness may prove counterproductive in the long run, and you'll have to unpick it later.

So what do you say when the actor says 'Why?' The
essential thing is to answer in the most simple and direct
way: 'To get yourself another drink from the fridge', 'To look
out of the window to see if your son has arrived', 'To stick the

knife in deeper', or whatever. These are specific, concrete actions, the building blocks for the actor's performance. An actor can only play one motivation at a time, so the continuous clarification of these moments of motivation is the most useful thing you can give him.

Sometimes, however, even the most precisely defined motivation doesn't help. This is most likely when the actor disagrees with the motivation you've given him: 'But I wouldn't go over to seduce her at this point, because I don't want to seduce her yet', or 'If I get a drink from the fridge now, what'll I do later in the play when my character says "I'm thirsty"?' and so on. These objections may be valid and you may find you've been giving the actor a bum steer. Alternatively you may come to realise there's a real disagreement, which should be clarified by going back to the individual work on language, story and character.

Sometimes the best answer to 'Why?' is to ask the actor what he would like to do instead. This will at least encourage him to start thinking through the problem for himself, and not wait to be told. And sometimes he'll have a good idea.

Telling the story

The best blocking tells the story by physically articulating the action in the most eloquent way possible.

The moment when Nora finally leaves in *A Doll's House* should be as simple as possible. We need to see her exchange rings with Torvald at the table, place her house keys somewhere, stand up, put her coat and hat on, pick up her case, finish her conversation and leave through the hall door. Moments later, when she's walked down the stairs, we need to hear the front door to the apartment block close. Every step of the way must be carefully charted and the whole episode has to go with fluidity, pressure and strength. If it's too fussy, it'll take too long and lose dramatic power and meaning. If any of the moments are fudged it will go for nothing. You have to block it step by step, beat by beat, second by second.

Another example – from the beginning of a play – is Lear's first entrance. Shakespeare tells us nothing except that

Gloucester says, 'The King is coming'. Does he enter with all three of his daughters, or with just Cordelia or with none? Do they enter first, and are they prepared to receive him, and if so how do they know they should be there? And then, when he divides up his kingdom, how can the blocking show that he's already divided it up in his head? You need to answer each of these questions, which are not made clear by the text. And the blocking should make these answers clear.

You need to work out what story you are going to tell, before you try to stage it.

Expressing social relationships

The blocking needs to express the relationships between the characters. Class, age and status as much as emotional or family connections inform these relationships.

An actor will sometimes say that he can't play 'kingly', but that regal status is given by the way other characters behave towards him. Thus, when King Lear enters you need to find ways of expressing the court's attitude towards him. Do they bow when he enters (Gloucester announces his arrival) or do you want to show that contempt has already set in? When Rosencrantz and Guildernstern arrive, how can the blocking show their mixture of chumminess and deference to the Prince (whom they have been asked to spy on)?

Similarly, in naturalism, you need to be careful of the nuances of drawing-room manners – or coal miner's kitchen manners for that matter. If the maid gets too close to her mistress she looks insolent. Should Osvald stand up – as a young man should – when Pastor Manders walks in, or does it say more if he doesn't? How does the working-class Joe behave with his sister-in-law, the middle-class Minnie, in D.H. Lawrence's *The Daughter-in-Law*? You need answers to all these questions.

Relationships across the classes take on a particular physical shape in any particular historical moment. You need to be constantly alert to this: 'Don't come too close to the beggar, he smells', 'Lower your head, she's a duchess', 'Keep looking down, if the Baron sees you looking at him he may kill you' and so on. You need to make sure that your staging makes the underlying truths of the society concrete.

Naturalistic blocking

The hard thing about blocking naturalistic drama is that in real life people stay sitting in the same chair for much longer than an audience can bear. Of course, the best naturalistic writers incorporate these moves into their stage directions: towards the stove for warmth in Ibsen, to the range to make tea in D.H. Lawrence, to the bar for a drink in Sean O'Casey and so on. But sometimes you need to find motivation for a move of some sort, if only as a way of creating a variation that will engage the audience. This can feel artificial, but is sometimes essential.

The other challenge when blocking naturalistic work is how intricately connected each move is. Once you've moved the conversation from the sofa to the kitchen table, you may hit a problem when a third character has to come in and eat his tea at the table. In other words, you need to keep an overview of the physical demands of the entire scene, thinking several pages ahead, while articulating the shifts in atmosphere and tone through appropriate positioning and moves.

Creating images

One of the more intriguing aspects in blocking is the creation of visually compelling stage pictures. Edgar's first appearance out of the hovel as Poor Tom, Peer Gynt lying in his mother's lap like a *pietà*, Lear carrying the hanged Cordelia in his arms, the brother and sister in Sam Shepard's *Fool For Love* hurling themselves across their motel room: each is a powerful image in its own right, with its own particular iconography and resonance.

The precise manipulation of the figure in the picture frame can create images of extraordinary strength: I remember looking at Piero della Francesca's painting of *The Baptism of Christ* and thinking, 'If I could block like that my audiences would be moved to tears.' The tilt of the head, the glance to heaven, the quality of the embrace, the bent back or the haughty brow, all make for the most powerful visual imagery.

Making this kind of thing happen on stage is a complex business, and the best actors tend to resist being manipulated like puppets. You need to bring every ounce of diplomacy to this, and appeal to their intelligence ('It expresses the moment brilliantly') as much as to their vanity ('You look great when you do that'). The best thing, sometimes, is to be sly in creating these images so that the actor doesn't realise you're doing it.

But you have to be careful about creating stage pictures. I've sometimes felt a contradiction between striking physical images, and shaping a scene with fluidity and dynamic life. The fact is, real actors bring on more awkward, energetic, idiosyncratic physicality than any number of card figures in a model or drawings by a designer. In other words when it's done well, blocking must be a three-dimensional and dynamic expression of unfolding action, rather than a series of beautiful and resonant snapshots.

Focusing the action

I've sometimes found a scene isn't working because the audience's attention isn't on the right actor. Audiences will most readily look at the person who is facing them most directly.

Thus, for example, when directing *Love's Labour's Lost*, I allowed too much of Berowne's beautiful speech ('Have at you then, affection's men-at-arms') to go off sideways into the wings. I'd asked the actor to address his three friends who were all sitting to his left. A quick rearrangement, placing Berowne in between his three interlocutors – two on one side, one on the other – allowed him to make his speech – and his emotions – available to the audience. Similarly, in directing the difficult scene in *King Lear* when Lear comes back from hunting, I found I could only focus it properly when I asked Timothy West to sit on a little bench. This gave a focal point to a bustling, quick-firing scene, with the knights rushing back and forth on either side. By 'anchoring' Lear, I gave the audience a clear centre around which their gaze could revolve.

One of the best ways of sharpening up the focus is to have characters placed behind the speaker looking downstage towards him: whenever the audience's eye wanders off the speaker it's encouraged to return to him by the actors behind him. This is particularly valuable in big crowd scenes, such as the last scene in a Shakespeare play, for example. I found something intriguing in directing Alexandra Gilbreath as Hedda Gabler: as she prowled the perimeter of the room watching the other characters, she came in and out of focus. The way she watched the action affected to what extent she was the centre of our attention.

Stage directions

Different writers have different attitudes to stage directions.

Only a handful of Shakespeare's stage directions survive, and even then it's difficult to know which are his, and which are taken from the prompt copies. It's not until nineteenth-century drama, with the development of theatrical natural-ism and the boom in publishing plays, that stage directions deserve close scrutiny.

With naturalistic stage directions you need to decide which are useful, and which you want to ignore. Ibsen's are particularly vivid. Look at the opening stage directions for *John Gabriel Borkman*:

> *Mrs Borkman's drawing room, furnished rather grandly, but now old-fashioned and faded-looking. An open sliding door upstage leads out to a conservatory with windows and a glass door, beyond which can be seen the garden. It is twilight, and a snowstorm is blowing. In the right-hand wall is a door leading out to the hall. Further downstage is a large old-fashioned iron stove, in which a fire is burning. At upstage left is a single, smaller door, and downstage on the same side is a heavily curtained window. Between the window and the door stands a horse-hair sofa, with a small table in front of it covered with a cloth, and a lighted lamp on the table. There is a high-backed armchair by the stove. Mrs Borkman is sitting on the sofa, busy*

with some crochet work. She is a woman in late middle age, of
a chilly, aristocratic demeanour – somewhat stiff, with a severely
controlled expression. Her thick hair is streaked with grey, and
she has very delicate, almost translucent hands. She is wearing
a heavy dark silk dress, at one time elegant, but now rather
shabby and threadbare. She has a shawl over her shoulders.
She works at her crochet for a while, sitting upright and very
still; the sound of bells is then heard from a sleigh drawing up
outside, and Mrs Borkman looks up, her eyes bright with
pleasure.

Every detail is meaningful, whether it be the snowstorm
outside, the description of the overheated interior, the furniture, the sound of the sleigh-bells, the stove, or Mrs Borkman
herself. It can all be ignored, if you like, but it's important
that you are aware of what you are rejecting.

Look how the scene develops once the dialogue starts:

MRS BORKMAN (*whispers*) Erhart! At last! (*She rises and goes over*
to look out through the curtains. Then, disappointed, she returns
to the sofa and resumes her work. After a few moments the maid
comes in from the hall with a visiting card on a little tray.)
MRS BORKMAN (*immediately*) That wasn't Master Erhart, was it?
MAID No, ma'am. But there's a lady outside . . .
MRS BORKMAN (*laying down her crochet*) Oh, that'll be Mrs
Wilton –
MAID (*approaching*) No, ma'am – it's a stranger.
MRS BORKMAN (*taking the card*) Let me see – (*She reads it,*
then rises abruptly and stares hard at the maid.) Are you sure
this is for me?
MAID Yes, ma'am – as far as I understood, it was for the
mistress.
MRS BORKMAN And did she actually ask to speak with Mrs
Borkman?
MAID She did, ma'am.
MRS BORKMAN (*tersely, decisive*) All right. You can tell her I'm
at home.

Everything needs to be registered and communicated:
Mrs Borkman is eagerly expecting her son Erhart and is

disappointed to see someone else's sleigh; she's amazed to read her estranged sister's card; she eventually gives the maid instructions to 'tell her I'm at home'. From these brief moments can spring an entire understanding of the play, its atmosphere and its characters. If you can direct these apparently incidental moments convincingly, you're on your way to making the whole thing work.

Some playwrights use extensive stage directions to do much more than describe the set or the actions of their characters, but to express what is not in the spoken text itself. Bernard Shaw's stage directions say much more than is strictly necessary for dramatic realisation and are little essays in their own right. As are John Osborne's (*'He wears glasses and has a slight stoop, from a kind of offhand pedantry which he originally assumed thirty years ago when he left one of those minor public day schools in London, which have usually managed to produce some raffish middle-class adventurers as well as bank managers and poets'*). Sometimes this is useful; at other times you should ignore it. There are no rules, but the important thing is to have worked out the consequences of either choice.

The theatre publisher Samuel French has produced a set of 'acting editions' for commonly produced plays from the popular repertoire. These are illustrated with diagrams which show how the set should be designed, where the furniture should be placed, and where the characters should stand. They also include property plots, lighting cues, costume changes and so on. They have been designed for amateur groups (are they really useful, I wonder?) but I found myself joking that I wished they had produced one for *King Lear*.

Many modern writers use stage directions very sparingly. Brecht used hardly any, and his disciples, Manfred Karge and Heiner Müller, cut them out altogether, with just numbers to mark the beginning of each new scene. When I direct Shakespeare, I prepare a rehearsal script which dispenses with stage directions altogether. I prefer the actors to work them out from the spoken text. After the initial confusion, the result can be electric.

Upstaging

A phrase that often emerges in blocking rehearsals is 'upstaging'. Upstaging can take many forms but basically means an actor being positioned in such a way that the audience looks at him, instead of the person who is speaking.

Some actors are good at getting themselves into positions where they upstage others, and this is sometimes a conscious strategy. I've heard of a famous leading actor who used to slowly nudge his chair three feet upstage; as a result the young actress he was playing opposite spent most of the scene with her back to the audience. A lesser, old school actor I worked with had an uncanny ability to find himself in the middle of the stage, whatever else was happening in the scene, even when he was playing a minor supporting role in a great Shakespearean tragedy.

Upstaging, however, is usually entirely innocent, and I've found that inexperienced or badly trained actors are often unaware of the impact of what they're doing. A sudden gesture, a move when another actor is speaking ('on his line'), an expression that's a bit forced: all of these can 'pull focus'. But saying 'Just stand totally still and don't do anything at all' can make things even worse: the artificial tension in a 'frozen' actor's body will be just as upstaging as an actor with his arms flapping about. Quite often, you have to explain carefully what the problem is and teach an actor the rudiments of stagecraft. I've even resorted to standing on stage demonstrating what he's doing wrong.

The best writers revel in scenic contradiction. In Act Four of *The Cherry Orchard* Chekhov insists that Yasha drinks all the champagne and gets drunk during Lopakhin's crucially important last conversation with Trigorin. In my production, the actor playing Lopakhin was understandably worried that what he said would go for nothing and was convinced that the actor playing Yasha could have done less, or drunk the champagne quicker. I found it very hard to focus this two-minute episode.

Blocking set pieces

There comes a moment – often in the third week of rehearsal – when the most important thing is to get the big scenes in the play blocked, efficiently, elegantly and accurately. This is when you turn into a traffic policeman: 'If you go stage left on that line – to get yourself another whisky – the door will be clear for Annabel's entrance', 'Can the three of you stay upstage for another two moments, and only come down stage when it gets really nasty?', 'Can you take a step left so we can see Cordelia when she's talking and, Albany, can you nod deferentially, not bow, when the King refers to you by name?' You have to handle all this with charm and tact, while at the same time remaining forceful and clear. The actors will have their own opinions, and you need to listen to each one and see how it might help, while having the confidence to decline when you feel it will hinder. Personally, I find this phase of rehearsals – what I call 'the coalface' – the hardest, both physically and mentally

Then you need to establish the important 'lines of access'. Where do people come on? How do they get to the centre of the scene? When do you need an entrance which announces itself, and when do you need someone to just appear from the side? And 'access' means eyeline as well as physical passage: in other words, who needs to be able to look at whom, if everything is going to work? This is particularly important when a character has to come on stage and not immediately notice a second character. It is even more important in comedy than it is in tragedy, and in farce it's essential.

But what are the keys to blocking a big set-piece scene, particularly one with lots of people on stage – the last scene of a Shakespeare play, for example? Most importantly, you need to have a clear sense of the heart of the scene's action – what it is that must be shown. Isabella's decision to kneel beside Mariana and beg the Duke to have mercy on Angelo's life is one of the central moments in the last scene of *Measure for Measure*. You need to give the Duke a position of authority (he's just asked for a chair). Mariana and Isabella need to be able to kneel in a place that has a connection with the Duke, but also allows us to see their faces. Angelo has to be in a place where we can see his face, which must also be accessible to both the Duke and the women. If the 'skeleton of the scene' is carefully enough constructed, you can build up the rest from it.

Some of the great scenes in drama are exceptionally complex: the quadruple marriage at the end of *As You Like It*, the Act Two Finale in Mozart's *Le Nozze di Figaro*, the dumb Katrin drumming on the roof to wake up the village in *Mother Courage*. Such scenes require relentlessly detailed work. Hour after hour of traffic policing is the only way to get them rehearsed. Extreme patience is essential.

It's important that you consider the expressive, visual qualities of good blocking, as well as the practical ones. The best visual images derive from a simple embodiment of dramatic action: Angelo standing by himself in disgrace off to one side of the stage; Lear raging against the storm, with only the Fool for company; Hedda Gabler moving around the room like a shark; Tesman with his head in his aunt's lap; Laertes' followers bursting in to attack Claudius and so on. Each of these dynamic images has to be built out of simple, practical elements.

The crucial point is that, however big the structure, the individual truth of each moment has to be made concrete.

Sightlines

It's crucial you don't forget the most important thing of all about blocking: to make sure that wherever the actors are placed on stage the audience can see them.

The main obstacles to clear sightlines are parts of the set or large pieces of furniture. Obviously, you need to avoid placing actors in places where they will be invisible: behind a wall, half way out of the door and so on (although I've occasionally asked actors to play a line or two offstage, particularly in naturalistic work, where people often start talking in the hallway).

But sightlines are more complex than that: an actor seated behind a desk for too long can feel 'hidden' from the audience even if you can see his face quite clearly. An actress half way up the steps leading up on to the stage can feel obscured.

An actor placed very far upstage centre can seem too far away from the audience.

Perhaps more problematic – because they move – are other actors, and one of the big challenges in choreographing big, crowded scenes is to ensure that the audience can see all the faces they need to, whenever they need to. This can be very complex and requires all your ingenuity and skill to pull off successfully. Of course, there are no absolutes, and there are inevitably moments when an important character will disappear out of sight for a moment: but the right balance needs to be struck.

And then individual theatres present their own sightline challenges. Before its renovation the Royal Court had very difficult sightlines: the only place on stage where an actor could be seen by everybody in the audience was upstage centre. Shakespeare's Globe is difficult too: not only is the audience almost all round, as well as above and below, but there are two large pillars on either side of the stage which make certain places on stage invisible to either side. The Old Vic by contrast has brilliant sightlines – as well as acoustics – and is one of the most rewarding theatres I know to direct in.

Five blocking sins

There are five 'blocking sins' that often arise and you need to keep an eye out for them.

THE DOWNSTAGE CROSS This is when an actor walks across the front of the stage in front of another one, particularly an actor who is speaking or sitting down. This can be ugly. More importantly, it interrupts the audience's clear view of the actor upstage to the benefit of the one downstage.

THE SCISSORS This is when two actors cross the stage in opposite directions. This splits the audience's focus and is considered inelegant. You should only let this happen when you're consciously making the point that the actors are going in opposite ways.

EVERYBODY IN A LINE This occurs when you have three or four actors standing side by side across the front of the stage, like soldiers on a parade ground. Such an artificial arrangement should be avoided: a line can be broken up fairly easily.

PEELING OFF THE WRONG WAY This is when two actors are having a conversation and one of them leaves. If he turns his face away from the other one on his way out, and breaks contact, our eyes follows him off to the door. Whereas if the same actor turns inwards instead, facing the other one, our eyes return to the one left on stage, who may well have something to say.

FLYING GEESE This consists of two actors crossing the stage in the same direction, but one slightly later than the other. This gives the impression of automated movement and can feel unnatural as a result.

It's important to stress that all these rules exist to be broken and are often done so to brilliant effect. When I directed *King Lear* I found that a 'scissors' in Act Five, Scene One was the best way of showing Regan and Albany going off one way, with Goneril following Edmund the other, before Goneril is stopped by Regan's insistence that she follow her and Albany. Peter Gill sometimes places a line of characters across the front of the stage side by side ('everybody in a line'), but in dramatic connection with each other, and the effect is like a Greek frieze. Linda Bassett did a brilliant 'downstage cross' in *John Gabriel Borkman* which allowed the audience a more intimate insight into her character's inner pain. And 'flying geese' creates a sense of a group of people moving together and can be very powerful.

The important thing is to trust the evidence of your own eyes: look at the actors carefully, and if it feels awkward or artificial, have the confidence to change it.

'Don't stand too close to each other'

Sometimes actors want to stand very close to each other on stage, perhaps because it gives them a stronger sense of intimate contact and communication. Sometimes this can be effective, and certainly a grouping with two people close together on an empty stage can be very striking. But it should be used sparingly. In Shakespeare it's particularly important to open up the distances between the actors, for two reasons: it allows characters to have easier 'lines of communication' with each other, and it encourages the actors to open their voices and commit themselves to the words they're speaking.

Faces and backs

The face is by far the most expressive part of the human body.

The director needs to ensure that the audience can see the actor's face when it's necessary to do so. The best way of doing this is to place the speaker further upstage and move the other actor downstage. Of course, the first one upstages the second one, and sometimes you should place both actors facing each other on the same line on the stage. This then puts both actors into sharp profile, which can be striking, but can feel excluding for the audience.

In badly directed work you sometimes see all the actors facing out towards the audience all the time. This is not simply dull to look at, and breaks the illusion, it dampens the electric charge that's generated when actors look each other in the eyes. You should try to avoid this, and change it when you see it occurring: 'Tom, take a step upstage, Mary, turn to look at John, and Michael, would you mind sitting on the sofa?'

Some actors love working with their backs to the audience. Turning backs to the audience at strategic moments can create a powerful illusion of depth and three-dimensionality. I remember being mesmerised by John Malkovich in *Burn This*, playing the first twenty minutes with his back to the audience. When he finally turned round we were so relieved that we forgave him anything, including the banality of the play. When I directed Ken Stott in Peter Arnott's *White Rose* I found it almost impossible to persuade him to face the audience at all, but Ken expresses more with his back than most actors do with their entire body.

Groups and crowds

Some plays – such as *Coriolanus,* Ibsen's *An Enemy of the People* or Dürrenmatt's *The Visit,* or any Greek tragedy for that matter – are concerned with the relationship between the individual and the masses, and provide a particular challenge for the director, both in terms of blocking and characterisation.

A group is made up of individuals, each with his own particular set of strengths and weaknesses, fears and desires. When these individuals come together they make up a mass, and that mass gains its own particular psychology, its own way of behaving as a crowd. And so in directing such scenes you need to start with the individuals in that crowd. I always ask people in a crowd to invent their character's name, job, love life and so on. From these individual details you can build up the way they operate as a group: 'Who's the timid one?', 'Who's the rabble rouser?', 'Who's serious and who thinks it's all a laugh?' and so on. They can move together as a group, but without their moves feeling automatic or lacking in individuality.

When you work with such a group on stage you can create a crowd that has great power and strength, but is also rich with detail and character. And so, when the heroic individual is confronted by society, we can see the complex reality of the obstacle he's facing, while also recognising it as a group, and not merely a group of disconnected individuals.

Movement and physicality

Central to the theatre experience is the sight of bodies moving round in a space, in a dynamic physical relationship with each other, expressing emotion and thought in a way which is almost as powerful as spoken language. However naturalistic the setting, however much furniture there is on stage, audiences look at the actors and read meaning in their physicality. It is an essential part of the theatre, and you must address it as the director.

The best actors develop an acute sense of the kind of physicality that they're going to bring to the part. When I directed *Ghosts*, Daniel Evans found an extraordinary physicality – half dissipated and destroyed, half cocky and aroused, his left leg trailing and his chin jutting forward – which caught brilliantly the particular nuances of the part of Osvald. Also in Ibsen – and it's fascinating to see such physical expressiveness in the most naturalistic surroundings – Alexandra Gilbreath as Hedda Gabler discovered a strangely powerful, glazed haughtiness as she glided imperiously around her living room.

It's important to encourage your actors to bring this physical playfulness to their parts. You can use physical games if you like, but most creative actors will bring that playfulness to rehearsals anyway, so long as you've created an atmosphere in which it's enjoyed and accepted as central. I sometimes say to actors things like 'Be tall' or 'Be heavy' or 'Play from your chest' or whatever. The tone is playful and suggestive and the actors need to discover the answers for themselves.

Occasionally, you'll find yourself confronted with an actor who is reluctant to move, who has a sort of physical paralysis and is 'rooted to the spot'. This can be frustrating but is usually just a symptom of nerves. Look at what he's doing very carefully, moment by moment, impulse by impulse. Try and help, but be patient: it will almost certainly come out in the wash.

I'm increasingly convinced that actors only make interesting and striking shapes with their bodies when they're acting well. It's only then their movements feel inhabited, and their energy isn't forced. Ultimately, physicality has to come from within, and you must be careful not to impose it from the outside.

Movement skills

There's a strong feeling among some directors that the British theatre is too text-based and that British acting is all 'talking heads'. These directors are interested in exploring a kind of robust physicality that has little relationship to 'naturalistic' portraits of everyday life. Their work draws on the traditions of the *commedia dell'arte* as well as clowning and slapstick. It has its roots in the Parisian drama school founded by Jacques Lecoq. Such an approach has its own complex codes and conventions and can be seen at its best in the work of Complicite and its many imitators. This movement has sometimes been labelled 'physical theatre'.

Other directors, working within more naturalistic conventions, are fascinated by the physicality of the ordinary: the tension in the typist's shoulders, the weight of the peasant woman's plough, the delicate poise of the Elizabethan courtier. Certain periods are characterised by their own physicality; the clothes and the attitudes lead people to move in different postures: Elizabethan codpieces deliberately make the wearer feel as if he's thrusting his genitals forwards, while the white ruff holds his head as if on a plate. Eighteenth-century aristocratic clothes inevitably demand a physicality that's elegant and aloof; peasants in Brueghel have a very different physicality from nineteenth-century archbishops. And so on

Good actors feel these things instinctively, but you need to encourage them. Physical expressiveness is an essential part of the theatre director's palette and must not be ignored, however 'textual' your work may be. I sometimes give actors some actual indication of how I imagine their character's physicality: 'Don't do it like me,' I always say, 'this is just a caricatured indication of how I think he might move.' But whether you're directing *commedia dell'arte* or naturalistic minimalism, be alert to the production's physical life: it's essential to a production's success.

Gesture

Hamlet is clear about what actors should do with their hands:

> Nor do not saw the air too much with your hand, thus, but use all gently; for in the very torrent, tempest, and, as I may say, the whirlwind of passion, you must acquire and beget a temperance that may give it smoothness.

This is intended as a corrective to the kind of bombastic acting style that the young Shakespeare would have seen. It's not hard to imagine what this would have looked like – endless arm-waving, big gestures and so on – and productions of *Hamlet* often send it up with the performance of the Player King ('The rugged Pyrrhus ...'). But it's a mistake to think Hamlet was expecting modern television acting. Furthermore, this acting style outlived Hamlet's most savage mockery: one has only to think of the style of theatre that was widespread in the nineteenth century before the 'naturalistic revolution' of the 1890s.

The history of most twentieth-century theatre practice has been the elimination of unnecessary theatrical gestures, and the reduction of acting to the most minimal, unemphatic naturalism. And so one of the most helpful things you can do is help actors edit their gestures: 'Use one pointing moment, not three', 'That gesturing to the gods is too much', 'Two gesticulations in that scene are fine; five is over-egging the pudding' and so on. Young actors sometimes don't know what to do with their hands: 'As little as possible' is usually the best advice.

However, the more classical work I direct, the more I want the actors to find precise and expressive gestures, which capture the powerful, often mythical, nature of the dramatic moment. Thus in *King Lear*, Nick Fletcher as Edgar enhanced his disguise as Poor Tom in the wilderness with hand gestures drawn from the iconography of the suffering Christ; Emma Cunniffe found a simple but powerful chopping gesture to accompany her talk about the Vikings as Hilde Wangel in *The Master Builder*.

This is a difficult thing to negotiate, particularly in Britain, where most experienced actors resent being given an external 'gesture'. The more intelligent ones will respond, if you give them a careful description of the iconography you're trying to achieve; just be careful to bring it out from within, and don't impose it.

Mark-outs

The moment when you ask the stage management to do a taped 'mark-out' provides an important change of tempo, so it's important you choose it carefully. I tend to avoid a mark-out for the first week, so the actors don't get fixated on the minutiae of the production too early. A good mark-out carries all the information about the set: where the doors are, where the windows are, where the trap is, where the stairs are and so on. It should be carefully taken from the designer's ground plan and must be accurate. In a production with different sets for different scenes this sometimes becomes a jungle of different coloured tape: 'Yellow is Act One, blue is Act Two, the dotted line is the "iron line", and those little green rectangles are the stairs.'

The point of a mark-out is to give everybody a clear sense of the space in which the production takes place. When you're blocking you need to keep an eye on it, and remind yourself and the actors of the physical constraints in which they're working. It's not just plays with doors and walls that need mark-outs: the best blocking has an acute awareness of the relationship between the characters and the frame of the 'empty space' in which you're working – which is only possible by using the mark-out in rehearsals.

But you need to approach the mark-out with a sense of humour. I remember years ago getting worried by an experienced actor who kept walking across the yellow tapeline, and not through the carefully marked out door. When I finally said, 'Tom, you keep walking through the wall,' he turned, smiled and said, 'Yes, dear, but I won't do that when there's a real wall, will I?'

Rehearsal set and furniture

When you're directing a production with walls and doors, you should try to persuade the production manager to provide you with rehearsal doors (which stand independently). These are particularly valuable for timing entrances and exits in comedies and farce. One of the most endearing things some older actors do is walk through an imaginary door, stamp their heel, and create the 'beat' that's realised with the shutting of the door on the set. A rehearsal door saves everybody the trouble.

I always ask for as much of the set as possible in rehearsal. My production of *King Lear* took place on a simple but very handsome raked wooden floor. We had it in rehearsal from the second week and by the time the production hit the stage it felt like home to everybody. For *Romeo and Juliet* we had the floor but not the balcony in rehearsals.

The other thing that's essential – particularly in the last two weeks of rehearsal – is to work with the real furniture that you're going to use. This is both practical – every piece of furniture has its own unique dimensions – and artistic. An Arthur Miller play (*The Price*) needed a sofa (amongst a huge amount of other furniture): we spent the first two weeks rehearsing on three plastic chairs placed next to each other. It was only when we got the real sofa in the third week that the acting began to have any physical life.

This is sometimes difficult for the theatre to provide – furniture hire and rehearsal set transport can be horrendously expensive. But it's worth asking for.

Blocking in different kinds of theatres

It's much easier to create memorable stage images in proscenium arch 'front-on' theatres, than in the round, and I prefer working in those theatres for that very reason. Proscenium arch theatres are often criticised as being too formal, and lacking in intimacy. But there's an enduring value in such theatres that is too easily dismissed. Above all they ensure that all members of the audience share the same view of the production.

By directing many touring productions I've learnt that in the best nineteenth-century proscenium theatres (usually designed by Frank Matcham or one of his pupils), the focus point (the place on stage where an actor can be best seen by everybody in the theatre) is too far upstage to achieve the kind of intimacy that most modern directors want. This is because these theatres were designed to have an orchestra pit just in front of the proscenium arch. But when you pull the action downstage of the proscenium arch you discover that the sightlines are difficult, particularly from the circle.

Theatres-in-the-round like the Stephen Joseph Theatre in Scarborough or the Royal Exchange in Manchester require a particular skill. The director needs to find ways of keeping the characters moving, so as to avoid having one section of the audience stuck with a good view of the back of an actor's neck. Farce is almost impossible because you can't include sudden entrances or rely on the audience having a unified view. In Shakespeare the soliloquies are particularly difficult: how many moves can you find in 'To be or not to be'? Small-cast naturalistic plays are even harder: a character sitting down in a chair for more than a minute can kill a scene dead; how do you keep it mobile while remaining truthful? I'm not a great fan of theatre-in-the-round, although many distin-guished directors are: they enjoy the sense of intimate eaves-dropping that it can provide.

You will probably get your first directing experience work-ing in a small studio theatre, a little black box with the audi-ence on two or three sides. I cut my teeth at the Traverse Theatre in Edinburgh and learnt a huge amount working in such a tiny restrictive space: above all, about detail and 'truth'. At their best, such theatres allow for an almost embarrassing sense of intimacy, and it's essential that you work in one at some point in your development. Although the shift to bigger stages – which require more commanding *mise-en-scène* – can be a challenge, such theatres are the best way to learn about actors.

Different attitudes to blocking

There are many different attitudes to blocking.

Brecht was a remarkable director who blocked brilliantly. He had three key principles. Firstly, he discouraged actors from moving until the action demanded a move. Secondly, he thought that the audience should be able to understand the basic dynamic, social and emotional action of any moment by looking at the disposition of the characters and their gestures. Thirdly, he wanted the blocking to capture the *gestus* of each moment – the character's precisely expressed attitude to each other.

The German director Peter Stein is a master of blocking. His productions have tremendous fluidity and freedom, while at the same time carry images and groupings that strike a deep chord. Stein has a notion of expressing the cultural subconscious in his staging and his productions have the ability to hit you in the solar plexus. It's as if you're looking at a great classical painting, but are not quite sure which one. This isn't directing as *tableaux vivants*; it's a highly sophisticated art that conveys the profound meanings of the play with great flair and understanding.

Mike Alfreds regards blocking as anathema, and asks his actors to find new, fresh moves every night. Certain basic imperatives are laid down, but a huge amount is left to chance and inspiration. This drives some actors mad, but can produce startling results. It helps avoid the kind of staleness that's such a problem in a long run, though chaos often ensues.

Look at the actors!

I once assisted Peter Gill, and was sitting at the back of his rehearsal room looking at the text. He walked up to me, snatched the script from my hands and joked that I was 'not in a university seminar now'. Like many young directors, I'd made a fundamental mistake: I was spending the rehearsals with my head in the script while the actors were up there rehearsing in front of me.

Of course, it's important to have the script readily available. But it's even more important to look at what is unfolding in front of you. Nowadays, I rehearse for hours without ever looking at the script, just glancing at my assistant or the DSM occasionally if there's something not clear in my mind. I know that if the play makes sense in front of me, it's beginning to work in the right way; if it doesn't, then the evidence of my own eyes will tell me. The point is that what you're rehearsing is something to be watched as well as heard, and you need to look as much as you listen.

16

Rehearsals 7: Specialists

Even the most experienced theatre director recognises there are times when it's best to bring in a specialist. This can come as a great relief, in that somebody else takes on some of the responsibility. Most specialists are good in their particular area, and know their contribution must fit into your overall conception and the demands of the play. Occasionally, however, their involvement requires careful management. It's important to brief specialists carefully, and give them a clear sense of what you want them to do.

Movement directors

In the last twenty years movement directors have been successful in challenging the dominance of language in so much British theatre.

Movement directors are most useful when you're directing a play set in a world very different from our own, with its own clothes, codes and manners. The way people move is a result of the world in which they live, and a period production that doesn't understand the physical movement of the period hasn't grasped the world that it's trying to portray. One example is the way that Elizabethan clothes for men were centred round two key areas – the intellect (the brain) held up on a white ruff, and the instinct (the genitals) thrust forward in a codpiece. Another is the extravagant display of eighteenth-century manners: all bowing and scraping, flowery gestures and hand movements. A third example is the stiff fabric and corseting of nineteenth-century costume drama. Each period has its own physicality.

Good movement directors can help actors develop their own physical expressiveness, whether through their walk, their posture, or physical gesture. Modern psychological actors tend to be rather cautious in their use of gestures, and movement directors need to treat them carefully. If they work from 'the outside in' ('Lift your arm like this, hold your thumb and your forefinger together' and so on), they may well encounter resistance. But if they can respond to the actor's sense of the character's inner life, they can help him gain a physical and gestural power that he didn't know he had.

Of course, in some productions, especially 'physical theatre', the movement director has a much more central role to play: he's there at every rehearsal, is the director's chief collaborator, and makes a whole range of important decisions, particularly about scenes which require a dynamic physical energy. And as such he can be an important creative figure in his own right.

I feel, however, that you need to be wary of allowing the movement director too much sway. There's a story about a movement director directing *A Doll's House* and spending the whole of the first week of rehearsals working on the tarantella, Nora's dance of death in Act Three. Ibsen's great play isn't an excuse for a dance: the physical is only one aspect of the theatre and, despite occasional claims to the contrary, isn't the dominant one.

Work with movement directors, but ensure that your production doesn't become an excuse for 'movement'.

Choreographers

Classical comedies often require dances, usually at the end, as a way of expressing the return of harmony. And some plays require dances as part of the action, be it the fiendishly difficult Act Three of *The Cherry Orchard* or a couple of dance steps in *The Beaux' Stratagem*. For these you need the help of a choreographer.

Crudely, there are two kinds of choreographers in straight drama (as opposed to opera or musicals). The good ones see dance as an essential part of the drama. They come to rehearsals having read the play, listened to the music, researched the period, looked at the model of the set, and with an outline of what kind of choreography they want to achieve. The bad ones are only interested in dance *per se*, not in the drama as a whole. They want a choreographic perfection, quite alien to the complexities of spoken drama.

Mind you, choreographers in the spoken theatre sometimes have to work with fairly uncongenial raw material. Some
actors, often the most talented, are physically unfit. Very few
of them feel immediately comfortable with dancing, and
some actively hate it. There are always young actresses who
are good at dancing (often having taken ballet training in
their youth) and infuriatingly pleased with themselves as a
result. The best choreographers will find ways of working
with all of these: helping the insecure ones gain self-confi-
dence, allowing the unfit ones a break now and again, even
working their breathlessness into the play.

Dances need to be handled with care. There was a time
when every self-respecting production of a Shakespeare
comedy ended with a knees-up, usually to the accompani-
ment of a live band, which would carry through into the
curtain call. At its best this would generate a kind of infectious energy which audiences love. At its worst, productions
of classical plays felt like musicals, in which the darker colours
would be painted out in the pursuit of relentless jollity.

Dance rehearsals take a long time. Steps need to be taught
in painstaking detail. A top choreographer once told me it
takes three hours to rehearse five minutes of stage dancing.
But little in the theatre is as life-enhancing as a brilliantly
choreographed dance.

Voice coaches

Perhaps the greatest challenge of the classical theatre is that the
actor has to come on stage, address a large number of people
sitting in an auditorium, often with an unforgiving acoustic,
be heard by everyone without resorting to shouting, and
convey information and emotion. Think of the opening
speech of *Much Ado About Nothing*: 'I learn in this letter that
Don Pedro of Aragon comes this night to Messina' – so much
information has to be conveyed with such modest means.

Good actors have good voices: volume, musicality, tonal
variety and resonance. All these different qualities impact on
their overall 'listenability'. Well-trained actors are fully aware of
the technical aspect of their voice. They talk about 'support',
'breathing', 'relaxation' and so on. They know how to be loud

without shouting, how to be expressive without singing, how to find enough breath to support a long speech. Most importantly they know how to 'centre' their voice in such a way that what comes out is a direct expression of the emotions and thoughts that they have discovered in rehearsals.

The actor's voice is his most important asset, and needs to be looked after, trained and developed. Sometimes, however, actors get into vocal trouble. Their voice is trapped, they're not resonating properly, they're shouting instead of speaking with 'support' and so on. Because many actors do the majority of their work on television, they find the vocal demands of the theatre difficult. And when a play is performing every night in a long run – especially if the part is long and vocally demanding – even the best voices can get tired and croaky.

When you're working with trained, professional actors, their voice is their responsibility and they should know what they're doing with it. But theatres are increasingly drawing on the services of voice coaches, who work with the actors to develop their technical skills. The good voice coaches come with all kinds of vocal exercises and can make an enormous contribution. They're especially useful when you're working with badly trained, inexperienced actors, who need the voice coach to give them the tuition that they should have received at drama school. Work with voice coaches, whenever possible.

The best books on voice are by Patsy Rodenburg, Cicely Berry, Michael McCallion and Barbara Houseman.

Dialect coaches

In Britain, especially, you can tell a huge amount about a person – not simply where he comes from, but also his class and education – by the way he speaks. As a result, actors are often required to perform in accents not their own (although in casting it's often useful to find actors whose native accents are appropriate): Mancunian, Glaswegian, Scouse and so on. Most actors have a good ear, but taking on a difficult and remote accent can be a major challenge (try reading the above in Geordie).

Many plays in English are written in dialect – from the medieval Mystery Plays through to contemporary drama –

and dialect has its own powerful poetry. Consider, for example, the following speech from Sean O'Casey's *Juno and the Paycock*:

> What was the pain I suffered, Johnny, bringin' you into the world to carry you to your cradle, to the pains I'll suffer carryin' you out o'the world to bring you to your grave! Mother o' God, Mother o' God, have pity on us all! Blessed Virgin, where was you when me darlin' son was riddled with bullets, when me darlin' son was riddled with bullets? Sacred Heart o' Jesus, take away our hearts of stone, and give us hearts o' flesh! Take away this murdherin' hate, an' give us Thine own eternal love!

This isn't quaint 'Oirishness'; it's a devastating expression of a powerful and real emotion. And you need to develop an ear for it.

The best thing to do is employ a dialect coach. The good ones come to early rehearsals, listen to the actor, go through the key principles of the accent, leave tapes and phonetic descriptions behind, and come back regularly to give detailed notes. Most dialect coaches are excellent. But be careful: there are bad ones around, who treat the actors with disdain because they can't master the dialect of a South Shields fisherman in a day, or, more dangerously, want to direct the actors' intentions, rhythm and understanding.

Fight directors

Plays often require fights, from formal sword fights to shocking acts of domestic violence.

A famous example is the blinding of Gloucester in *King Lear* (sometimes nicknamed the 'Moorfields scene', after the Eye Hospital): Gloucester's hands are tied to the chair, the chair is pushed over backwards, the first of Gloucester's eyes is stamped out ('Upon these eyes of thine I'll set my foot'), the servant mortally wounds Cornwall, Regan kills the servant, Gloucester's second eye is gouged out ('Out, vile jelly') and Gloucester emerges eyeless, with blood streaming down, to be led away by the surviving servants. All this needs to be handled with consummate skill if it's to avoid unwanted comedy. The blood needs to be applied in such a way that the audience doesn't see it happening. Crucial dramatic actions take place amidst the blood and gore, and need to be made visible. Most importantly you need to stun the audience with the sight of the recently blinded Gloucester:

> All dark and comfortless. Where's my son Edmund?
> Edmund, enkindle all the sparks of nature
> To quit this horrid act.

All this requires staging skills of the highest order if it's to be convincing.

Stage fights have to fulfil two apparently contradictory demands: a powerful illusion of danger on the one hand, and complete safety for all involved on the other. In the amateur theatre the director arranges the fights, to the best of his abilities. In the professional theatre, however, you need to work with a qualified fight director, and many actors wouldn't be prepared to perform a fight that had not been rehearsed by one. I've always got on well with fight directors (and tease them about which violent hot spot they held their annual conference at, or ask them with a straight face how to do a 'completely safe' decapitation). Fight directors have their own registry, and the best thing to do is to contact it and find someone appropriate for the production.

Fight directors have different qualities. The good ones recognise that stage fighting is an expression of the action of the play and the psychology of its characters. They know that it has a realistic function, and want to discover what has brought the characters to the point where violence takes place. This analysis can have a great impact on the way the fight is staged: does 'the noble Laertes' resort to even more dirty tricks in his fight with Hamlet, or is the poisoned sword enough? How much of a ghastly botch is the end of the play, or should it maintain its stateliness to the end? In *Henry IV, Part One*, does Falstaff make an attempt to fight Douglas or is it funnier if their swords don't even touch? Does Hal get 'down and dirty' in his fight with Hotspur, and if he does, is that a crucial moment in the development of his character? All of this matters and a good fight director will respect it.

[195]

There's another kind of fight director, however, who regards fighting as a form of choreography, with a great deal of
dazzling movement, the illusion of danger, and the athletic
thrill of a complex, muscular dance. Of course, not everything
you direct can be a 'shocking exposé of the realities of violence' (to use the standard critical terms), and a staging of
The Three Musketeers that didn't have some astonishing, 'high-
wire' sword-fighting, would be disappointing. I just feel that
stage fights should be dramatically meaningful too.

Rehearsing stage fights takes a huge amount of time. When
I directed *Hamlet*, I was astonished that five minutes of stage
time (the fight between Hamlet and Laertes) could take up so
many rehearsals. In addition to the many sessions with Terry
King, in which the two actors worked out the basic moves
and strokes, they used to practise every morning for half an
hour before rehearsals. Safety needs to be endlessly drilled.
I remember Terry telling them that they should be boring
but reliable, explaining that when an audience fears for the
actors' safety they lose contact with the fiction and respond
as human beings concerned about a fellow human being.
And so the illusion is broken.

Magic consultants, pet handlers, chaperones, flying consultants and other quacks

It amazes me the range of specialists a production can require.

In Act Three of *The Cherry Orchard*, Chekhov asks that
Charlotta Ivanovna should be able to do magic tricks, including putting Anya behind a blanket and then making her
disappear. We brought in a magic specialist, Paul Kieve, and
I won't tell you how he did it lest he gets expelled from the
Magic Circle, but it was fascinating watching him at work. I
asked him to do a few card tricks so the actors might feel the
strange sensation of having witnessed something they really
couldn't understand. It was important for keeping the scene
as fresh as possible.

You sometimes need to bring in expertise for particularly
complicated – and dangerous – technical tricks, of which the
most complicated is flying a person. For this kind of effect
you must bring in a flying specialist, who can take everybody

through the routines that make it reliable and safe. You'll certainly need a flying specialist when you come to direct *Peter Pan*.

Marty Cruickshank's play *A Difficult Age* needed two live ducks on stage in a cage (they were to be eaten later). Because of the law about cruelty to animals, we couldn't take the same ducks on tour and used to have different ones at every theatre. We also had to employ a fully-trained animal handler who would be responsible for their welfare. I remember bitterly joking that it cost more to tour two ducks than to employ an extra actor.

But nothing is as expensive, or specialist-intensive, as having children in a production. Their parents' worries need to be soothed, chaperones paid for and schools pacified. Adult actors have to be on their best behaviour (no swearing). And then getting the kids to remember their lines, be loud enough, and bring some level of spontaneity to what they're doing requires extraordinary patience, and – sometimes – the help of a specialist. The old adage about 'not working with children or animals' is spot on. It's impossible to stop them upstaging the adults.

Specialists are useful; just make sure they don't take over: 'On tap, not on top,' as Churchill used to say.

17

Rehearsals 8: Manners

In putting on a play many people, from very diverse backgrounds and skills, are brought together and put into an emotional and psychological pressure cooker. The director is the person who needs to deal with all those complex feelings, set the tone, defuse the tension and understand the kind of pressure they are working under. As a director, you have to be much more than an egocentric and demanding artist: you need to be a well-equipped, psychologically sophisticated nanny.

Tone of voice

The crucial thing is the tone of voice.

You need to convey tremendous authority, while also allowing the space for contradiction and questioning. I remember one weekend teaching a group of young directors, spending most of the first day watching them work with young actors. At the end, I found myself saying to nearly all of them – before we had begun to discuss the artistic, theatrical or practical challenges of the play they had chosen – that I was shocked to see just how rude they had been to the actors. They were assuming an authority that was hardly justified by their experience and some of them had addressed their actors with undisguised contempt.

It's essential to remember that although as the director you have the last word about many things, there are limits to what you can and should say. You need to develop a sense not only for when to speak, but also when to hold back, when to be forceful and when to use a light, almost imperceptible touch. Tact is essential, and the best directors will show respect to their actors at all times, however challenging or pressurised the work may be.

The point is that actors need to give you permission to direct them, as much as you give them permission to act. This is an unspoken contract, but as a young director I once found myself in a situation where – for whatever reason – the actors simply refused to be directed by me: my tears and despair hardly helped convince them otherwise. I had to be taken off the production, and I nearly gave up directing as a result.

I don't get into these sort of scrapes any more: but I'm acutely (perhaps too acutely) aware of the kind of nuanced diplomacy you need to employ with experienced, demanding actors, if the production is to be a success.

How to interrupt

One of the hardest things is to know how and when to interrupt.

In the early stages of rehearsal – reading and analysis – you'll need to interrupt frequently. You need to ask questions as much as offer answers and point out details in the play, its characters and its language. You're expected to lead these discussions, and interruptions are only natural. In the mid-stage of rehearsals – language, character, blocking – you'll want to interrupt fairly frequently: 'Why don't you come downstage of the sofa on that line?', 'Do you see how obsessed he is with money?', 'Try using the caesura more heavily, to show up the contrasting elements in the line' and so on. But as the production begins to take shape, and you begin to run sections, and the acting starts to take off, you need to be careful not to disturb the actors in mid-flow, breaking their concentration and sense of dramatic development. Each of your interruptions must be carefully judged.

But, of course, there are no rules: stopping a final run-through which has got off to a bad start, or interrupting a scene because the actors have forgotten the blocking, may be necessary, and letting them continue counterproductive. The important thing is that interrupting must be done with sensitivity and care. Developing a performance is an organic process, and actors in rehearsal need careful tending if they're to flourish.

Talking too much

One of the mistakes many young directors make is talking too much.

Young directors are full of things to say: they care passionately about the theatre, they've read widely and they've thought deeply. But some of them have jumbled, overcrowded minds, and they forget to organise their thoughts before they open their mouth. They desperately want to express themselves and fear makes them talk too much to disguise it.

The fact is the more you talk, the more you confuse. Be concise and to the point: your actors will thank you for it.

Awareness of everything

To direct well you have to be aware of everything that's going on in the room, and not just in the marked-out area. A raised eyebrow from a senior actor sitting looking at the paper; a pair of actresses jealous of each other's figures; a tired stage manager; a distracting noise from an open window and so on. By being aware of all this, you develop an understanding of how everything has an impact on the work itself.

Of course, it's all too easy to let this induce paranoia: 'That quizzical look must be a direct result of my incompetence', 'She's yawning because I'm boring' and so on. Sometimes, of course, your paranoia will have caught a basic truth, and you can adjust your behaviour accordingly. At other times, though, the important thing is to understand what is going on, and plough on regardless, with your convictions intact.

It's important to remember that many things are best expressed physically. As a director you need to find a way of expressing yourself beyond the words you speak, and you must develop an understanding of the way your own physicality affects the people you're working with. And so I never sit behind a desk in rehearsal. Sometimes I'm very still; at other times I prowl around the room. Directing is an intuitive business and you need to be aware of what you're communicating with every part of your being: your *body* language, not just your words.

Putting an arm round

I find that I can often say more physically than through hours of talk: a pat, a hug, an arm round a shoulder and a touch on the arm. One of the things such fleeting physical contact can do is allow the performer to appreciate your sensual apprehension of the scene, not just your intellectual understanding, and intuitive actors will often respond well.

Of course, you have to be careful. A director inevitably has a kind of personal power, and actors and actresses can easily misunderstand your intentions. I remember putting my arm round a young actress who immediately misinterpreted my motives, and I had a lot of explaining to do before she accepted that I'm just a 'touchy-feely' person. There are stories of directors abusing their authority and young actresses imagining that sleeping with the director might help their career. But there are as many stories about actresses feeling betrayed and preyed on by those directors, whose reputations have slumped as a result.

The fact is, however, that the best theatre is always driven by a kind of libido, and directors without any sensual undertone or erotic frisson are likely to produce dull work. A director who is physically tense is unlikely to be able to release performances that are centred and have a physical life. But you need to find out your own personal style in this: every director is different and you need to work out who you are – not just as an intellectual, or a skilled craftsman, or a manager or a coordinator, but as a sensual, physical presence.

Temper tantrums

Occasionally, just occasionally, somebody loses his temper.

Temper tantrums come at the most surprising moments, from the most unlikely people and take a range of different forms. Some people shout, storm off and come back ten minutes later; others disappear into the blackest of black moods. A temper tantrum can be difficult to handle, but it's important the director doesn't surrender to this kind of behaviour. I tend to sit quietly and let the whole thing take its course, and then, when the outburst is finished, calmly and carefully call a break to the work. I think that anybody who loses his temper should apologise to all concerned – just as you would in your private life. Anger is a destructive emotion which makes people retreat into a position of fear and caution, and is counterproductive. A temper tantrum needs to be acknowledged for what it is.

Yet it's always worth trying to work out what it was that triggered the flare-up. It's usually because the actor is feeling insecure, or because he's finding another actor (or the director) difficult to work with. And so if you need to bring about reconciliation and a dialogue between the two actors, so be it.

An older actor in one of my productions lost his temper with a young actress who would never play the scene in the same way twice. He felt that it was impossible to build on what had been achieved the last time. She was being serious and inquisitive, constantly exploring her part and refining her performance in the best possible way. What she didn't understand, however, was that the older actor needed to repeat the scene exactly so he could memorise it. His frustration erupted in anger; the anger was an overreaction but the cause was real.

Patience

The best directors have a low boredom threshold. They want to get things done quickly and become restless when something is slow, undramatic or plain dull. Their impatience is valuable.

But you have to be capable of great patience as well, and there are many moments in rehearsal when your patience is sorely tested. In the early stages you have to allow actors the space to talk, even to talk about ideas that you know will lead to a dead end. They have to find their own way through. And sometimes it's infuriating: 'Why do they have to do all this talk?' you ask yourself, 'Why don't they just cut to the chase?' At other times they seem incapable of hearing what you say over and over again – some strange resistance has built up, and you need to find a way through, drawing on all your intuition and tact. Occasionally, you can't believe how complicated actors want to make it. This frustration is understandable, and to an extent useful. But stern-eyed patience is even better.

Up until the 1950s, actors would come to the first rehearsals with their lines learnt. (Opera singers still learn their score before the first day of 'production rehearsals'.) Then, in the 1960s, it was argued an actor who had learnt his lines before rehearsals would be stuck in a particular rhythm and emphasis, and actors were encouraged to come to rehearsals open to discoveries. In many ways this was right, and most actors don't have much difficulty in learning their lines. But some actors, occasionally out of laziness but usually because of age, find it very difficult, and sometimes even mar the first few performances by struggling to remember. The best ones know they have a problem and either try to get ahead before rehearsals, or have invented complicated mnemonic systems. Some actors use their moves as a way of providing a physical correlative to the line, which is the cause of tremendous resistance if you want to change the moves after the first week or two. But sometimes you just wish they would 'get on with it'. 'Why is it taking so long?' you think, 'Why can't they just remember their lines? That's their job. Why can't they do it?' Judging when actors should have learnt their lines ('be off the book' is the usual phrase) is complicated, and varies from actor to actor. Young actors who take a long time to learn their lines irritate me the most; I feel they have no excuse. I tend to be more understanding with older actors. In a four-week rehearsal period I expect the actors to be 'off the book' by the last week: it usually works out like that.

There always comes a moment in rehearsals when you feel you're just waiting for the actors to catch up, not just on their lines, but on the more interesting problems of character, emotion, pace and dramatic flow. In other words, you've done all the work on the scene – all the analysis, all the imaginative work – but it still isn't really working. It's at that point you have to sit on your hands and let the actors find their own way through. And in that phase, patience is all.

Losing your temper

Directing is a pressurised activity and patience can snap. As the opening night looms, more and more decisions have to be made, just as more and profound problems start to appear. Inevitably, some directors become tetchy, take on a kind of 'schoolmaster' tone of voice, and even lose their temper and shout and scream. Others like to find a 'whipping boy', somebody they can pick on and bully, or they use teasing as a way of maintaining their own elevated position.

But such behaviour isn't just cruel, it's counterproductive. There must be some kind of morality in theatre directing – some shared, but unspoken contract between director and actor that certain personal boundaries won't be crossed, that certain things will be accepted and respected. It's one of the least appealing phenomena of the contemporary theatre that, in pursuit of the passionate and the expressive, morally dubious means are used. It's a mistake to think it's only older directors who are tyrannical monsters. If anything, it's a new generation of directors, drunk on the idea of their own genius, who most often behave badly.

The theatre is full of passionate temperaments working under considerable pressure, and it's not surprising that sometimes people don't behave like saints. But don't become one of those directors whom everybody dismisses as a bully. The critics may like the noisy energy of your work, but you'll be loathed and rejected by your peers.

It's not worth it, I promise you.

Homework

It's easy at this stage in rehearsals, when you're working very hard, to leave the script in the rehearsal room at the end of the day, go to the pub or get some dinner, and forget all about it until the morning. In many ways this is wise: rehearsals shouldn't take over your life. But when things get difficult – as they always do – it's worth spending an hour or two with the text in the evening, re-reading it, and reminding yourself of the characters' objectives as well as the play's practical and artistic challenges. This is helpful even when you feel confident about what you want, but are worried about why an actor is finding it so difficult. Homework lets you go back into rehearsals the next morning fresher, sharper and of more use to everyone. It's particularly valuable when the alternative is a sleepless night that makes you even less useful the next day.

18

Rehearsals 9: Running it

There comes a moment in rehearsals when you need to 'run' the action of the play: first just 'units', then scenes, then acts and finally the whole play.

Your aim is two-fold. First, you're trying to get the actors to navigate their way through the play, to act with some sense of purpose and pleasure, and to develop a sense of through-line and momentum. Second, you're trying to discover those moments when the action seems to go soggy, when the energy comes up against a brick wall and when things don't seem to be coming together. This allows you to draw up your agenda for further work.

Rhythm

An essential part of the director's job is to control and shape the pace of the production.

I've watched orchestral conductors at work and increasingly feel the theatre director's role is analogous. Like a conductor, you can't change the writer's 'score', but your control of the shifts in *tempi* makes or breaks the evening. This is an essential element of your interpretation, and a badly 'conducted' production is as poor as a badly designed, cast or blocked one.

Pacing is a complex task. At times you need to encourage the actors to slow down, to feel every moment of the shifting emotions and unfolding narrative action. Brecht had a useful phrase – 'play one thing after another' – and I often encourage actors to distinguish between the different impulses, step by step, moment by moment. I remember watching Peter Stein's production of Heinrich von Kleist's *The Prince of Homburg*, mesmerised at the way the Elector signed, dried with sand, and sealed the letter that released the Prince from his death sentence. The actor did this with such immaculate attention to detail that you understood a bit more of the world in which the play was set. The letter became a hugely important object, whose contents affected the whole subsequent action of the play.

At other times, it's essential you tell the actors to speed up, catch fire and drive the action on to its inevitable conclusion. You find yourself frustrated: 'Everything seems to be going too slowly'; 'If she could cross the stage with a spring in her step everything would work'; 'Why can't he just grab the hammer and bang in the nail?' And that's when you have to insist on pace, above everything else, ruthlessly and forcefully. You sometimes come up against resistance: an actor enjoys playing all the subtleties he's discovered, and is enjoying a languorous pace. The trick is to hint that the audience will get restless as a result. But you also have to be merciless on your own work too: 'Those extra moves I got you to put in – that hesitant bow before you leave – interesting and revealing as it seemed when we first created them, mean that the scene is losing pace. They have to go!' Having the courage to jettison one of your most treasured ideas is the mark of a good director.

Pace and rhythm should be dictated by the overall shape of the evening. It's often a good idea to get the actors to go slowly at the beginning. This makes things crystal clear and gives the audience the time to enter into the world of the play. But then, three quarters of the way through, you need to drive the play relentlessly along to its climax. Ibsen has an astonishing trick of suddenly speeding up the action in the last minute or two before the end of each Act. In Shakespeare, Act Four (the England Scene in *Macbeth*, Claudius and Laertes in *Hamlet*, Lear and Gloucester on Dover Cliff in *King Lear*) is often the hardest act to get right, because the writing tends to open up and be at its most philosophically investigative; if you've not paced the whole evening well, it can seem interminable.

Running units

Quite early on in rehearsal (maybe the second week) I ask the actors to run a section (sometimes called a 'unit'). This allows you to gain some of the benefits of a full run-through, while at the same time giving you time to adjust things section by section.

What are you looking for? Crucially, you're witnessing the results of the decisions you've already made being played out in real time. You can see where you've been too fussy, where your direction is slowing things down unnecessarily, where an all-important moment is being slid over and so on. You can then tighten the focus, adjust the rhythm and shape the scene in the way that's needed. 'Stretch that pause there, it'll hold', you say, 'Please come on stage a beat earlier, there's a dead moment', 'You need to hit a higher emotional level at the end: it's not quite carrying' and so on.

Running sections also gives you an all-important perspective on the acting. You'll find that when you watch a scene that isn't quite working, it may be because one of the actors isn't clear about his motivation. More likely, at this stage, an actor is failing to deliver from a technical point of view: he's too slow, or too quiet, or simply lacking in the right kind of energy. Sometimes, though, the problem is the opposite: the actor is too loud, too fast or pushing it: running the scene makes all that clear.

Sometimes, you realise that the problem is of your own making. If you show you're prepared to admit when you've misdirected a scene, the actors will be more prepared to listen when you tell them they've been taking a scene down a blind alley. As usual the process is mutual. But it's here you need to be most careful, particularly with older actors, who may well be treating running sections as a way of getting things fixed in their memory – too many last-minute changes can cause mayhem.

If I'm directing a big classic I may – in the last week – run the first half of the play first thing in the morning, work on the sections that need attention, and run it again before lunch. I'll then run the second half after lunch and do the same thing during the afternoon. The advantage of this is that it allows you to get through the whole play in a day, but work on the sections that need attention too.

When to start running the play?

It's difficult to know when to call the first complete run-through.

If you insist on a run-through too early, you risk damaging the actors' confidence ('We're just not ready for it'). But a fairly early run-through often releases all those energies that you've been trying to free, and resolves some of those detailed problems that you've been struggling with. Everybody learns from a well-timed run-through and it's an essential step in the rehearsal process.

In a four-week rehearsal process I try to get two run-throughs in the last week, the first maybe on the Thursday, and a final run-through on the Saturday morning.

The final run-through

Getting to the point where the actors can give a fluent final run-through in the rehearsal room is crucial. I schedule the last week with this as a definite objective.

I make sure that the atmosphere for the final run-through has a certain formality, a kind of tension that brings out the best in people. I sometimes make a point of turning up with just seconds to spare before it's due to begin: 'You've got to do this thing without me' is the subliminal signal I'm trying to send. I also insist on silence, and an atmosphere of concentration and stillness in the rehearsal room. I start the run-through myself, and insist on quiet ('No chatter') in any moves of furniture that are required.

I also invite the rest of the creative team to attend. I will already have had extensive conversations with the lighting, music and sound designers, but this is an ideal moment for them to work out whether their initial ideas are the right ones. Sometimes a musician or sound designer will want to play the cues. I tend to discourage this – unless we've been working with the cues for weeks (for a dance, for example, or underscoring some text, or something intrinsic to the action) – because I don't want the actors to be suddenly confronted by the kinds of issues that await them in the technical rehearsal.

The point of the final run-through is that if the actors can get the show right in the rehearsal room, it stands a reasonable chance of transferring creatively and successfully on to the stage: the next and perhaps most daunting moment in the whole journey to date.

How to give notes

Once you start running sections of the play, or the entire play, your relationship with the actors changes. You've become more objective, your eye is now on whether it's beginning to work as a whole, and you've moved beyond both the analytical and the creative phase. You're now polishing and sharpening those decisions that have already been made. And if you're really going to help the piece flow, you'll have to find a way of keeping quiet until it's time for you to give your feedback: this is when you start to 'give notes'.

It's essential that when you assemble the actors after a run-through you give your notes quickly and effectively. There's nothing more draining for an actor than to sit for hours waiting for the director to say perhaps only one thing that affects him. Actors need you to be helpful, and the best thing you can do is to be encouraging and specific. Say things like: 'That's excellent, but there's a quality of melancholy in that line which I feel you're not quite expressing'; 'I think you've got Act One, but you need to bring in more inquisitorial energy in Act Two. The audience should learn about this dysfunctional family through your eyes, but I don't feel you're looking carefully enough yourself'; 'The thought's not particular enough on that line, can you be more precise: you're not asking him to marry you, you just want him to be more honest' and so on.

Always check the actor has understood your point ('Do you see what I'm driving at?'). If he hasn't, you may have to move on and say, 'Can I come back to you later on that?' One of the things I always dread about note sessions is when people say, 'Can we work on that a bit?' In many ways they're right: the only way to solve a problem is to rehearse it. The difficulty is that actors hardly ever understand the kind of time pressure you're working under, and if you worked on every section they wanted to look at, you would never get the show opened. You need to discriminate here between what genuinely needs detailed rehearsal, and what is just a cry for attention. Occasionally, I'm afraid, you need to fob someone off with a promise.

It's finally time to leave the rehearsal room for the last time, and make your way into the theatre itself.

19

Putting it onto the Stage

The moment when you first walk into the theatre and see the set under 'working lights' can come as a terrible shock. It usually looks rather tawdry and more physically constrained than you expected it to be – more like a scruffy pile of wood and metal than the thing of beauty you dreamt up with the designer. You've got a lot of work to do now and putting the show on stage is when you really earn your money.

Technical schedule

A good production manager will have drawn up a 'production schedule' long before the production week and will want to check this through with you. In discussing a schedule it's important to understand how much time is needed: to get the set up and working, rig and focus the lights, prepare the wings, sort out the side masking and so on. In addition you need extensive technical rehearsal time and, ideally, two dress rehearsals.

There'll be a wide range of variables in this – from the total time available, to the theatre's staff and budget, to the scale of the set and the lighting rig. An outline schedule for my production of *King Lear* gives a flavour of the amount of time I think a 'middle scale' production of a Shakespeare play should take:

SUNDAY AND MONDAY Get in the set
TUESDAY Rig and focus the lights
WEDNESDAY Plot the lights and sound and start the technical rehearsal (one session)
THURSDAY Continue technical rehearsal (three sessions)
FRIDAY Finish technical rehearsal (three sessions)
SATURDAY First dress rehearsal
SUNDAY Day off
MONDAY Second dress rehearsal in the afternoon and first performance in the evening

In some theatres you get much more time, in others far less. The crucial thing is that you've got to get a lot of work done in a limited amount of time.

The creative team

At this point it's important to remember you have a team around you: designer, costume designer, lighting designer, sound engineer (or sound designer), production manager and so on. Ultimately, you have to lead them, but you should recognise their own particular areas of expertise. One of the best responses I got from a lighting designer when I was struggling with the technicalities of a particular effect was when he said: 'Tell me what atmosphere you're after. Let me work out how to do it. I'm the lighting designer, after all.'

A powerful bond can build up within the creative team during the technical and dress rehearsals. You all sit in a darkened auditorium, cut off from the actors, trying to be objective and critical, working together, cracking jokes, and being friends. In the tea break you wander front of house while the actors are in the green room. All this can produce its own kind of creative energy.

Lighting

Lighting is a great and complex art, and the more I direct, the more I see how it affects the way the audience watch the play.

You need to have talked to the lighting designer at least three weeks before you start on the technical rehearsals. Good lighting designers look at the model of the set, come to the read-through, attend rehearsals, talk to you about their ideas, and generally become involved in the production as it develops. Briefing a lighting designer shouldn't be very different from briefing a set or costume designer. In other words, what kind of theatre are we creating? Is it subjective and expressionistic, or cool and objective? Is the style natur-alistic, or is it theatrical? And if so, what kind of theatricality? If we want atmospheric lighting what is the particular atmosphere we're after? Just how much naturalistic inform-ation do we want the lighting to give? And so on.

But lighting is also a practical task. If the production isn't lit well the audience will not be able to see the actors and if they can't see the actors they won't listen to the play. An underlit scene will quickly lose its audience's attention (and 'kill the laughs' in comedy) while one that's too bright makes everything look cheap and tacky. There are psychological reasons for this which you and the lighting designer need to understand. But it's essential that the lighting designer remembers to illuminate the action.

The lighting designer has to have designed the rig before you get on stage. This means he has to have worked out where to hang the lanterns, chosen what kind he'll use, and focused them. The outline of the lighting is usually done at a plotting session, which takes place without any actors (the Wednesday morning on the chart above), but with a stage manager (or another body) to do the 'walking' (standing in the places where the lighting designer needs to see the effect of his lights). The mistake is trying to do this in too much detail; it's much better to sketch a feel of the various lighting states, a 'rough plot' for each scene, which should illuminate the areas needed in the action, if without much art or subtlety. Once the actors come on stage in costume and move around, the most careful and elaborately plotted lighting tends to look wrong, and so the best time to get into detail with the lighting designer is in the technical and dress rehearsals.

I've developed my own set of principles in lighting. I joke that coloured light is 'immoral', that gobos (the little patterned things which make light look as if it's coming through trees, or church windows, or whatever) are 'wicked', and that if I notice the lighting changing in the middle of the scene it's 'badly lit'. Most directors bring their own prejudices, and these happen to mine. Other directors think differently, and lighting designers have to be flexible.

Such beliefs do, of course, have their roots in certain theatrical and aesthetic principles. For example, if you light the leading actor more brightly than the servants, what does that say about your view of hierarchy? I've a code with one of my favourite lighting designers: 'Light the messenger' means light all the people equally, regardless of social class or centrality in the story. And if the stage goes pink at the end of a

Shakespeare comedy, doesn't that suggest you see its resolution in a distinctly romantic, almost slushy way? Like everything in the theatre, your approach to lighting has a relationship to your approach to life.

Sound

With modern technology the potential for sound is enormous, and recent years have seen the emergence of sound designers who are creative artists in their own right. Subliminal soundscapes are possible: dogs barking in the distance, trains going by, aeroplanes flying overhead, a washing machine churning in the kitchen – all reproduced with startling authenticity. Sound designers get their sound effects from a whole range of places – the BBC's sound library, the Internet, as well as their own recordings.

Different kinds of plays need different attitudes to sound. Tweeting birds can be marvellous in a naturalistic play but counterproductive in Shakespeare, where I think it's often wise to have only those sound effects which would have been used at the Globe: thunder, door knocks, off-stage cries and so on. But even in work as naturalistic as *The Cherry Orchard* you have to be careful. Chekhov evidently became exasperated with Stanislavski's over-enthusiastic use of sound effects, which evidently included a whole menagerie of wildlife. In a letter he pointed out:

> Hay-making takes place June 20–25, by that time the corncrake's rasping cry is no longer heard, the frogs are also silent by then . . .

But in Act Two, Chekhov himself writes:

> *Suddenly a far-off noise is heard, as if in the heavens – like the sound of a breaking string, dying away, sadly.*

He then follows this with the following cryptic dialogue:

RANEVSKAYA What's that?
LOPAKHIN I don't know. Possibly a coal-tub broken loose
somewhere, down the mines. A long way from here, anyway.

GAEV Could be some sort of bird, like a heron.
TROFIMOV Or an owl, perhaps . . .
RANEVSKAYA (*shudders*) It's horrible, whatever it is.

Try to imagine a sound that can satisfy Chekhov's stage directions, allow for both Lopakhin's and Gaev's comments, and not make Trofimov seem ridiculous or Ranevskaya hysterical, and you'll see just how difficult Chekhov has made it. The different interpretations say something about the characters (Lopakhin's industrial roots, Gaev's mild prettiness, Trofimov's gloominess, Ranevskaya's fear) but the sound used must not make it impossible for them to say their lines. And then at the end of the play Chekhov asks for the following:

> From far away, as if coming from the sky, the sound of a breaking string – a melancholy, dying fall. Silence descends then, and the only thing we hear is a distant axe, striking a tree in the orchard.

It's a beautiful idea – but what is it really meant to sound like?

Good plays sometimes have sound effects that are essential to their meaning. These are often the hardest to get right. A famous example is the door slam at the end of Ibsen's *A Doll's House*. I eventually discovered that this was best done with an actual 'door slam', not a tape, though I sat in a sound studio for hours listening to 'a door slamming in the hall'. I faced a similar problem in *The Master Builder*. The noise I was offered of Solness falling through the trees and 'smashing his head on the stone-pile' was just too comical; but how could the basic information be put over otherwise? The sound designer eventually created a sound that had the right kind of shocking impact but was not literal – a slightly abstracted crash. In retrospect, I think this too failed to capture Ibsen's precise intention. At such times, Ibsen's stage directions can only be fully realised in film.

Listening through headphones in a sound studio to the noise of a door closing, or footsteps walking about upstairs, or the cherry orchard being cut down, can be very difficult: 'Is that all it is?' you think, listening to it out of context. Played in the theatre, however, at an appropriate level and from the right place on stage, surrounded by the action that it's meant to support, it all sounds perfect. But you sometimes come across the opposite: what seemed right in the studio sounds ridiculous in the theatre, and you need to know when to cut it, or at least ask it to be changed.

The most important thing is to develop a strong working relationship with your sound designer (ironically, they're always the quietest people in the business). Together you can make the sound right.

Music

Ever since the Greeks, music has been a fundamental part of the theatrical experience.

Music in the theatre can be divided into two kinds: 'realistic' music that the characters are meant to hear (an offstage band, the Fool's songs in *King Lear*, a wind-up gramophone) and 'theatrical' music that's part of the overall production. Music can express and develop the inner emotions of the individual characters, and help us feel, in the most direct way, what it is they're experiencing.

But music can also make a major contribution to the story-telling: hurrying a scene change along, giving it a particular atmosphere, commenting ironically and so on. This can be very effective, and gives the audience a more direct access to the emotion and dramatic power that's being deployed. Directors sometimes like to have music underscoring certain speeches and even entire scenes. When I directed *Measure for Measure*, I asked the composer to highlight the moment of decision in Isabella's speech 'To whom should I complain?' with a series of delicate notes played on the piano.

But underscoring needs to be handled carefully. Increasingly, actors resent the desire to turn spoken drama into musical drama, and you may find that such underscoring simplifies the emotion and obscures the thought. Directing Ibsen's *Ghosts*, I asked the composer to write a few seconds of 'catastrophe music' to catch and underline the play's extraordinary ending. When we tried this in the technical rehearsal both Diana Quick (Mrs Alving) and Daniel Evans (Osvald) were unhappy – 'I would hope that if we're doing it properly we wouldn't need this' – and I quickly realised they were right. It was much better to end the play in aching silence.

I tend to use music most often as a way of bridging the gap between the scenes, particularly in a Shakespeare play. One scene might end with an upbeat, driving energy, but the next needs to start with a mood of quiet contemplation. I love it when a composer finds a way of making one scene dovetail with another. In Shakespeare, scene changes should be as quick as possible; with *King Lear* I told the composer that no scene-change should last longer than four seconds.

I enjoy commissioning composers and sometimes give them surprising and challenging briefs: 'Schoenberg put through an industrial accident with pop songs thrown into the mix', 'Elizabethan madrigals dripping with acid put through a spin-dryer', 'The *Songs of the Auvergne* set against the rumble of a gathering storm' and so on. Good composers tend to respond well to such contradictory, complex briefs: it gives them a feel of what's looked for without being too prescriptive.

Ideally, all music in the theatre should be played live: it gives a richness of sound and an immediacy of effect that's irreplaceable. At the RSC and the National Theatre, the Musicians Union has insisted that live musicians should always be used. But very few companies can afford this and most music is recorded or written on and played by sophisticated computer programmes.

It's of little use having specially commissioned music if it's not played through a high quality sound system. This differs from theatre to theatre and company to company, but the involvement of a good sound engineer is often crucial in making the musical and sound world of the play work successfully.

Technical rehearsals

The technical rehearsal (always called 'the tech') is a crucial time, in which you need to make a wide range of important decisions which radically affect the way the production works. I love techs because I enjoy the plastic nature of the theatre, and I work harder in the seven or eight tech sessions than I do in the rest of the rehearsal period. This is when all your best-laid plans are first tested, when everything you did with the actors in the rehearsal room has to be made to work on stage, and when all the work of the creative team has to cohere. The tech requires you to be at your most decisive, yet most receptive, your most organised and yet most open-minded, to look with the greatest attention to detail, but with the firmest grasp of the whole show.

The best run techs are very thorough, and will last two or three full days for a three-hour play. The aim is that by the end everybody involved knows exactly how every second of action works on the stage. From out front, you're in charge of co-ordinating the impact of a whole range of different elements, and are seeing them together for the first time – actors, furniture, doors, props, lighting and sound cues, revolves, trucks, costumes, etc. Meanwhile, the deputy stage manager writes every decision down in 'the book'. The wardrobe mistress works out how to do quick changes. The props tables are set out in the wings and the props placed in the right order. The stage management and crew work out how to do quick set and furniture changes, the fly-men discover how to handle the flying pieces, and the whole thing is made reliable, safe and capable of repetition.

The extraordinary thing is how much detail is involved. Working out how to start a play is always hard. Should the houselights go down before the stage lights come up and should the music come in before or after the first stage lighting state is complete? How loud should the opening music be, and is it possible to set a sound level accurately in an empty theatre? And then when the butler comes in, what happens when he can't put the tray down on the lower table because his collar is so stiff? When the phone needs to ring, what is the exact cue for the sound, and does it really seem to come from the phone, when you know it's coming from a speaker behind the wall? The fact is that every single one of these problems needs solving, often in collaboration with another member of the team. But as the director you have to make the final decisions.

After twenty years of doing techs, I've just begun to know how I like to run them. I think it's crucial you don't jump up and down on to the stage every two minutes since it's important that you maintain some kind of clear-eyed objectivity. I rely on the Company Stage Manager standing on the forestage with headphones ('cans') on, relaying and interpreting my decisions. I insist on obsessive detail and repeat everything over and over again. I know there's no point in trying to do a tech too quickly. I remember being astonished that the business of an actress opening a French window and firing a shot at somebody walking through the garden (in *Hedda Gabler*) took about an hour of technical time to get right: 'How does the gun work?', 'Where's the door handle?', 'What's the best angle for the shot?', 'Do we have a plan B if the gun gets jammed?' (they always do) and so on and so on. But I also know that there are certain matters – particularly lighting and sound levels – that are very difficult to judge before the first dress rehearsal, when you see those decisions unfold in real time.

One thing that often needs attention is the detail of the costumes. However brilliant the costume designer is, a shirt that looked superb in the fitting can now seem too bright on stage. Or a detail that had seemed subtle and sophisticated is now illegible. Clothes often look too clean, too stiff and starched, and I often talk to the costume designer about 'breaking them down', making them feel worn and used. Occasionally it goes further than that, and it becomes obvious that one of the costumes is just plain wrong, badly conceived, shabbily executed and needs to be changed. For Mozart's *Don Giovanni*, Mark Bouman had made Elvira a very beautiful, entirely characteristic, carefully researched travelling hat, which was to be worn at a rakish angle with a feather on the top. The problem was that when she came on singing 'Ah che mi dice mai', the audience saw a walking hat, and the singer – who was a fine actress – was obliterated by it. I cut it, but it wasn't easy. Of course, a decision like this is hard to broach, particularly when somebody has spent days making the discarded item and the budget has been spent, but occasionally unpopular decisions need to be made and you need the clarity of vision and guts to insist on them.

The other thing you have to do at the tech is look at the acting from a technical point of view, and this needs to be handled with some care. I quite often draw the actors' attention to the acoustic of the theatre, the kind of projection that's needed, the degree of articulation and so on. This occasionally comes as a shock to the actors – particularly the inexperienced ones – who feel that all their carefully worked out details are going to be jettisoned. Of course, more experienced actors know these are simply technical challenges that need to be mastered, and will usually help the younger ones.

And you need to keep an eye on sightlines. Sometimes even the most carefully rehearsed production feels badly blocked when you first put it on the stage. In *Love's Labour's Lost* a dining table running up and down the stage obscured the actor sitting at the upstage end, and it was only when we turned the table with its length running across the stage that you could see Holofernes. The more experienced you are, the more likely you will avoid these kinds of problems. But it's difficult to predict, and you need to be prepared to make drastic last-minute changes. Your actors may grumble, but within an hour they will have forgotten all about it if the decision is right.

One of the more gratifying things about a tech is when you suddenly have an insight that changes everything, when a small artistic decision becomes enormously powerful. When Emma Cunniffe playing Hilde Wangel came on for her first scene in the tech of *The Master Builder*, I suddenly saw a swooping, hawk-like move that encapsulated her role in the play. I asked her to do it, and many people commented on how brilliant that moment was. In the tech for *Le Nozze di Figaro* the singer playing the gardener Antonio didn't know where to put his broken, muddy carnation pot. When he just plonked it down on the cream sofa in the Countess's boudoir I suddenly saw that the meaning of the scene (and the opera itself) had been caught. In seconds I was encouraging Antonio to sprinkle more earth around the pristine white room. Creativity can happen in an environment full of talk about 'ten-second fades', 'FX cues' and 'quick changes'.

One of the hardest things is to get the tech finished on time. I give myself clear targets ('The end of Act One by lunchtime on Tuesday'), but you often find that something goes faster than you thought, while something else needs a surprising amount of time. You need to keep one eye firmly on the clock.

Scene changes

Most plays require a change of location at some point in the evening; some plays – particularly by Shakespeare and Brecht – require dozens of them. If the evening is to flow easily and dynamically the necessary changes have to happen fluently and at speed, and quite often in full view of the audience. They usually have music playing over them, and are lit in interesting ways that distinguish them from the action of the play. Sometimes these changes can be very simple – a chair needs to be brought on, a curtain needs to be drawn. At other times the change is much more complex, and needs choreographing with care and attention to detail.

In some productions the scene changes have a whole life and attitude of their own. In a 'Brechtian' production, the scene changes encourage a feeling of the ephemeral nature of each scene. Directors sometimes ask the actors to participate in the scene changes themselves, sometimes in 'character', in full view of the audience. I once turned the scene changes in a new play into pieces of ballet in their own right.

Whatever you want the scene changes to be, you must form a view and rehearse them properly during the tech. I've become increasingly impatient with long scene changes, and work carefully with the designer on making sure they're as elegant and simple as possible. Nothing can kill an evening in the theatre more easily than dull, interminable, badly organised scene changes.

The First Dress Rehearsal

I find it valuable to lower everybody's expectations prior to the first dress rehearsal. I tend to talk about it as a 'technical dress rehearsal', as the first 'stumble-through' on stage, telling the actors that 'I won't be looking at them anyway', that the point of the rehearsal is 'to recap, at performance speed, all the work that was done in the tech.' The 'tech dress' gives you a chance to look at the production, not at the acting. You can now make a few more critically important decisions.

You need to realise that you are, for the first time, looking at the production unfolding in real time. All the work you did so painstakingly in the tech has now all got to run together. Lighting changes that seemed graceful now look over-dramatic. Sound effects that in the tech seemed appropriate suddenly feel over-elaborate. You notice that one of the actors seems to spend the whole of the first act facing left, or that the colour of a hat is so bright that it blows the colour balance in the rest of the costumes. The raked stage, which seemed to be quite possible in the tech, now feels much too steep for the actors, and you can tell that you are going to have to re-rehearse the fight to make it safe, as well as rework that awkward entrance into Act Five. The first dress rehearsal makes all this clear.

You need to remember that the first dress rehearsal – the technical dress rehearsal – is the stage management's first attempt at running the play on set and with all the cues, and this is an opportunity for everyone to get the technical side of the production right.

The Second Dress Rehearsal

The crucial thing about the second dress rehearsal is to encourage the actors to start to reclaim the stage. After days of 'teching', they need to be reminded that the challenges aren't all technical; and they must now remember the drama, the people and the artistry that they spent four weeks working on in the rehearsal room.

Before the second dress rehearsal I often go round the dressing rooms and tell the actors that I'm now going to be looking at the acting again. And so I usually go and sit by myself in the theatre, away from the production desk, with its endless conversations about lighting levels and missed sound cues, and try to focus on the performances.

You're sometimes helped in this if the production photographs are taken in the second dress. The actors know that they're being photographed and, curiously, this brings out the best in them. The sound of the whirring reflexes reminds them that an audience is coming to watch *them*, living a human drama, not a revolving stage that always gets jammed, or a 22-second lighting cue.

Sometimes, a few friends and colleagues may join you in the auditorium for the second dress rehearsal. I encourage this since it reminds the actors they're playing for a live audience, and it's quite possible the audience might even respond in ways which are helpful – especially laughing, if it's a comedy. You have to be careful if the theatre's artistic director comes to the second dress rehearsal and has a lot of notes for you and your cast: this new perspective may be genuinely helpful, but can be confusing at such a late stage.

Whoever else is in the auditorium, you must concentrate on formulating those key notes that will make everything so much better. Sometimes these are technical issues ('You've got to be louder'), sometimes rhythmic ('You're gabbling in Act One, and leaving us behind'), sometimes character-based ('I still don't understand why you get quite so angry with her'). But this is your opportunity to see what is working and what isn't.

Curtain call

One of the last things you have to do is to arrange and rehearse the curtain call. I tend to do this at the end of the second dress. It's very easy to forget all about it, but a good stage manager or assistant director will remind you. Before you start you need to work out exactly how you're going to structure it. Don't underestimate the delicacy involved: the curtain call makes a statement to the audience and to the theatrical profession about the relative status of the actors. If you change your mind halfway through, things can get difficult.

I tend to arrange a 'company call', with all the actors spread out evenly across the front of the stage. They then bow together (usually twice – three times always feels like asking for too much) and go off, ready to come back on again if there's sufficient demand. You need to get them to bow together and they should take their cue from one of the actors near the front and in the middle. It's sometimes good to reverse the positions on the second call, so someone who was on the side now bows in the middle and vice versa.

In some plays a 'company call' doesn't seem appropriate. In *King Lear* I divided up the cast into six groups (Knights; Cornwall, Albany and Oswald; Edgar, Edmund, Kent and the Fool; the sisters; Gloucester; Lear), each of whom took a bow, followed by a group bow. Occasionally, I will go for an additional individual call (Alan Cumming took his own bow in *Hamlet* as did Timothy West in *King Lear*). Occasionally, for example in *The Cherry Orchard*, I found it useful to divide the company up into two groups and have the leading eight bow first, and the rest later. And then you need to work out which order they're on stage: by tradition, you put the leading actor in the middle, and try to divide it up by gender, in some order of 'rank' on either side. The front row of *The Cherry Orchard* was – from left to right – Simeonov-Pishchik, Trofimov, Anya, Gaev, Ranevskaya, Lopakhin, Varya and Firs.

You need to decide when the actors should return for more. It's important to nominate someone to do this (usually the stage manager, sometimes the leading actor). But you need to be careful. Some DSMs kill the applause by bringing up the house lights too early, and you need to find someone who can judge this well.

A good curtain call is a tightly managed event, and needs to be properly rehearsed. There are all kinds of tricks you can play to make the production feel like more of a triumph: pushing the lights up, getting the actors to come on with energy and élan, playing music loudly, 'bouncing the tabs' (getting the curtain to come in and out very quickly) and so on. The most successful directors spend a surprisingly large amount of time and effort making their curtain calls work.

Each theatre culture has its own attitude to curtain calls. They're taken much more seriously in opera and abroad. When I worked at the Traverse Theatre in Edinburgh we had to explain to companies from Russia, Germany or France that getting a British audience to clap for more than a minute is almost impossible. They were used to five-minute standing ovations and were inconsolable.

Final notes

You must be careful how and when you frame your final notes.

Note sessions usually take place on stage, straight after the second dress rehearsal, or in another room in the theatre if the technical team need to work on the stage. But you need to be careful about assembling all the actors together for a long notes session at this point: people are usually very tired, and sometimes the best thing is to find an individual actor and give him your notes by himself. I sometimes do this on the phone.

Directors occasionally make the mistake of giving actors a 'big note', such as 'I don't think we know who you are' or 'Your acting isn't up to much' or 'God, it's boring', after seeing the dress rehearsal. But this betrays naïveté: the actor is going through hell and needs to close down certain options in his mind if he's to get through to the first preview in one piece.

The best final notes are straightforward technical ones: 'It's a bit quiet from the back of the stalls', or 'Can you tighten up those two entrances in Act Four because things are getting a bit slow?' 'Grandstanding', or any kind of self-serving sweeping judgments, are counterproductive at the best of times and catastrophic just before the first performance. If you're really worried about an individual performance, the audience will tell you – and the actor – whether you're right and, if so, what it is that's so bad about it. Sometimes the wise thing is to let the actor discover his own mistakes in the frankest and most terrifying rehearsal room of all: the stage in front of a paying audience.

20

Opening

It's easy to forget that the point of all this work is to present your production to a paying public.

I sometimes experience an alarming discrepancy between the energy that I've invested in the show, and the largely indifferent audience who turn up to watch it. 'Don't they have souls?' I think to myself, 'How can they be talking about their mortgages as they come to see my production of *Hamlet*?' The fact is that everybody involved in rehearsing a play can become self-absorbed, introspective and blind to the rest of the world. This happens in the very best companies, and the challenge you now face is to ensure that your production goes out to meet its public with confidence and élan, but also ready to learn and develop. The audience is the real test.

Cards and flowers

The first night has its own ritual and atmosphere that can be charming, and can be deeply irritating. People send each other cards saying things like 'It's been such a pleasure working with you'. Actors get flowers from their agents. One of them has bought everybody involved little presents; somebody else leaves a big box of chocolates in the green room and messages of goodwill are stuck up on the notice board.

As the director you're expected to participate in this, and should probably give people cards and/or presents, particularly if it's your first production. I don't always get round to it, and have never felt that it was taken amiss. What is important is that if you're going to do anything, do it for everybody involved and not just the stars. Recognise the huge amount of work that *everybody* has put in. The wisest thing I ever did was to give a bottle of whisky to the crew, and take all the stage management out for a curry.

Don't be scornful of the first night palaver, but don't get too involved in it either. You've got a more important job to do.

First performance

There's no more extraordinary moment for a director than sitting with an audience waiting for the lights to go down on the first performance of a new production. You're a bundle of nerves, sometimes joking with your assistant, sometimes locked in solitary loneliness with your notebook on your lap. Finally, the houselights dim, and your production begins its first of many long journeys in front of an audience.

You'll often be disappointed that the audience isn't as gripped by the first minute as you were in rehearsal. And that's when you start to realise that the actors are going too slowly, or too quietly, or gabbling their lines, or that they're nervous. You sit there trying to work out what exactly is the problem. Half of your brain is focused on that, while the other half is flooded with adrenalin and has lost its analytical capacity. You twitch nervously and look at the audience ('How can that woman be looking at her programme?', 'Why's that man not laughing at that gag?', 'God, some people are boring' or even 'Isn't that girl gorgeous?'). And all the time the play is unrolling in front of you, and you realise to your horror that it's your job to get this thing to work.

Of course, the most valuable thing is to sit still and learn from your audience, and let them be your master. If they're restless in one section, it's probably because the dramatic tension is missing. If they're bored, then you need to work out why. If you feel that something fundamental isn't being grasped, then you need to understand the reason. And sometimes the truth is unpalatable. But if you try to sense what the audience feels, it will be your most useful teacher.

Taking notes

Taking notes in a dark auditorium can be a difficult business. Some directors have note pads and hold little penlights so they can see what they're writing. Occasionally I scribble in the dark and spend the next day trying to interpret my scrawl. Sometimes, if the house isn't full, I sit in an empty area of the auditorium with a torch. Assistants can help, remembering my muttered comments or writing them down. These days I simply try to remember the key points and re-reading the script the next morning triggers my memory.

But what are the things you should look out for? Essentially, there are two different areas: production notes and acting notes. When you feel that a sound cue is too loud, a music cue too late, a lighting state too bright, or an actor too quiet, these are production notes. Acting notes tend to be about noticing when an actor's objectives are not clear, or when he's skating over an important moment, or making too much of something trivial. Sometimes, you sense that the actor's performance is becoming too theatrical, or too sentimental, or too vulgar: it's lost the quality of truth you spent so long searching for.

You have to watch the show with as much critical intelligence as you can muster, sometimes pleasurably and sometimes in anguish. You need to be careful that your faculties are not clouded by relief that the show is on at all. At the same time you need to accept that some problems have to be left to resolve themselves, through the process of repetition under performance conditions. If you're unhappy with the way the production is working, you need to find the 'head space' to reflect on your own mistakes and other people's frailties, and somehow construct a plan to improve things, even though it's almost certainly too late to alter the basic ingredients. And at this point the actors' perspective can seem very different. Sometimes they think everything is fine, when you know it's not; at other times they're deep in despair, when you feel that everything is going swimmingly. And it's at this stage that you can start to feel very lonely.

Giving notes

Big note sessions after the first performance can be very valuable, but they are difficult to do well. It's important to choose the right moment – the afternoon after the first performance may be premature – and sometimes the best thing is to let the production bed in for a few performances. Some of your notes may sort themselves out without you giving them, and by watching the show several times you'll come to a clearer analysis.

A note session usually consists of the actors gathered together in the front of the auditorium while you sit on the stage or stand in front of it. It's essential that you prepare for this very carefully. You must take the time not only to interpret the previous night's scribble, but also to work out exactly what you want to say. And here you need to be careful about being too technical. It's much more constructive to say that you feel the character should have a 'more positive energy' at a particular moment, rather than that he's 'too quiet'; better to say you feel 'the character should be more agitated', when what you really want is for the actor to 'go faster'.

Furthermore, each note needs to be tailored to the particular anxieties and resistances of the individual actor. Sometimes you get this wrong: you imagine an actor won't be able to accept what you're saying and are amazed when it's all taken on gamely; but then another actor rejects a note which you thought was uncontroversial.

I avoid long notes sessions, because I think they can be draining for all involved. I prefer to find an actor in the bar afterwards, or in his dressing room in the hour before the performance, or in the mad rush as he gets out of his costume at the end. Occasionally I might ring an actor on his mobile, just to give some quick response. The crucial thing to understand is that it's now time for the actors to get into their stride and make the show their own. As with bringing up children, there comes a moment when you need to relinquish your grip.

Rehearsing on stage

Instead of giving long note sessions, I prefer to rehearse (and re-rehearse) scenes on set; I sometimes even insist on the actors wearing their costumes rehearsing it under the lights. This allows me to see the scene under performance conditions, which is particularly useful when the problem isn't about analysis but delivery. This is sometimes difficult to organise, because it needs the involvement of the technical team, as well as the actors, but it can be tremendously useful. It also allows you to 're-tech' a moment you're not quite happy with, to nudge a sound level, to ask the lighting designer to think again about a particular effect and so on.

I then sit quite far back in the stalls, calling out to the actors when the energy seems to lag, or the moment has been fudged, or the point has not been put across cleanly. This can be particularly useful with young, inexperienced actors, especially when you're working in a big theatre. With older actors it's usually better to forbear. I also find that rehearsing on stage gives me greater clarity, and I suddenly understand the problem of a scene which I've spent weeks consistently misunderstanding.

The critics

Understandably, young directors are keen to attract national critics to their productions, but it's not always a good idea.

Press nights have their own, uniquely awful atmosphere. In big London theatres, it's not unheard of for forty or fifty critics to appear, along with their wives and partners. When they arrive, the press agent meets them from behind a little desk, where they're given their free tickets, a copy of the programme, and maybe a drink. The atmosphere is like being at a funeral: people talk about anything except the show itself. And then they race off home at the end before the applause has died away.

The critics of the national papers are a complex group of people. Some are charming, even gentlemanly. Others are unpleasant, arrogant and vain. Theatre practitioners, especially directors, sometimes speak of critics with loathing behind their backs, but are reluctant to confront them in public or in print. The crucial thing to remember is that critics are, first and foremost, journalists, whose main duty is to their newspaper. And if you find you consistently disagree with a newspaper's political commentary, you're likely to find its cultural opinions objectionable. Critics are important, but many of them are hacks at heart.

British critics are increasingly powerful, and London is becoming more and more like New York, where one or two critics can turn a production into a hit, or close it in a week. They affect audience numbers, particularly when theatre tickets are so expensive, and there's such a huge range of theatre to choose from. Critics can also affect people's careers. The infuriating thing is that they exercise the harlot's pre-rogative – power without responsibility – while the theatre profession goes on trying to please the very critics they despise. They're probably best seen as a necessary evil.

Some theatres employ the services of a press representative, whose contacts and single-minded commitment to press coverage can be extremely useful. Some directors do this work themselves: chatting up the press, taking them out to lunch, making them feel that they're part of the whole process. Artistic directors speak of making their companies 'critic-proof', and certainly one of the most difficult challenges you face is how to get them 'on side'. My limited experience of attempting this has always been more pleasurable than I'd imagined it would be.

Reviews

Newspaper reviews ('notices' as they're sometimes called) tend to appear in dribs and drabs: two one day, three the next, and then a break till Sunday when there might be another two. Some reviews appear much later, sometimes – astonishingly – once the play has closed. Many actors talk about not wanting to read the reviews, particularly while the show is on, and they're probably wise: a young actor I directed was slated by an important London critic, and his performance collapsed as a result. It took weeks to rebuild his confidence.

I'm afraid I'm a masochist. I used to rush out eagerly and buy all the papers; I now look them up on the Internet (this at least means you don't have to spend money on them). I used to look for the review with some optimism (and I've had some good ones along with the bad); but I've finally learnt that the only way to open the papers is with an absolute conviction that however much you like the production, they will hate it. This at least means that when the notice is lukewarm you're pleasantly surprised. Unless you're lucky, the reviews will be mixed, with some praising your work, others hating it.

Occasionally – and most directors have experienced this – all the reviews are bad. But don't expect much sympathy. Richard Eyre has conjured up an image of a herd of gazelles pretending not to notice one of their brothers being dragged to the ground by a group of wild dogs. A dozen bad reviews in all the national papers is a difficult thing to deal with, and it's not surprising some directors book a holiday straight after the opening night.

It's hard to know whether it's worth responding to bad reviews. I've sometimes penned letters, and occasionally sent them, as much in defence of somebody else's work as in defence of mine. I can't pretend that it has helped, and the best advice is to rise above even the vilest *ad hominem* abuse. One of the most baffling things is when there's evidently a contradiction between the press's poor opinion of the production and what your audiences are telling you. That's when you wonder whether it's worth inviting them to see the work at all.

Oscar Wilde should be given the last word: 'Critics have often spoiled my breakfast, but never my lunch.'

The aftermath

Some directors insist on coming to see every performance of their play. This shows admirable commitment, but isn't necessarily the best thing for the production. One of the hardest things to do, once a play has had its Press Night, is to leave it alone for a while. Productions that have been carefully rehearsed and are well cast develop nuances of their own in performance, and such nuances make a huge difference. I find that if I see my production too often, I lose objectivity: tiny things that are not quite right take on a significance that are entirely disproportionate. The best thing is to go away for a while and come back fresh: it's then that you can give positive and useful notes.

A word of caution, however: giving notes to a production that's well run-in has its own particular challenges. After a week or two, actors develop a rather proprietorial attitude to the production and the work. They know how the audience has been reacting, and they may well regard your opinions with a degree of scepticism and distance. The key, I think, is to give notes on areas where their intention isn't quite communicating itself, or where it has become too internalised: 'I love what you're doing but I think if you took a momentary pause before "let them anatomise Regan", we would see Lear's development in the storm more clearly.' As ever, the best thing you can do is to be concrete and precise.

Once a production has opened – regardless of the reviews – I often get a wave of depression, which is usually to do with the demands of everyday real life reasserting themselves, and the inevitable consequence of exhaustion. Suddenly everything feels rather grey. And then of course you have to consider what is going to happen next. If you're lucky you may be booked up for the following two years. More likely you'll be looking at an empty diary with a little bit of drama school teaching scheduled three weeks later. If the reviews are bad, you'll no doubt be convinced that you'll never work again. If they're good, you'll be depressed to discover that nobody who matters has read them.

There's no way to avoid it: being a theatre director can be a tough and lonely challenge. At other times it's the best job you can imagine. But you have to keep going. As the greatest of all modern dramatists, Samuel Beckett, said: 'No matter. Try again. Fail again. Fail better.'

21

Hamlet, Konstantin
and the Radical Young Director

One of the key characteristics of all great directors has been their desire to further the theatre, to use it for radically new, often highly political, purposes, to purge it of 'irrelevance' and 'mere entertainment'. As a result they have changed it in radical, fresh ways.

Young directors

The role of the director is a recent invention and it's important to realise that it's still evolving fast. And it's young directors who are, as ever, leading the charge. But two of the greatest dramatists, Shakespeare and Chekhov, got there first. *Hamlet* and *The Seagull* give us a powerful insight into many a young director, drawn with great affection and admiration, but also hedged around with essential irony. It's almost as if these two great dramatists have got to the heart of what it's like to be a young theatre director today.

Hamlet

Hamlet's 'advice to the players' (3.2) gives us a useful insight into the Elizabethan theatre at work:

HAMLET Speak the speech, I pray you, as I pronounced it to
  you, trippingly on the tongue. But if you mouth it, as many
  of your players do, I had as lief the town crier spoke my lines.
  Nor do not saw the air too much with your hand, thus, but
  use all gently; for in the very torrent, tempest, and, as I may
  say, the whirlwind of passion, you must acquire and beget
  a temperance that may give it smoothness. O, it offends
  me to the soul to hear a robustious periwig-pated fellow
  tear a passion to tatters, to very rags, to split the ears of the
  groundlings, who for the most part are capable of nothing
  but inexplicable dumbshows and noise: I would have such

a fellow whipped for o'erdoing Termagant; it out-herods
Herod: pray you, avoid it.

FIRST PLAYER I warrant your honour.

HAMLET Be not too tame neither, but let your own discretion
be your tutor: suit the action to the word, the word to the
action; with this special observance, that you o'erstep not
the modesty of nature: for anything so overdone is from the
purpose of playing, whose end, both at the first and now,
was and is, to hold, as 'twere, the mirror up to nature; to
show virtue her own feature, scorn her own image, and the
very age and body of the time his form and pressure. Now
this overdone, or come tardy off, though it make the unskilful
laugh, cannot but make the judicious grieve; the censure of
the which one must in your allowance o'erweigh a whole
theatre of others. O, there be players that I have seen play, and
heard others praise, and that highly, not to speak it profanely,
that, neither having the accent of Christians nor the gait of
Christian, pagan, nor man, have so strutted and bellowed
that I have thought some of nature's journeymen had made
men, and not made them well, they imitated humanity so
abominably.

FIRST PLAYER I hope we have reformed that indifferently with
us, sir.

HAMLET O, reform it altogether. And let those that play your
clowns speak no more than is set down for them; for there be
of them that will themselves laugh, to set on some quantity
of barren spectators to laugh too; though, in the meantime,
some necessary question of the play be then to be considered:
that's villainous, and shows a most pitiful ambition in the
fool that uses it.

The young, highly intellectual student is trying to persuade
these professional actors to play in a new way: with more
naturalness and smoothness, less rhetoric and gesture, and
more meaning and commitment. Like many a modern
director, Hamlet is trying to be 'innovative'. The irony is that
for all his 'radical chic', he is confronted with a tradition rich
with its own unshakeable value and appeal.

Hamlet's role in the presentation of *The Mousetrap* is as
much producer as director (after all, he's commissioned the
performance and rewritten the story for his own ends). Seeing

the theatre as a political tool, not just an aesthetic object, he's determined that it should play a critical and radical role in society. His 'production' of *The Mousetrap* is designed specifically to catch 'the conscience of the King' (even if it doesn't make it any easier to purge the state of its rottenness).

But look how suspicious of the professionals Hamlet is. He thinks they will undermine the seriousness of his plan with their ad-libbing, ham acting and laughter. Modern audiences tend to side with Hamlet in his tirade against melodramatic acting. But he's going against the grain. You can almost hear the players saying: 'Look, guv, you get on with being a prince, and we'll do what we're good at, making people laugh.' It's a comment that can still be heard in many a rehearsal room.

Konstantin

Likewise, Konstantin in *The Seagull* (which is thick with references to *Hamlet*) wants the theatre to be different. He feels the need to condemn out of hand the theatre as it exists, so as to dream up a new kind of theatre which will communicate directly to its audience. But Konstantin's (Kostya's) avant-garde play turns out to be pretentious twaddle and is cruelly laughed off stage by the other characters, including his mother Arkadina, the professional actress. Kostya's rage (which is against his mother's emotional dominance, as much as against the theatre) is deliberately and ironically overstated by Chekhov, who leaves us wondering whether Sorin's uncomplicated objection carries an ocean of commonsense behind it:

KOSTYA As far as I'm concerned the theatre of today's stuck
  in a rut, boring and conventional. When the curtain goes up
  on that room with those three walls, and its artificial light,
  and we see those great geniuses, those high priests of the
  sacred art, miming how people eat, drink, make love, walk,
  wear their jackets – when they try to fish some sort of moral
  out the most banal scenes and lines, some pathetic reach-me-
  down maxim that'll come in handy around the house – when
  they serve up the same thing over and over again in a hundred-
  and-one variations – well, I just take to my heels, the way

Maupassant fled from the Eiffel Tower, which weighed down his brain with its sheer vulgarity.

SORIN We can't do without the theatre.

KOSTYA It's new forms we need. We need new forms of theatre, and if we can't have them, we'd be better off with nothing.

The Radical Young Director

Shakespeare and Chekhov are infinitely wise dramatists who present us with a compelling paradox. The theatre desperately needs radical young directors, full of reforming zeal, passionate, committed, prepared to look foolish, to knock the theatre out of its habitual complacency. And it's not just the theatre that needs their challenge – it's society, the status quo – whether it's the political corruption of Elsinore, or the disastrous indolence of the Russian upper-middle classes before the Revolution. These young men want to change the world, and we should celebrate their vision.

'And yet, and yet . . .' both writers seem to be saying, 'This is how it always is, and disaster and humiliation is never far off.' The resistance that both Hamlet and Kostya come up against is part of the complexity of the world, and isn't easily dismissed. The fact is you can't change the theatre simply by thinking it should be changed. The great challenge of making it into a living art form that speaks to its audience is a lifelong struggle.

The lessons for today's 'radical young director' are many. Part of the point of this book is to show some of them, and help the young director avoid the humiliation that Shakespeare and Chekhov seemed to understand so intimately, and which so many modern directors (myself included) have lived through and filed in a drawer marked 'experience'. Theatre directing is a hard and challenging job. But it's still true that if you devote yourself to it, develop your skills and hone your art, bring all your humanity and your passion to it, you're not just changing the theatre, you're changing the world.

Endnotes

1 What it takes

Other useful books on directing include: *Directors on Directing: A Source Book to the Modern Theatre*, ed. Toby Cole (Simon and Schuster, 1963); William Ball, *A Sense of Direction* (Drama Book Publishers, 1984); Don Taylor, *Directing Plays* (A&C Black, 1996); Harold Clurman, *On Directing* (Simon and Schuster, 1997); Michael McCaffery, *Directing a Play* (Phaidon, 1998); *On Directing*, ed. Gabriella Giannachi and Mary Luckhurst (Faber, 1999); *Stage Directions*, ed. Stephen Peithman and Neil Offen (Greenwood, 1999); *Stage Director's Handbook*, ed. David Diamond and Terry Berliner (Theatre Communications Group, 2000); Anne Bogart, *A Director Prepares* (Routledge, 2001); Michael Bloom, *Thinking like a Director* (Faber, 2002); and Polly Irvin, *Directing for the Stage* (RotoVision, 2002).

The three visionary productions I mention are David Storey's *Home*, directed by Lindsay Anderson, designed by Jocelyn Herbert (Royal Court Theatre, 1970); Shakespeare's *A Midsummer Night's Dream*, directed by Peter Brook, designed by Sally Jacobs (Royal Shakespeare Company, 1970); and Chekhov's *The Cherry Orchard* (*Der Kirschgarten*), directed by Peter Stein, designed by Karl-Heinz Herrmann, costumes by Moidele Bickel (Landestheater Salzburg, 1995).

2 What is a Theatre Director?

For a useful account of female directors – Joan Littlewood, Annie Castledine, Helene Kaut-Howson, Deborah Warner, Katie Mitchell, Di Trevis, Jenny Killick, Marianne Elliot, Phyllida Lloyd, Rachel Kavenaugh, Jude Kelly and others – see Helen Manfull, *Taking Stage: Women Directors on Directing* (Methuen, 1999).

The Directors Guild of Great Britain (Acorn House, 314-320 Gray's Inn Road, London WC1X 8DP; www.dggb.co.uk) represents directors' interests. It has worked hard to increase pay levels and secure intellectual property rights, but its power is limited.

3 Starting out

Drama schools offering directing courses include the Drama Studio, London (Grange Court, 1 Grange Road, Ealing W5 5QN); the Bristol Old Vic Theatre School (Downside Road, Clifton, Bristol BS8 2XF); and the Central School of Speech and Drama (Embassy Theatre, Eton Avenue, London NW3 3HY). The National Theatre Studio, among others, runs an annual Directors' Course (Royal National Theatre, Upper Ground SE1).

For a crash-course in the 'classical' repertoire, I would recommend Nicholas Wright's *99 Great Plays* (Methuen, 1992); NHB's Drama Classics list; my own *Pocket Guide to Shakespeare* (Faber, 1997) and *Pocket Guide to Twentieth Century Drama* (Faber, 2001); Richard Eyre and Nicholas Wright's *Changing Stages* (Bloomsbury, 2000); and *The Continuum Guide to Twentieth-Century Theatre*, ed. Colin Chambers (Continuum, 2002). Also useful is the *Oxford Concise Companion to the Theatre*, ed. Phyllis Hartnoll and Peter Found (Oxford, 1972) and the *Penguin Dictionary of the Theatre*, ed. John Russell Taylor (Penguin, 1966). For plays written by women, see Susan Croft's *She Also Wrote Plays* (Faber, 2001). One of the most remarkable resources is Ken Tynan's *List of Prospective Plays for the National Theatre* which can be found on the Columbia University website: http://www.columbia.edu/~tdk3/tynan.html.

As for new writing, London's Royal Court, the Bush, Hampstead, and the Soho Theatre; the Rep Studio (the Door) in Birmingham; the Royal Exchange in Manchester; and the Traverse Theatre in Edinburgh are currently the leading 'new play theatres'. Touring companies such as Out of Joint, Paines Plough, Shared Experience, The Red Room, 7:84, Oxford Stage Company and English Touring Theatre all produce new work as well. There are two useful recent books on modern British playwriting: Dominic Dromgoole's *The Full Room* (Methuen, 2002); and Aleks Sierz's *In Yer Face Theatre* (Faber, 2001). The main publishers of new British plays are Nick Hern Books, Faber and Faber, Methuen and Oberon. The best bookshops for plays are the National Theatre Bookshop, French's and Offstage, all in London.

Current training schemes for directors include, at the time of writing: the Carlton Television/Donmar Warehouse Traineeship (The Donmar Warehouse, 41 Earlham Street, London WC2H 9LD); the Arts Council Regional Theatre Initiative (ACE, 14 Great

Peter Street, London SW1P 3NQ); the Jerwood Scheme at the Young Vic (66 The Cut, London SE1 8LZ); the Cohen Bursary with English Touring Theatre (ETT, 25 Short Street, London SE1); the National Theatre Studio (RNT, Upper Ground London SE1); and the Channel 4 Theatre Director Scheme. The Caird Company also has a strong commitment to developing young directors.

4 Contexts and Colleagues

The best book on the Royal Court in the 1960s is by Philip Roberts: *The Royal Court Theatre and the Modern Stage* (Cambridge, 1999). See also William Gaskill, *A Sense of Direction* (Faber, 1988).

5 Choice of Play

Manfred Karge's *Man to Man* and *The Conquest of the South Pole* (p. 34) were premiered at the Traverse Theatre in Edinburgh, and transferred to the Royal Court (Methuen 1987). Brecht's thoughts on approaching the classics (p. 36) are taken from *Classical Status as an Inhibiting Factor* in *Brecht on Theatre*, ed. John Willett (Methuen, 1964). Jan Kott's *Shakespeare Our Contemporary* (Methuen, 1965) influenced Peter Brook's productions of *King Lear* (RSC, 1962) and *A Midsummer Night's Dream* (RSC, 1970). Harley Granville Barker's *Prefaces to Shakespeare* have been reprinted by Nick Hern Books. George Steiner's *After Babel: Aspects of Language and Translation* (Faber, 1975) is as good a starting place as any for the complexities of translation. Kenneth McLeish's outstanding translations of Ibsen include *Peer Gynt* (1990), *A Doll's House* (1994), *The Master Builder* (1997), *Hedda Gabler* (1995), *The Lady from the Sea* (2001) and *Rosmersholm* (2002). Following McLeish's death, Stephen Mulrine continued this work with translations of *Ghosts* (2002) and *John Gabriel Borkman* (2003). All of these translations are available in NHB's Drama Classics Series.

For works in copyright, the main literary agents are listed in *Contacts*, the most important index of agents, theatres, casting directors, relevant publications, companies, producers, costume hire stores and so on. I refer to it almost every day of my working life. It is published annually by Spotlight (7 Leicester Place, London WC2H 7RJ).

6 Preparation

For various historical contexts, see Orlando Figes's *A People's Tragedy* (Pimlico, 1996); the same author's *Natasha's Dance* (Penguin, 2002); and John Willett's *The New Sobriety 1917–1933* (Thames and Hudson, 1978). For knowing the writer, see Bertolt Brecht's *Work Journal* (Methuen, 1993) and *Poems* (Methuen, 1987); Michael Meyer's biographies of *Ibsen* (Pelican, 1974) and *Strindberg* (Random House, 1985), Donald Rayfield's *Chekhov* (Harper Collins, 1997), Richard Ellmann's *Oscar Wilde* (Hamish Hamilton, 1987), and Philip Hoare's *Noël Coward* (Sinclair-Stevenson, 1995); and John Osborne's two volumes of auto-biography, *A Better Class of Person* (Faber, 1981) and *Almost a Gentleman* (Faber, 1991). For Shakespeare, see Park Honan, *Shakespeare: A Life* (Oxford, 1998) and Ted Hughes, *Shakespeare and the Goddess of Complete Being* (Faber, 1992) (which discusses the 'rival brothers').

On original stage-practice and reception, see Peter Thomson's *Shakespeare's Theatre* (Routledge, 1992) and *Shakespeare's Professional Career* (Cambridge, 1992); Andrew Gurr's *The Shakespearean Stage, 1574-1642* (Cambridge, 1970) and *Playgoing in Shakespeare's London* (Cambridge, 1992); Michael Pennington's *Hamlet: A Users's Guide* (NHB, 1996) and *Twelfth Night: A User's Guide* (NHB, 2000); the Faber *Actors on Shakespeare* and Cambridge *Players of Shakespeare* series; Strindberg's 'Preface' to *Miss Julie*, translated by Kenneth McLeish (NHB, 1995); Michael Billington, *One Night Stands* (NHB, 1993); and Kenneth Tynan, *Profiles* (NHB, 1989).

A longer version of my summary of *The Cherry Orchard* can be found in my *Pocket Guide to Twentieth Century Drama* (Faber, 2001). For examples of cutting, see *King Lear*, ed. Stephen Unwin (Oberon, 2002) and *Romeo and Juliet*, ed. Stephen Unwin and Michael Cronin (Oberon, 2003). Examples of innovative rearrangements of Shakespeare's histories include *The Wars of the Roses* (RSC, 1962–3), *The Plantagenets* (RSC, 1988–9), and *Rose Rage* (Newbury, 2002).

7 Casting

There are exceptions to every rule. Although the idea of modern royalty acting in plays is faintly worrying, Prince Charles's Macbeth, at Gordonstoun School, evidently had a certain strange force, above all because the audience were fully aware that this was a man who really was destined to be king. And while eyebrows were raised in some quarters at my casting of Tilda Swinton – an old friend from Cambridge – in Manfred Karge's one-woman show *Man to Man*, the production went on to become a huge success both at the Traverse and the Royal Court.

On integrated casting, see the Arts Council's Eclipse Report of 2002, which paints a worrying picture of the racism latent in subsidised theatre, and suggests ways of addressing it.

For building up a database of actors, *Spotlight* is the essential tool: *Spotlight* is an eight-volume directory of actors and actresses, also available on CD-Rom, from Spotlight, 7 Leicester Place, London WC2H 78P (020 7437 7631; www.spotlightcd.com). Because these are updated every two years, theatres or casting directors will often give you their old copies – if you ask nicely. For casting directors, see www.castingdirectorsguild.co.uk.

8 Design 1: Creative

The Designers' Register is available on www.theatredesign.org.uk. Art schools committed to running theatre design courses include Wimbledon School of Art, the Slade, Trent Polytechnic, Central St Martin's, Central School of Speech and Drama. The Linbury Biennial Prize for Stage Design is run by the Linbury Trust and administered by Kallaway Ltd (www.linburybiennial. org.uk). For Caspar Neher's designs, see the Berliner Ensemble's *Modellbuch*; for Jocelyn Herbert's, see her *Theatre Workbook* (Arts Books International, 1993). Chloe Obolensky's book is *The Russian Empire: A Portrait in Photographs* (Jonathan Cape, 1980). D.H. Lawrence's *The Widowing of Mrs Holroyd* was published by Penguin in 1969. Brecht's poem to Neher, 'The Friends', is included in his *Poems 1913–1956*, translated by Michael Hamburger (Methuen, 1976).

10 Rehearsals 1: Starting out

On the perils of one's fellow actors having other ideas, Peter Brook tells the story of the read-through of *Measure for Measure*. After only two lines, John Gielgud (playing the Duke) turned to Brook and enquired whether the actor playing Escalus intended to play his first line ('My lord') 'like that'. See Brook's 'The Two Ages of Gielgud' in his *The Shifting Point* (Methuen, 1989).

11 Rehearsals 2: Establishing Facts

Timothy West's scrupulous analysis of *The Cherry Orchard* can be found in his *A Moment Towards the End of the Play* (NHB, 2001). Some answers to my own questions (p. 114): An 'ancient' is an ensign (the military rank between sergeant and captain). Denmark had a complicated system of elected monarchy. A 'master builder' is the equivalent of a modern contractor: although less skilled than an architect, he would commission an architect to design the buildings he had conceived. Lopakhin has made his money through land speculation and Ranevskaya has spent her money living too well – and too long – in France.

12 Rehearsals 3: Warm-ups, Improvisations, Games and Theories

Some crucial books: Viola Spolin, *Theater Games for Rehearsal: A Director's Handbook* (Northwestern University Press, 1985) and her *Improvisation for Theatre* (Northwestern University Press, 1998); Clive Barker, *Theatre Games: A New Approach to Actor Training* (Methuen, 1977); Chris Johnston, *House of Games* (NHB, 1998); Keith Johnstone, *Impro* (Methuen, 1979); Antonin Artaud, *The Theatre and Its Double* (Calder, 1970); Jerzy Grotowski, *Towards a Poor Theatre* (Methuen, 1969); Peter Brook, *The Empty Space* (Pelican, 1972), *The Shifting Point* (Methuen, 1988), *There Are No Secrets* (Methuen, 1993) and *Threads of Time* (Methuen, 1998); Konstantin Stanislavski, *My Life in Art* (Methuen, 1980), *An Actor Prepares* (Methuen, 1980) and *Building a Character* (Methuen, 1979). On Brecht, see John Willett, *The Theatre of Bertolt Brecht* (Methuen, 1977), *Brecht on Theatre: The Development of an Aesthetic* (Methuen, 1978) and *Brecht in Context* (Methuen, 1984), as well as John Willett and Ralph Manheim's outstanding Methuen editions of the Plays, Poems, Songs, Letters and Workbook. For 'actioning', see Max Stafford-Clark's excellent *Letters to George* (NHB, 1989).

13 Rehearsals 4: Language

Text: Peter Hall, *Advice to the Players* (Oberon, 2003); David Mamet, *True or False* (Faber and Faber, 2000). Reference books: *A Shakespeare Glossary*, ed. C.T. Onions (Oxford, 1986); Ben and David Crystal, *Shakespeare's Words* (Penguin, 2002); *The Penguin Dictionary of Classical Mythology* (Penguin 1990); *Who's Who in the Bible* (Penguin 1998). Obscenity: Eric Partridge, *Shakespeare's Bawdy* (Routledge, 1947). Speaking Shakespeare: Patsy Rodenburg, *Acting Shakespeare* (Methuen, 2002); John Barton, *Playing Shakespeare* (Methuen, 1985); and see also James Fenton *An Introduction to English Poetry* (Penguin, 2003). My three modern examples (pp. 133–4) are from Edward Bond's *Saved* (Methuen, 1966), Harold Pinter's *No Man's Land* (Methuen, 1975) and Samuel Beckett's *A Piece of Monologue* (Faber, 1979).

14 Rehearsals 5: Character

Quotations in this chapter are from translations by Stephen Mulrine of Chekhov's *The Cherry Orchard* (NHB, 1998) and Ibsen's *Ghosts* (NHB, 2002); and by Kenneth McLeish of Ibsen's *Hedda Gabler* (NHB, 1995). On the Method, see *Strasberg at the Actors' Studio*, ed. Robert Hethman (TCG, 1965) and Uta Hagen's *Respect for Acting* (Macmillan, 1973) and *A Challenge for the Actor* (Macmillan, 1991).

The pleasures of such speculation about characters extend to John Osborne's revisiting of his *Look Back in Anger* in *Déja Vu* (Faber, 1991), where Jimmy and Cliff are still angry, thirty years on and in middle age, but about different things, and still cracking jokes (even if they aren't as good). Brian Friel did the same with Chekhov in *Afterplay* (Faber, 2002), which imagined Andrei from *Three Sisters* meeting Sonya from *Uncle Vanya* in the 1920s.

A cautionary note about Brecht's theories: when Brecht's widow Helene Weigel came to London to see a production of *Galileo*, she was asked by an eager cast whether they had understand the 'alienation effect' properly. She laughed derisorily and said: 'Oh, that was just a silly phrase Bert came up with to stop his actors from over-acting.' Of course, this was deliberately disingenuous, but it does help put this term into some context.

15 Rehearsals 6: Blocking and Movement

Many of Pamela Howard's drawings for *The Cherry Orchard* are reproduced in her *What is Scenography?* (Routledge, 2000). On movement skills, see Jacques Lecoq, *The Moving Body* (Methuen, 2000); and on an earlier tradition of gesture, see B.L. Joseph, *Elizabethan Acting* (Oxford, 1951, now, sadly, out of print), which reproduces a series of hand gestures, each representing a separate emotion, with which Shakespeare's contemporaries were evidently familiar.

The 'iron line' (p. 186) is where the fire curtain (the iron) sits when it's down; in most theatres you're not allowed to place anything on the iron line that can't be easily moved by the stage management if there's a fire.

For an example of Brecht's use of blocking and *gestus*, in his production of *Mother Courage*, each time Courage lost one of her children, her cart was placed between her and the respective child, thus literally blocking her view and metaphorically implying that the wagon – her business – came between her and her children. The Berliner Ensemble produced a number of *Model Books* (now out-of-print collectors' items), which recorded Brecht's finest productions and were intended as tools to teach other theatre directors something of Brecht's intentions. Richly illustrated, with photographs of every scene, and furnished with accompanying texts, they are remarkable theatrical documents, which show how his productions unfolded on the stage, moment by moment.

From the sublime to the ridiculous: there's a famous story of John Barton directing *Twelfth Night* with his head so deep in the text that he didn't notice Judi Dench pulling faces in the pauses allowed in Viola's great speech 'I will build a willow cabin at your gate.'

16 Rehearsals 7: Specialists

Useful books on movement: Rudolf Laban, *Mastery of Movement* (Macdonald, 1980); John Hodgson, *Mastering Movement: The Life and Work of Rudolf Laban* (Routledge, 2001); Jean Newlove and John Dalby, *Laban for All* (NHB, 2003); Litz Pisk, *The Actor and His Body* (Methuen, 1998); and Kelly McEvenue, *The Alexander Technique for Actors* (Methuen, 2001). (Period specialists don't always hold all the answers: when John Malkovich was filming *Les Liaisons Dangereuses*, he pointedly refused to use one of the many period bows that the production's movement director had offered him, and instead invented his own.) Useful books on voice: Patsy Rodenburg's *The Right to Speak* (Methuen, 1992) and *The Actor Speaks* (Methuen, 1997); Cicely Berry, *Voice and the Actor* (Harrap, 1973); Michael McCallion, *The Voice Book* (Faber, 1988); and Barbara Houseman, *Finding your Voice* (NHB, 2003). For fight directors, visit www.badc.co.uk.